101 BEST SMALL BUSINESSES FOR WOMEN

Priscilla Y. Huff

PRIMA PUBLISHING

Dedicated to my family, for their love and support; to the memory of five young persons no longer with us: Tim Slemmer, Billy Kirkner, Tommy Dorfis, Christopher Marx, and Jenny Wilson; and to the children of America—one in five of whom lives in poverty. May we, the women of the world, work to fulfill our aspirations and also the dreams of children everywhere.

Library of Congress Cataloging-in-Publication Data

Huff, Priscilla Y.
101 best small businesses for women : everything you need to know to get started on the road to success / Priscilla Y. Huff.
p. c.m.
Includes bibliographical references and index.
ISBN 0-7615-0580-6
1. Self-employed women. 2. Women in business. 3. Small business—Management. 4. New business enterprises—Management.
5. Entrepeneurship. 6. Success in business. I. Title.
HD6072.5.H84 1996
658.02'2'024042—dc20   96-28166
                                         CIP

97 98 99 00 01 HH 10 9 8 7 6 5 4 3
Printed in the United States of America

How to Order
Single copies may be ordered from Prima Publishing, P.O. Box 1260BK, Rocklin, CA 95677; telephone (916) 632-4400. Quantity discounts are also available. On your letterhead, include information concerning the intended use of the books and the number of books you wish to purchase.

Visit us online at http://www.primapublishing.com

Contents

Preface

Owning and running one's own business is seldom a 9:00 to 5:00 routine. For many, the hours are more like 5:00 A.M. to 9:00 P.M. There are numerous business owners who work even longer hours in their pursuit of financial independence. As their businesses get established, the time they invest may or may not decrease. It is somewhat like raising a child whose needs change with each stage of growth, including many attendant small and large crises. With persistence, faith, love, prayer (a lot with teenagers!), and dedicated attention, the child will grow into a responsible adult—someone to help care for us in our old age.

A new venture also makes tremendous demands on our time, money, and energy. The rewards may not always be what we expect. There is little chance of being bored, as no two days will be the same. You will constantly be learning new skills, making new contacts, and facing new challenges. Of course, you will make your share of mistakes, but I believe that a mistake is only foolish if you do not learn from it and thereby repeat it!

At the very least, being in business for yourself gives you a feeling of empowerment. Instead of letting others dictate the direction of your life, you can begin to take control and make decisions that will help you to reach your goals.

Even if you lack the money or time to start a business now, there is nothing to keep you from doing research on businesses that interests you. In fact, it is wise to read business books and trade publications, network and talk with other entrepreneurs, take a course, or even work part-time or volunteer in a business similar to the one you are thinking of starting.

Do this realistically, weigh the pros and cons, and consider whether this business will be the best choice for you and your lifestyle. This way you will have a much better picture of what to expect in a business, not to mention some valuable information and experience that you can use in your venture. With this preparation, you will be more likely to succeed and better able to adapt to the twists and turns your business will take. Best of all, you can say, "I did that!"

It is my hope that this book will be part of your initial steps toward becoming a business owner. Come join us; there is nothing quite like it!

Best wishes in your endeavors,
Priscilla Y. Huff

Acknowledgments

I want to thank all of the representatives of the many trade associations with whom I spoke, the librarians at the Pierce Branch of the Bucks County Free Library, my local postal workers for their handling of the hundreds of letters sent and received, and all the business owners and women experts who kindly shared their time and helpful tips with me for this book.

I also want to express my thanks to Jennifer Basye Sander for her confidence in my ability to write this book, and to Andi Reese Brady for her patience with me in working on my last book.

Part I

GETTING
STARTED

⚐ 1 ⚐

Facts and Figures

> I will never ask for anything more because I
> am a woman, but never give me anything less.
> —Rep. E. Z. Taylor, Republican Caucus Secre-
> tary, Pennsylvania Legislature.

So you are thinking about starting a business? You are not alone!

A 1995 study conducted by the National Foundation for Women Business Owners (NFWBO) and Dun & Bradstreet Information Services (DBIS) reported that there were over 7.7 million woman-owned businesses in the U.S., providing jobs for 15.5 million people and generating nearly $1.4 trillion in revenues annually.

The U.S. Small Business Administration (SBA) estimates that women are starting businesses at twice the rate of men. Woman-owned firms continue to expand into "non-traditional" industries while maintaining their solid base in retail trade and services. The number of woman-owned businesses in construction, manufacturing, transportation, communications, wholesale trade, finance, insurance, and real estate is growing at significantly faster rates than the overall averages for those industries.

Since the eighties, the growth in woman-owned businesses has been constant. The numbers continue to grow as women gain more recognition and respect in all areas and fields of entrepreneurship.

Women's reasons for starting their own businesses are both common and individual. With which ones can you identify?

- child and/or elder parent care concerns
- lack of job security and few guarantees of job promotions
- threats of job loss with the national trend of downsizing
- frustration with office politics
- a desire to work for yourself
- the potential for an increase in earnings
- the wish to work at a job that you love
- wanting the power to make decisions concerning your own destiny
- a need for flexible work schedules

These are just a few of the many reasons why women want to become entrepreneurs. You can probably add a few of your own, but whatever the reason, it has to be something that you *really* want to do—a burning desire that motivates you into action. You will need this motivation, determination, and doggedness to drive and sustain you through this new way of life. It is both exciting to contemplate going into business for yourself, and frightening as you worry about the changes that a business will bring to you and your family's routine, not to mention the fear of possibly failing.

⚓ 2 ⚓

Personal Traits for Entrepreneurial Success

Make no mistake, it will take a lot of persistence to get you from a great idea to a profit-making venture. Here are some qualities that are common among successful entrepreneurs:

Professionalism

Whether you work out of an office, a business center, or your home, you have to treat your business as a business! This means "going to work" every day by having regular business hours, having business stationery, setting up an office and a bookkeeping system, treating customers and business contacts in a professional manner, staying current with the latest information in your trade, and conducting yourself in a manner that establishes you as an expert in your field.

Flexibility

While a professional must follow certain procedures in a business-like manner, you have to be open to unexpected opportunities that may arise. For example, I know a woman who has now started her fourth business. She began in a small shop that she shared with two other women, designing and sewing custom-quilted jackets. Then she went on to create hand-painted sweatshirts. When that market was flooded, she learned all there was to know about potpourri, and made her own recipes and related products. She then branched out into making herbal soaps. She now sells a variety of soaps and soap-making kits.

Another woman opened an antique shop in her remodeled barn. She decided to carry lace curtains and pottery. There was such a demand for the curtains that she now advertises them in several magazines and takes orders over her 800 number. She even put together her own mail-order catalog, which includes her curtains and other country-style items.

The point is that you may start to serve a certain market, but because of new or unexpected customer demands, your business may go in an entirely different direction than you expected. You have to be alert and ready to change directions, or at least consider new avenues. The survival of your business may depend on your willingness to change. If you are afraid—and almost everyone is afraid of the unknown—then explore your new markets a little at a time. Keep careful records of your profits and customer response to your new service or product. Then decide whether this is a worthwhile direction in which to invest your business time and money.

Persistence

> Press on! Nothing in the world can take the place of persistence.
> —President Calvin Coolidge

It really is true: if you want to succeed, you will have to persevere to reach your goals. If you need an answer concerning your business, the information you need is out there; someone somewhere can help you. Finding that information, of course, is the problem, but there is a plethora of sources—many of them free or low-cost—and people who can help you find solutions. You just have to be willing to press on until you locate them. It gets easier, too, because in your quest for answers you will inevitably make contacts with experts, other business owners, agencies, and trade associations that you can contact over and over again.

Self-Confidence

It is risky to start a business, but the more prepared you are, the more confident you will be in your ability to handle the tasks you must complete. A good business plan—a plan of action—will help you succeed. Take time to research the ventures that interest you. One young woman who runs a successful food delivery franchise took a full year to investigate this venture. You will probably not need this much time to do your research, but taking the time to learn what is needed to get your business up and running will help you overcome obstacles and achieve your goals.

Willingness to Learn

You may have expertise in your field or trade, but as a business owner you will have to be concerned with all the aspects of your business: market research, advertising, customer service, supplies, business finances, delivery of services or products, bookkeeping, banking, and many other areas of which you may know little. Again, tap your resources if you need help, and ask many, many questions. You may also need to take extra training in business management. If possible, talk to people in your line of business or a similar one. If you cannot find any in your area who are willing to help, check out similar businesses in another town where you will not be competing for the same customers. Be willing to learn all you can, and keep an open mind to any advice you receive. Then implement what you believe best fits your business, and file the rest.

Knowledge of Your Business

Of course, you need to *know* your business before you can *start* your business. You can do this through education and training, experience, or both. One of the best ways to get a working knowledge is to do just that: work in a business similar to one you want to start. If you feel that it is dishonest to work in a business with the purpose of opening your own, you can talk with the business owner about it. Chances are good that, if it is an established business, it will be difficult to compete for the same customers.

A better chance for success in a similar business is to find a niche, or area, that is not being filled by others, and have your business fill that niche. Often, established businesses will be happy to refer customers to you for services they really do not want to offer or are not equipped to handle.

Working in a business will not only give you skills, it will provide you with opportunities to observe marketing methods and customer service techniques, to become familiar with suppliers and other business contacts, and to generally learn how the business is run. You may be able to see where customers' needs are not being met, which you can then fill with your own business. Working in a similar business will also give you the opportunity to see if you really want to start a business like this. It's better to find out now than after you have invested time and money! Finally, you will be earning some money—even if it is at minimum wage—to support yourself and your family, and possibly to save for your future venture.

Organizational Skills

Set yearly, monthly, weekly, and daily goals, then break those down into the steps you need to take to reach each goal. Tackle the most difficult ones first, when you have the most energy. Make checklists and compliment yourself at the end of the day for how many things you accomplished, not how many things you did not get done. Set up a workplace that is comfortable and that enables you to find what you need in about a minute.

Until you can afford an office manager, you will be responsible for your own record keeping and paperwork. If you have trouble with this, hire a professional organizer or read some of the excellent books on organization and time management. Being organized will not only make you more efficient, it will help you to know how your business is doing financially and if it is going in the right direction.

Knowing How to Serve Your Customers

If you have started your business to fulfill a specific need for a certain group of customers, keep these tips in mind:

+ Do your market research (more on this in Part II) to be sure that you will have enough customers to support your business.
+ Know which advertising methods best reach your customers (word of mouth, classified ads, direct mail). Track your advertising or ask your customers directly how they heard about you.
+ Regularly poll your customers about your services. Ask them what they like and do not like. Also inquire about additional services that they might like to have.
+ Have an established policy about handling customer complaints and concerns. Respond to them as soon as possible, and in a professional manner.
+ Keep your business focused on your customer.

Networking Ability

"Networking" is another way to say "communicating and exchanging information with other business owners." For example, the Entrepreneur's Association (EA) in Austin, Texas, which began only a few years ago, is a city association of small and home-based business owners who meet regularly for information exchange, business seminars, and other forms of mutual support. EA recently acquired an office building that includes executive suites and office spaces to rent, individual workstations (for rent by the hour, day, or week), two conference rooms, and a service center (with copiers, mail room, receptionists, phone, voice mail, mailing address, and business counseling). Home-business owners or other members who want a presence at the EA building can use the EA receptionist, answering service, and mail drop.

Unfortunately, most of us do not have an EA near us, but you can network with other business owners through local Chambers of Commerce or via local, state, and national trade associations, or go to a "business incubator" (centers in your community set up to guide new entrepreneurs). Or you can have another business owner as a friend or mentor. Not only will it be comforting to share problems and bounce ideas off others in similar situations, but you may gain valuable tips and leads that will lead to more customers. You may even want to organize your own business networking group if there are none in your area.

Knowledge of Your Strengths and Weaknesses

Everyone has abilities and limitations in certain areas. Since you will be handling a multitude of tasks as a business owner, it is important to know what you can contribute to your business success and what may be detrimental to it. Maybe you are good at marketing, but poor at record keeping. Luckily, you do not have to know how to do everything for your business, but you do have to know people who can help you: experts such as an accountant, bookkeeper, business lawyer (specializing in small-business matters), insurance agent, printer, and business consultant. These experts will give you the professional assistance to prevent costly mistakes. If you have a network of business friends, you can pay or barter for their services. It is important that you have this "back-up team" of experts before you start your venture; don't start looking for them when there is a crisis.

⚹ 3 ⚺

Elements of Success

A sobering statistic from the SBA says that for every ten businesses that start, nine will fail within ten years. The good news for women, however, is that 75 percent of woman-owned businesses are more likely to have remained in business in the past three years than the average U.S. business, according to the NFWBO. What are some of the common elements you must have if you are to succeed?

A Good Business Plan

This is crucial for planning, implementing, and conducting a new business. It helps organize and direct the important steps for your venture and can mean the difference between success and failure. Where can you get help in writing a business plan? There are books, software, and business planning consultants, and the U.S. Small Business Administration's (SBA) Small Business Development Centers (SBDCs) will often provide free help in writing a business plan. Women's associations and business groups may also offer workshops on this. Part II of this book will discuss each of the major points of a typical business plan.

Clear Goals

Select the goals you want to concentrate on and the direction you will take to achieve those goals. Determine daily, weekly, monthly, and yearly goals for your business, and then make a "to do" list of steps that you will take to accomplish each goal (see Chapter 6: "Start-up Checklist").

Money

If you quit your job to start your business, experts recommend that you have the equivalent of six months to two years of salary in savings. That is just to cover living expenses. You will also need to determine your start-up costs, plus the estimated costs of conducting business. Again, your business plan will help you outline these costs. Then the question will be where to get this money—savings, loans from friends, bank loans? This topic will be covered in Chapter 11: "Financial Considerations."

To keep your business going, you will need to have a cash reserve for all your purchases, bills, and other expenses. You will need to charge enough for your services or products to enable you to make a profit. Keeping good records and consulting with financial advisors will all help you stay in business. Keep good records, and learn what the IRS requires of you.

Know Your Break-Even Point

Using your records and the advice of your accountant or financial advisor, watch for the point when your business begins to make a profit. Depending on the amount of money you have borrowed, it may take as many as two years before your business makes money. A service business, such as public relations or counseling, will generally require less start-up money than opening a small shop with inventory or another product-related business.

When your business does begin to make a profit, you will then have to make decisions as how to distribute the money—put it back into the business for equipment, purchase additional advertising, take some as earnings, and so on. You and your financial advisor will have to carefully evaluate these decisions.

Knowing your break-even point will also help you understand your cash-flow statement, which is the amount of money available in your business at any given time. Knowing and understanding these will help increase your financial control of your business by helping you make pricing adjustments to ensure profits.

A Marketing Strategy

If you have completed your market research, and you know who your prospective customers are, the next step is to choose the advertising methods you will use to let people know you are in business. Your strategies for reaching customers should be mapped and then assessed as to their cost and their potential effectiveness in increasing sales.

Family Involvement

Whether you are married or single, it is much easier to start a business if you have the support of your family. Your new venture is going to cause some changes in your life and in the lives of those close to you, especially if you are a primary caregiver. Your money and your time will be in shorter supply as you get going. Discuss the pros and cons of what it takes to be an entrepreneur, and encourage your loved ones to be honest and to express their concerns.

With many women today having to work, convincing your family of the value of your starting a business may not be as difficult as you think, especially if you emphasize the flexibility in your new work schedule. Do make them realize, however, that you probably will be working more hours.

Do not expect your family to be free employees. Many women business owners do involve their families in their businesses, but only to a point. You can pay them to assist you, but it may be wiser to hire employees or to subcontract work than to depend on your family. It will help eliminate tension among you.

You will still probably feel pressured or pulled in two directions at times by family demands. Many of us are of the "sandwich generation," having to care not only for our children, but sometimes for our parents as well. It may be easier for you to reorganize your lifestyle and streamline your schedule than to get your family to sacrifice theirs. I am not saying that you should be a martyr, giving up your leisure activities and not asking for extra help with household chores. I am just advising you to be realistic in your expectations of yourself, your family, and your business. I am a firm believer that everything takes longer than expected, and that, as Murphy's Law states, "if something can go wrong, it will." Focus on the important matters within your family and business, and save the extraneous activites (meetings, volunteer activities, etc.) for when you have some extra time.

Staying Focused

Remember the customers you are targeting, and focus on their needs. Do not spread yourself too thin and try to take on too many different projects at the same time. It is easier to keep good customers than to get new ones, and repeat business is one of the best indicators that your customers are happy. Focus on your basic services and only expand them when you are ready. If you do not keep trying to improve your business and give the best possible service, your competitors will be happy to steal your unhappy customers.

Good Employee Relations

If you do hire people, treat them with respect and value their suggestions. Make sure that they are in positions that best use their talents and that they are helping your business. Involve them in the decision-making process of your business and reward them accordingly.

Conclusion

These are just a few of the considerations you may face in starting a business. It takes courage and faith to succeed, but you stand to reap both financial rewards and the fulfillment of doing the work you enjoy.

4

Choosing a Business

Before you can *start* a business, you have to *choose* a business. The best business for you needs to combine your personal goals, philosophy, interests, talents, experiences, and training, while simultaneously filling a need for your customers. Here are some questions to ask yourself to help you decide which business is for you.

What Hobbies or Interests Do You Have?

Many people have begun with a favorite leisure activity and turned that interest into a profitable business. A hobby can give you crucial firsthand experience, skills, and knowledge, but that may not be enough to launch a successful business. You may need additional business management training to know how to run a business. However, starting a business in a field that you are already familiar with can improve your chances for success.

What Is Your Work or Business Experience?

Skills and education that you have acquired through your job, community volunteering, and schooling can often be parlayed into a spin-off business of your own. While on the job, you may have seen a certain customer need that was not being met, and you can fill that void with your own venture. A former employer of yours may even refer customers to you when he or she realizes that you are providing a service to customers that he or she really does not have the time or desire to serve.

Is There a Need for Your Business?

You must have customers who need your product or service. Even if you discover a niche that is not being filled, does your market research show that there are sufficient numbers of potential customers to support your business?

Can You Afford the Investment of Time and Money Needed to Start Your Particular Business?

Working out a business plan will help you determine if you can start your business now, or later when you obtain more start-up resources. It will help you decide on the best time to start, and evaluate whether your time can be divided between this new business, your present job, and other obligations. It is important to take your time in researching the potential risks and costs involved. You may be impatient to get started, but you need to look realistically at a business idea and the ramifications it can have in your life. Consult with business experts, and evaluate honestly what you can and cannot do at this time.

Do not be disheartened if you determine that the present time is not the best time to officially begin your venture. You can take the opportunity to get more training, experience, and money so that you will eventually be prepared to become the successful business owner you dream of being.

5

Franchises and Other Opportunities

Franchises

A franchise agreement involves a *franchisor* (the owner of the franchise, and also the *licensor*) who sells his or her trade name and business system to a *franchisee* (you, *the licensee*), who pays a royalty and often a franchise fee for the right to sell and distribute their products and use their trade name or trademark. Before you purchase a franchise you should ask the following questions:

Yourself

What are your strengths? What hours do you want to work? Do you like to work with people or behind the scenes? What capital do you have to invest and how will you get it?

The Franchisor

Based on your investment, what rate of return and break-even point can you expect? What costs do you have to pay before you make a payment to yourself? What support and training can you expect for yourself and your employees? What is the length of the contract, and can you renew it? What are reasons for disenfranchising (non-renewal of license and contract by the franchisor)? What are the company's future plans? What is the franchisee's mission statement?

These are just a few of the many questions you should ask, besides going to visit the headquarters and other franchises in operation. Some women research for years before investing in a franchise.

A franchisor is also required to supply you with a Uniform Franchise Offering Circular (UFOC), which covers 23 categories of information. Sometimes they will send you an FTC (Federal Trade Commission) disclosure document which contains much of the same information. (See "Organizations," below). Consult with an attorney familiar with franchise agreements if you do decide to purchase a franchise.

Resources

Organizations

American Association of Franchisees and Dealers (AAFD)
P.O. Box 81887
San Diego, CA 92138-1887

"This is a national, nonprofit trade association serving the interests of prospective and current franchisees." Supports and promotes AAFD Fair Franchising Standards and Legislative Advocacy. Membership benefits include consultations with attorneys, accountants, special discounts, subscription to newsletter, and more. Write for more information.

The Women's Franchise Network
International Franchise Association
1350 New York Ave., Suite 900
Washington, DC 20005

Helps women understand the diverse opportunities that franchising offers them.

Public Reference Branch,
Federal Trade Commission
Washington, DC 20580

Provides a package of information about the FTC Franchise and Business Opportunity Rule free of charge.

Books

Franchise Bible: How to Buy a Franchise or Franchise Your Own Business by Erwin J. Keup. 1995, The Oasis Press/PSI Research, Grants Pass, OR.

The Franchise Fraud: How to Protect Yourself Before and After You Invest by Robert L. Purvin, American Association of Franchisees and Dealers. 1994, John Wiley & Sons, Inc., New York, NY.

Franchise Opportunities Handbook, Superintendent of Documents, U.S. Government Printing Office, P.O. Box 371954, Pittsburgh, PA 15250; $21.

Small Business Franchise Made Simple by William Lasher and Carl Hausman. 1994, Doubleday Company, Inc., New York, NY.

Direct Sales

In a distributorship or direct sales, you distribute or sell another manufacturer's products. Such companies as Mary Kay, Amway, and Shaklee sell their products this way. If you like being independent and selling a well-known product directly to people, you may want to look into these ventures.

Resources

The Direct Selling Association
1666 K St. NW, Suite 1010
Washington, DC 20006-2808

Send a SASE for information about any companies that you are considering representing in direct sales.

The Selling from Home Sourcebook: A Guide to Home-Based Business Opportunities in the Selling Industry by Kathryn Caputo. 1996, Betterway Books, Cincinnati, OH.

Multilevel Marketing

Multilevel marketing (MLM) is a form of a distributorship in which you sell products and services through a chain of independent distributors. You make your profits by selling your company's products and by having other people buy from you and, in turn, selling the products. You are paid a commission from what you sell and from what the distributors below you sell. Again, investigate these companies and their opportunities thoroughly before you invest any money in them. The Direct Selling Association (see "Resources" under "Direct Sales," above) can also send you pamphlets about pyramid schemes. Send them a SASE requesting this information.

Telecommuting

Telecommuting means making an arrangement with a company to work at home in some related work. If you are classified as an independent contractor, you may do work for more than one firm. Check with your accountant as to whether you are an employee or an independent contractor for tax purposes.

There are advantages to working at home: no commuting, flexible hours, being with family. But there are disadvantages as well: you have to be disciplined, you can feel isolated, and you can have multiple interruptions. Independent contractors also enjoy working at home, but they have to pay for their own insurance and other costs that an employee in a telecommuter arrangement does not have to pay. An independent contractor is just that—independent—which has its own benefits.

Read, talk to other telecommuters who are independent contractors, and get an idea of what their working lives are like. You may just end up with the best of both worlds.

Resources

The Telecommuter's Handbook: Earn a Living Without Going to the Office by Debra Schepp and Brad Schepp. 1996, The McGraw-Hill Companies, New York, NY.

The Virtual Office Survival Handbook: What Telecommuters and Entrepreneurs Need to Succeed in Today's Nontraditional

Workplace by Alice Bredin. 1996, John Wiley & Sons, Inc., New York, NY.

Scams

Unfortunately, with the growth of entrepreneurship comes a growth in scams in both small-business and home-based business opportunities. Some are outright fraudulent deals in which you pay something and get nothing in return. Others are more subtle, selling you equipment and software, but nothing else.

For example, one older woman and her husband took out a $15,000 second mortgage to buy a computer and programs to run several home-based computer businesses. They bought these from a company offering a number of home-based computer businesses. Unfortunately, this couple did no research in their community to see if there was a market for these business opportunities, and they did not know how to market these businesses because they had no experience or training in running a business. The company gave them no support. But this company's activity is not considered illegal, because what they sold the couple was a business opportunity, not the guarantee of making money. Another man spent $45,000 on software from a similar company, but also received little support or training.

The message is very clear: "Let the buyer beware!" Do not spend a single dollar on any business investment until you have thoroughly researched it. It may take time, but you will be better off for it. Here are some other signs that a company is running business-opportunity scams:

❖ They promise that you can run this business in your spare time and make huge profits.
❖ They will not give you the names of others who have invested in this business opportunity.
❖ They ask you for money for work-at-home sources.

6

Start-Up Checklist

You want to be a business owner, but just where and when do you start? Here is a suggested timetable and checklist. Remember, it is just a suggested list. You will follow your own timetable and list as your schedule and resources permit.

One Year to Six Months Before Start-Up

* Collect ideas of businesses that interest you; visit the library and bookstore for business books, magazines, and other related business publications for brainstorming.
* Assess your skills, life and work experiences, investment capabilities, and personal and family obligations, and relate them to your business idea(s).
* Attend courses, seminars, and workshops on entrepreneurship; go to women business owners' group meetings; see if your state publishes a guide for new entrepreneurs (check with a nearby Small Business Development Center or a state legislator).
* Work or volunteer in a business similar to the one you wish to start. Visit similar businesses in regions outside your area and see what does or does not appeal to you. If possible, talk to the owners and ask about the positive and negative aspects of their businesses.

Four to Six Months Before Start-Up

❖ Start writing your business plan: study your target customers and decide what specific products and services your business will be offering.

❖ Study your competition and their strong and weak points.

❖ Choose and consult with the experts you will be using for your business:

Insurance agent: coverage for the building, equipment, liability, bonding, health, disability, and so on.

Legal consultant: filing for a fictitious name, deciding on a legal structure.

Bookkeeper, accountant: setting up a record-keeping system, organizing tax information, determining start-up expenses.

Business consultants: marketing, computer, business plan.

❖ Decide whether your business will be home-based or on-site (in a commericial district). If it will be in your home, check on the zoning requirements (The American Planning Association, 122 South Michigan Ave., Suite 1600, Chicago, IL, 60603-6107 is a nonprofit city planning organization that offers publications on zoning issues, including those for small and home-based businesses). If it is on-site, investigate the best (and most affordable) business location; take into account any applicable fire, environmental, and safety codes.

❖ Get licensed. If you need a license, permit, or resale number, or to fulfill other requirements, start the process.

❖ Join networking organizations: trade, national, state, and local business associations.

❖ Decide whether the business will be part-time or full-time. Add up your living expenses and the costs for the business. If you are the sole supporter of your family, you will have to have a cushion of cash to cover your living expenses, or else you can opt to start part-time, on the side, until you can "quit your day job."

Three Months Before Start-Up to Opening Day

❖ Finalize your business plan and begin to implement your advertising and marketing strategies: press releases, opening promotions, talks, seminars, various types of advertising.

❖ Arrange financing, if needed, and set up a business checking account.

❖ Set up the office and its equipment.

❖ Have promotional materials printed: business cards and brochures, stationery, advertising specialties.

❖ Network with your trade associations, other business owners, and local business groups to let them know when and where you will be in business.

Conclusion

This is only a general checklist. Yours will be much more detailed and geared to your specific business. It is important to take your time and learn as much as you can about your business and the skills needed to conduct a business before you open for business. Yes, you will learn much more once your venture gets going, but the more homework you do and the more resources you gather, the better prepared you will be for the ups and downs you are likely to experience as a business owner.

7

Resources

It is important to network with other women business owners. As mentioned before, other women business owners, either affiliated with an established group or on an informal basis, can provide a wealth of information. Many of these women both barter with and use the services of other women's businesses. A very strong bond can be formed this way, and it is one way to keep from feeling isolated, especially in a one-person business.

See also the section "For More Information" in each chapter, as well as the "General Resources" section at the back of this book.

Start-Up Books

How to Start a Business Without Quitting Your Job: The Moonlight Entrepreneur's Guide by Phillip Holland. 1992, Ten Speed Press, Berkeley, CA.

How to Start & Manage Your Own Business by Jerre G. Lewis and Leslie D. Renn. 1991, Lewis & Renn Associates, Interlochen, MI.

How to Start Your Own Business, Keep Your Books, Pay Your Taxes, and Stay Out of Trouble by Bernard Kamoroff. 1993, Bell Springs Publishing, Laytonville, CA.

Mid-Career Entrepreneur: How to Start a Business and Be Your Own Boss by Joseph Mancuso. 1993, Dearborn Financial Publishing, Inc., Chicago, IL.

Running a One-Person Business by Claude Whitmyer and Salli Rasberry. 1996, Ten Speed Press, Berkeley, CA.

The Small Business Start-Up Guide by Hal Root and Steve Koenig. 1995, Sourcebooks, Inc., Naperville, IL.

The Smart Woman's Guide to Starting a Business by Vickie Montgomery. 1994, Career Press, Franklin Lakes, NJ.

Start-Up: An Entrepreneur's Guide to Launching and Managing a New Business, 3rd ed., by William J. Stolze. 1994, Career Press, Franklin Lakes, NJ.

The Start-Up Guide: A One-Year Plan for Entrepreneurs by David H. Bangs, Jr. 1995, Upstart Publishing Company, Dover, NH.

Start Your Own Business for $1,000 or Less by Will Davis. 1994, Upstart Publishing Company, Dover, NH.

Steps to Small Business Start-Up by Linda Pinson and Jerry Jennett. 1995, Upstart Publishing Company, Dover, NH.

A Step-by-Step Guide to Starting and Running Your Own Business by Ted Nicholas. 1995, Upstart Publishing Company, Dover, NH.

A Woman's Guide to Starting a Business, 2nd ed., by Laurie B. Zuckerman. 1995, Upstart Publishing Company, Dover, NH.

A Woman's Guide to Starting Her Own Business: How to Turn Talent into Profit by Cynthia Smith. 1994, Carol Publishing Group, New York, NY.

Entrepreneur Magazine Group,
2392 Morse Ave.
P.O. Box 57050
Irvine, CA 92619-7050

Many business and idea guides for specific businesses, including *The Entrepreneurial Woman's Guide, Small Business Encyclopedia,* and others helpful to the new entrepreneur. Call (800) 421-2300 for a "Small Business Development Catalog."

Business Idea Books

100 Best Retirement Businesses by Lisa Angowski Rogak. 1994, Upstart Publishing Company, Dover, NH.

199 Great Home Businesses You Can Start (and Succeed In) for $1,000 by Tyler Hicks. 1993, Prima Publishing, Rocklin, CA.

The Best Home Businesses for the 90's, 2nd ed., by Paul and Sarah Edwards. 1994, Jeremy P. Tarcher/Putnam Books, New York, NY.

1,001 Business Profit Making Ideas. Success Publications, 3419 Dunham Road, Box 263, Warsaw, NY 14569; $7 booklet.

Finding Your Perfect Work: The New Career Guide to Making a Living, Creating a Life by Paul and Sarah Edwards. 1996, Putnam Publishing Group, New York, NY.

The Ideal Entrepreneurial Business for You by Glenn Desmond and Monica Faulkner. 1995, John Wiley & Sons, Inc., New York, NY.

Miscellaneous

Office Clutter Cure by Don Aslett. 1995, Betterway Books, Cincinnati, OH.

Checklists and Operating Forms for Small Businesses, 19th ed., by John C. Wisdom. 1995, John Wiley & Sons, Inc., New York.

Pacific Bell has worked with the SBA to publish an annual magazine, *Small Business Success.* It is free, and it helps entrepreneurs with business planning and other concerns. It has an excellent listing of resources in the back of the magazine. Call (800) 848-8000 to receive an issue.

Part II

YOUR
BUSINESS PLAN

⚹8⚹

What Is a Business Plan?

This part of the book discusses the components of a business plan. Why is a business plan so important? A business plan is a combination of statements and figures that tells you what your business is, what it does, where you want to go, and what financing you will need to consider. A business plan gives you a direction in which to take your business. It is your road map to guide and steer your business on the right path.

Business plans can run from 20 to 60 pages long. Charts, diagrams, ad samples, and product photos can all enhance a plan and help you be more effective in getting financial help. You do not need to be a business expert to write a business plan, and there are plenty of resources available if you need assistance: business plan consultants, small-business development centers, books, and software (see "Business Plan Resources," at the end of this chapter).

Even if you do not plan on opening a business for a year or two, you should write a business plan now. It will give you a better idea of how much your start-up costs will be and what steps you will have to take before you officially open for business. Most importantly, the market research involved in a business plan will help you determine if there are customers who will want or need your business in your area. You can have the greatest business idea in the world, but without any customers, it will never succeed. A business plan is not just for start-up purposes. Regularly reviewing and updating your business plan will keep you from being sidetracked from the main goals you established in the beginning. Thus, creating the business plan may be the most important step in starting a new business, so take your time to do a thorough job. It will help to guarantee your business success.

Business Plan Resources

Books

Anatomy of a Business Plan, 3rd ed., by Linda Pinson and Jerry Jinnet. 1996, Upstart Publishing Co., Dover, NH.

Business Planning Guide, 2nd ed., by David H. Bangs, Jr. 1995, Upstart Publishing, Co., Dover, NH.

Business Plans Handbook, 2nd vol., by Gale Research, 1996, Detroit, MI. Twenty-four business plans.

How to Write a Business Plan by Mike McKeenen. 1994, Nolo Press, Berkeley, CA.

The Total Business Plan, 2nd ed., by Patrick D. O'Hara, Ph.D. 1994, John Wiley & Sons, Inc., New York, NY.

Your First Business Plan, 2nd ed., by Joseph Covello and Brian Hazelgren. 1996, Sourcebooks, Inc., Naperville, IL.

Federal Government

Business Plans for Small Manufacturers, Construction, Retail, Service and Home-Based Businesses. SBA Publications, P.O. Box 4651, Denver, CO 80201-0031.

U.S. Small Business Administration: (800) 827-5722; or on the World Wide Web at *http://www.sbaonline.sba.gov.* Get the numbers for the nearest SBA office, SBDC, or relevant state agency.

SCORE (Service Corps of Retired Executives) has chapters around the U.S. Call the SBA for the office nearest you.

Business Plan Software

Jian
1975 El Camino Real
Mountain View, CA 94040

Microsoft Corporation
One Microsoft Way
Redmond, WA 98052-6399
(800) 426-9400

Palo Alto Software
144 E. 14th Ave.
Eugene, OR 97401
"Business Plan Pro" or "Business Plan Toolkit."

9

Your Business Description

Your business plan needs to contain a detailed description and summary of what your business is and does. In the first few drafts of your business plan, you will specify what tasks or services your business will perform, or products your business will create. Later, after you have completed your plan, you will be better able to give an overview of your business, as the plan will better define your business' goals. Your business description can help you concentrate on certain target markets and not try to be "all things to all customers." It will also be important to people such as a banker who is evaluating your business plan for a possible loan.

Of course, as mentioned in previous chapters, your business description may totally or partially change according to who actually become your customers, or there may be a directional shift in the products or services that you produce. No matter what direction your business takes, though, you still need a basic description from which to start.

Product or Service? Your Niche

When you are brainstorming for business ideas, ask yourself whether you want your business to sell a product or a service. A product, such as a handicraft or food, will typically require more of an investment because you need to purchase supplies to produce your product, or purchase and warehouse the product. In a service business, you are the business; you help individuals or other businesses accomplish tasks that they either do not have the time or resources to do.

Usually, a service business costs less to get started, and can show a profit faster than a product-based business. Remember, though, that either type of business will take from six months to two years to make money, so be prepared with savings, a part-time job, a back-up job, or a loan or grant to help support you until you make a profit.

Once you have decided whether to sell products or services, you have to find your "business niche"—what your business can offer that no others can. Better customer service, personal delivery, money-back guarantees, and free estimates are all ways to attract customers from larger businesses.

Your business niche also pertains to a market not yet tapped. For example, craft supply houses often require a minimum order of a certain size from wholesale customers, making it difficult for the beginning crafter to buy. You could offer a no-minimum-order policy with next-day service for those "little" persons.

In the service-business realm, larger companies may not want to do smaller jobs for individual customers, but prefer to work with other companies. Your service could pick up those consumers, often with referrals from the big companies. Thorough market research (see Chapter 10) will help you determine who your customers are and where your business niche will be.

Business Structure

There are four basic business structures from which you can choose in setting up your business:

Sole Proprietorship

You are the sole owner of the business, which also means that you are responsible for all aspects of your business, including any liabilities and debts that your business may incur.

Partnership

You may want to enter into a partnership for the advantages of sharing work and costs, but each of you will then be responsible for debts and other responsibilities of the business. You should have a written contract defining each partner's responsibilities and the terms of dissolution in case one of the partners decides to pull out.

Incorporation

Many businesses start out as sole proprietorships and later become incorporated as their growth warrants it. A separate legal entity is created by incorporating, which decreases your personal liability, but regulations, taxes, and organizational costs may increase.

Limited Liability Company

This a newer trend that limits liability like a corporation, but allows you to take advantage of partnership tax considerations. If you are in doubt as to which structure is best for your business, consult an accountant and/or a business dictionary.

Business Goals

Norman Vincent Peale once said, "A dream plus a plan equals a goal." Listing your business goals is good, but listing the specific steps you plan to take to reach those goals is better. Be specific but realistic. Saying that you want to have a desktop publishing business making $100,000 a year is a nice goal, but you have to plan to take desktop publishing courses if needed, get financing to purchase your basic equipment, find your customers, and produce the work before you ever make your first dollar in profit. Set little goals upon little goals; they are more attainable, and will give you the incentive to accomplish more. Small successes will build upon one another to help you realize that dream.

Selecting a Business Name

What's in a name? Quite a bit, when it comes to selecting a name for your business. It is important to make your business name:

Unique
Make your name stand out from those of other similar businesses.

Descriptive
Your name should tell potential customers what you do ("Computer Tutor," for example).

Simple
Do not make your business name too long.

Easy to Recall
One or two words or initials make it easier for your customers to remember you.

A Good Fit
Your name should fit your business without being too cute or ridiculous, unless your type of business warrants it. "Whoopsie & Daisy" is appropriate for the two women who run this clowning business. But a more serious-minded

business name should be given to an accounting service, for example, and should befit its nature.

Legal

Your name should be original. Check local telephone books, consult your county clerk and state commerce office, or get advice from an attorney who is familiar with registering business names and performing trademark searches. You may also want to protect a logo associated with your name. Online services such as Genie and CompuServe offer trademark and trade-name databases if you wish to do the searches yourself.

Register your business name and get a certificate of doing business under an assumed name, or DBA ("doing business as ..."). Check to see if your state requires you to register your business name whether you are operating under another name or not.

Business Cards

After you have decided on a name, you will want to design business cards, which are one of the best (and least expensive) ways to start advertising your business. You can hire a local graphic artist to help you design yours and then take the design to a local print shop. Or you can use software, pre-designed papers from paper supply companies, or books with royalty-free designs.

Resources

Books

Names That Sell: How to Create Great Names for Your Business by Fred Barrett. 1995, Alder Press, Portland, OR.

Trademark: How to Name Your Business & Product, 2nd ed., by Stephen Elias. 1996, Nolo Press, Berkeley, CA.

1,000 + Stationery Designs by Val Cooper. 1991, Point Pacific Press, Hollywood, CA. Design tips plus royalty-free logos and symbols.

Paper Companies
Idea Art
(800) 433-2278

Company Colors
NEBS, Inc.
500 Main St.
Groton, MA 10471
(508) 448-6111

Software
"Easy Business Cards for Windows," Claris, (408) 727-8227.
"My Advanced Brochures, Mailers & More: CD for Windows,"
MySoftware Co., (415) 473-3600.

🔅 10 🔅

Marketing

Market Research

This may just be the most important part of your business plan. It will define where your market is and just who your potential customers are. You can find this information in several ways:

Primary Resources

You can contact potential customers through direct-mail questionnaires, telemarketing, or personal interviews. Networking with local business groups and even friends and family can give you feedback as to the suitability of your business in your community.

Secondary Resources

These include:

❖ Public sources of statistical and demographic information found through local, state, and federal data books, statistical abstracts, and studies, often found in the reference sections of public libraries.

❖ Trade sources, such as your specific business trade association, and research firms, found in *Encyclopedia of Associations,* by Gale Reseach.

❖ Studies conducted by universities and colleges. Searches on the Internet can bring you many research studies on specific businesses.

Your Marketing Plan

First, let's distinguish between marketing and advertising. Marketing is determining where and to whom you will sell your goods or services. Advertising is the method you will use to publicly acquaint your customers with your goods or services in order to get them to buy what your business is offering.

After you do adequate market research, you want to evaluate the information you have gathered, set business goals and objectives, then plan your marketing strategy. Start with target advertising (advertising to the customer most likely to buy your products or services) you can afford, then evaluate the customer response after several months. If that advertising approach wasn't productive, try another tactic or consult a marketing adviser. There are free resources available through the Service Corps of Retired Executives (SCORE) or local Small Business Development Centers (SBDCs) (see "General Resources," at the end of this book).

Resources

Do-It-Yourself Marketing Research, 3rd ed., by George Edward Breen. 1989, McGraw-Hill, New York, NY.

Marketing Research, 5th ed., by David A. Aaker and George S. Day. 1995, John Wiley & Sons, Inc., New York, NY. An 800-page marketing book that may be found at colleges offering business degrees.

Marketing on a Shoestring: Low-Cost Tips for Marketing Your Products or Services, 2nd ed., by Jeff Davidson. 1994, John Wiley & Sons, Inc., New York, NY.

Grow Your Business with Desktop Marketing by Steve Morgenstern. 1996. Order through *Home Office Computing*, Box 10214, Dept. 77507, Des Moines, IA 50380-0214, or call (800) 411-7354.

Advertising and Sales

Start with the free or low-cost advertising methods: press releases, referrals, business cards, flyers, donations to charity events, and so on, and then with ads targeted to your market.

Track any paid advertising with a code, or ask customers where they heard about your business. Try local and national advertising, and then evaluate and plan your advertising budget based on those results.

Some Other Effective Advertising Methods

Trade Shows

The right trade show can be well worth the investment. Research the trade shows that would be best for your business. When you have decided on the best shows for you, send out pre-show mailings to people on your mailing list and be sure to follow up on any leads you get during the shows.

Newsletters

A promotional newsletter to your customer mailing list can keep your business in your customers' minds, give them tips on how to use your products or services, and alert them to upcoming sales or new products.

Résumés

A résumé can help your new business by stating your business philosophy, your qualifications, and your experience. It can project your confidence in your ability to complete a job, or substantiate your claims of being an expert. If you are

selling a product, your customer may be interested in the
"story" behind your item, and what training and education
enabled you to be able to create it.

Resources

Books

Advertising for a Small Business Made Simple by Bernard Ryan,
Jr. 1996, Doubleday, Inc., New York, NY.

*The Advertising Handbook for Small Business: Make a Big Impact
with a Small Budget,* 2nd ed., by Dell Dennison. 1994, Self-
Counsel Press, Bellingham, WA.

How to Get the Most out of Trade Shows by Steve Miller. 1995.
NTC Business Books, (800) 323-4900.

The Internet Business Primer by Wayne Allison. 1995, Sourcebooks, Napierville, IL.

Power Networking: 55 Secrets for Personal & Professional Success
by Donna Fisher and Sandy Vilas. 1991, Discovery Seminars, Houston, TX.

*Six Steps to Free Publicity: And Dozens of Other Ways to Win
Free Media Attention for You or Your Business* by Marcia
Yudkin. 1995, Plume/Penguin, New York, NY.

Trade Shows Worldwide, 1996 by Gale Research, Detroit, MI;
trade shows, show organizers, conventions.

Miscellaneous

Jeffrey Lant Associates
P.O. Box 38-2767
Cambridge, MA 02238
Jeffrey Lant sells publications and reports on advertising;
write for a catalog.

Trade Show Bureau
1660 Lincoln St., Suite 2080
Denver, CO 80264
This is the trade show industry association; it publishes *A Guide
to the U.S. Exposition Industry.* Send a SASE for information.

◢ 11 ◣

Financial
Considerations

Projected Income

Based on your market research, estimated customer response, costs, and so on, you can come up with a projected income for the next six months or longer. A potential lender will be interested in this to see if you are able to make loan payments. Keep careful records to substantiate this.

Additional Costs

In addition to equipment, rental, and promotional materials, do not neglect to include the following when you estimate your start-up costs:

* Reference books—how-to, pricing, and ethics guides.
* Association membership fees—important for networking, accreditation, industry updates, etc.
* Insurance—medical, life, accident, disability, liability, bonding requirements.
* Consultant/expert fees—budget for these in case they are needed in a crisis.

❖ Taxes—local, state, and federal.

❖ Loan payments—include credit card and loan payments in your monthly expenses.

Setting Prices

How to set prices is one of the most difficult decisions in starting a new business. You are afraid that potential customers will be frightened off if your prices are too high, but if you set your prices too low, your business will fail. A successful business professional continually monitors operating expenses, incoming revenue, and profit in order to evaluate pricing strategies, and other business decisions.

There are several ways to come up with a price for your product or service:

❖ Industry guidelines and standards—check with your business trade association for any rate-setting guides they may have.

❖ Location—being in an urban versus a rural area will affect prices.

❖ Competition—how much competition you have in your area and what they charge will guide you in setting rates, as well as indicating the demand for your services.

❖ Break-even point—using formulas found in such books as *Homemade Money*, 5th edition, by Barbara Brabec (1994, Betterway Books, Cincinatti, OH), and *Working from Home* by Paul and Sarah Edwards (Jeremy Tarcher/Putnam, New York), as well as SBA government booklets, can help you work out your final price.

Factors such as materials costs, your time, your profit percentage, and your overhead will all work together to determine your prices. Keeping up with your bookkeeping on a regular basis is also essential to tell you if you are making money or not.

Pricing for Profits is a report by Judy Smith that was written for sewing and craft businesses, but it is a good source for general product pricing as well. Send a SASE for listings to Success Publications, 3419 Dunham, Box 263, Warsaw, NY 14569.

Production

If you have a product-related business, you will have to make sure that your production can keep up with your demand without compromising quality. If you have a service business, you will have to estimate how long it will take you to complete a project or job. This will also help you set your prices and adjust them as needed. Some business owners charge by the hour or charge a flat fee for a service business. For a product business, the time required to make the product, plus your time as the producer, are also factored in your prices. A flat fee is often quoted so potential customers have some estimate of what a job will cost them.

Getting Financing

This is still one of the biggest obstacles for many women entrepreneurs to overcome. Thankfully, because of the number of women who are starting businesses, lenders and government sources are starting to realize that women are good financial risks. After you have totaled your estimated start-up costs, here are some financing methods you may want to explore:

The Government

Check with your state and SBA offices for loan programs for women, minorities, and persons with disabilities.

Credit Cards

Use credit cards at the beginning of a month, and you will have 30 days to pay back the amount if you wish. If you cannot, make regular payments and try to pay off the debt as soon as you can to reduce the amount of interest you will be paying.

Bank Loans
Go with a bank that is friendly to women and small businesses. Ask other women entrepreneurs in your area where they went for financing.

Personal Assets
Sell or borrow against personal assets and bank certificates.

Moonlighting
Get a part-time job and set aside whatever you can in a separate savings account. It will be an added bonus to you in terms of work experience if you get a job in the same industry in which you want to start a business.

Family or Friends
To prevent hard feelings, borrow from them only if you can work up a contract or loan payment plan. Sometimes you can also get your inheritance early.

Investment Companies, Nonprofit Groups, or Foundations
Seek venture capitalists (individuals who provide capital in return for a percentage of your profits or your business), or look into groups or foundations that give grants or low-cost loans for start-ups and small businesses.

Borrow from Insurance Policies, IRAs
Check with your insurance agent, or look into the policies regarding borrowing from your mutual funds or retirement account.

Bartering

Bartering for goods and services is one way to conserve cash and get needed products and services. For many business owners, bartering helps to expand their markets, increases their buying power, and increases the number of customers who pay cash by helping to spread the word about your business. For more information, send a SASE to the International Reciprocal Trade Association (IRTA), 6305 Hawaii Ct., Alexandria, VA 22314.

Resources

Office of Financial Assistance
U.S. Small Business Administration
409 Third St. SW
Washington, DC 20416
Can give advice about various available loans.

Small Business Development Centers (SBDCs)
1300 Chainbridge Rd.
McClean, VA 22101-3967
Or check your local telephone directory for the nearest SBDC.

Finding Money: The Small Business Guide to Financing by Kate Lister. 1995, John Wiley & Sons, Inc., New York, NY.
Free Money: For Small Business and Entrepreneurs by Laurie Blum. 1995, John Wiley & Sons, Inc., New York, NY.
"Smart Women, Foolish Bankers," *Working Woman.* March 1996, p. 29. This article discusses the problems of women entrepreneurs in getting financing, and lists a number of useful programs designated to help women get business funding. Look in the magazine index in your local library to find it.

Women's Collateral Worldwide
1529 Walnut St., 4th Floor
Philadelphia, PA 19102
(215) 564-2800
The group's mission is to provide access to qualified woman-owned or woman-led businesses, and to provide products and services to support those businesses. Publishes *The WCF Women's Business Directory*™. For women business owners in such cities as Philadelphia, Washington, D.C., San Francisco, Boston, Houston, Columbus, and other major U.S. cities.

Part III

BUSINESSES

This part of the book features both traditional and non-traditional businesses for women. This is the nineties, after all, and women should not stop themselves from entering into a particular venture just because it is not a traditional women's business (which should apply to men as well!). You must follow your interests and pursue what you really enjoy doing. That's what is so great about being your own boss: you get to do the work you like best with the bonus of getting paid for it. True, business owners typically work more hours than they would for an employer, but it is still your choice whether to work or not.

One of the biggest obstacles for women in starting a business, besides financing, is overcoming their fears. "What if I fail? Am I really qualified to start a business? What if people laugh at my idea?" These and many other self-doubts assail women, often more than men. In my opinion, part of this is to be blamed on our society, which lauds only the winners and not those who strive but sometimes falter. In school, we are punished with failing grades and considered less intelligent if we do not score well on that system's tests.

Time and time again, the ones who succeed in this life are those who persist despite some failures along the way. As a former special-education teacher, I always say: failure is not bad; it only becomes a detriment to us if we fail to learn from our mistakes. Prepare yourself as thoroughly as possible for your venture, but realize that you will make mistakes. Fortunately, there are experts, networking friends, and others who can help you through those business blunders.

To keep your business current and alive, stay informed about the latest business trends in your trade and keep improving your skills and knowledge. This will both help prevent mistakes from occurring, and help develop your self-confidence, which is vital. If your customers perceive that you have confidence in your capabilities, then they will have more confidence in you.

Even if your customers should present you with challenges (and they will!), you will learn to tap your network of resources to find solutions to meet their demands. If it turns out that your business cannot help them, be ready to give them referrals to people who can. Many will appreciate your honesty, and often return to you for products or services that you *can* deliver. In turn, businesses to which you refer customers may return the favor and refer customers to you. You, the other businesses in your network, and the customers can then all be satisfied.

Just never forget that the customers really are first and foremost. Listen to what they want, supply what they need, and you will be successful. You have heard this advice many times, but one of the reasons people have patronized small businesses over the years is for that personal attention—something that Big Business says it does, but when was the last time you talked to the CEO of a major retailer when you had a complaint?

As the owner of your own business, *you* will be the CEO, president, and decision-maker—something to remind yourself when you talk to the executives of companies with which you do business. You are the head of your business, just as they are, but you do not need to call a board meeting to make major decisions!

Remember, too, that this is not a complete listing of all the small businesses that women do. You may discover a business niche that no one has yet filled. No matter which venture you choose, it takes an inner drive to want to succeed—a "fire in the belly," as the popular saying goes—but if you do not give up, you will become the proud owner of a business!

If the opportunity comes along to help another entrepreneur, do not hesitate to give her some words of encouragement or a few helpful tips. Believe me, it really does come back to you if ever the time comes when you have to turn to someone for help. The following 101-plus small businesses cover a wide range of small ventures that women can run. Some may only earn part-time money, while others can earn quite a bit. In most cases, businesses start slowly and expand as the demand for a product or service warrants it. Some of the following businesses may seem a little odd for a woman to run—especially the ones traditionally run by men—but to the women who own them there is nothing peculiar at all in what they do.

All the best wishes for success in whatever entrepreneurial ventures you may decide to undertake!

Features of the Businesses

Each business profile in this book will contain most of the following details, depending on what information was available. I cannot possibly include all the information that exists on each business, but I have attempted to provide the basics to assist you in getting started in the business that interests you the most.

Description of the Business

Describes the activities involved in conducting the business featured.

Start-Up Costs

Estimated costs to start the business.

Pricing Guidelines

Gives an idea about what to charge for business services or products.

Marketing and Advertising Methods and Tips

Offers suggestions for bringing in customers.

Essential Equipment
Lists basic materials and equipment needed for the business.

Recommended Training, Experience, or Skills
Describes the knowledge, background, and/or training needed, as well as tips for gaining experience.

Income Potential
Estimates the potential earnings for the business featured (hourly, annually).

Best Customers
Gives an idea who is most likely to purchase your goods and/or services.

Helpful Tips
Advice from business owners to help make you successful.

Franchises
Lists of related franchises and/or business opportunities.

For More Information
Where available, lists publications, books, trade associations, home-study courses, business start-up guides, and other helpful resources related to this business.

Please note: many associations do not have start-up business information, but rather exist for membership networking. Where requested, please send a self-addressed, stamped envelope (SASE) to insure a reply to any information requests you may make. Many associations are nonprofit and are staffed by volunteers.

Additional Business Ideas
Lists any related business ventures.

Animal-Related Businesses

AQUARIUM SERVICES

In this business, you set up fish aquariums for individuals and businesses, and make periodic visits to clean and care for the tanks and fish.

Start-Up Costs
$1,000 for basic equipment—more if you want to purchase a computer for record keeping or other general business equipment.

Pricing Guidelines
❖ $30/hr for the first hour and $25/hr for each additional hour for maintenance. No charge to set up if they buy the aquarium and supplies from you. If they buy the equipment elsewhere, charge them your standard hourly rate.
❖ Any extra pads or chemicals used for each visit incurs an added charge.

Marketing and Advertising Methods and Tips
Yellows Page listings; flyers in pet stores; word-of-mouth referrals; classified ads in newspapers; exhibits at local business expos and pet shows.

Essential Equipment
Sponges, filter pads, hoses, nets, buckets, extra aquarium equipment and parts, a vehicle to haul equipment, and tanks if they order from you.

Recommended Training, Experience, or Skills
* Read reference books.
* Have your own aquarium.
* Work in one or more pet shops with fish aquariums so that you know how to care for the fish, clean the tanks, and learn who the suppliers are.

Income Potential
* $8,000 per year part time.
* $20,000 to $28,000 per year full time.

Best Customers
* Individuals
* Business offices
* Professionals with waiting rooms
* Retirement home reception rooms
* College offices

Helpful Tips
* Know your fish.
* Work in the industry and read books on the care of the fish and tanks.
* Sell aquariums and equipment; let your customers tell you what they want, and order it for them at a better price than the commercial pet stores.
* Know how to set up both fresh- and saltwater fish aquariums.

For More Information

Books

The Complete Aquarium by Peter Scott. 1995, Dorling Kindersley Publishing, Inc., New York, NY.

The Complete Aquarium Problem-Solver: A Total Trouble-Shooting Guide for Freshwater and Marine Animals by Kevin W. Boyd. 1992, Tetra Press, Blacksburg, VA.

Complete Fishkeeper: Everything Aquarium Fishes Need to Stay Happy, Healthy and Alive by Joseph S. Levine. 1995, William Morrow & Company, New York, NY.

Live-Bearing Fishes: A Guide to Their Aquarium Care, Biology and Classification by John Dawes. 1996, Sterling Publishing Company, Inc., New York, NY.

Looking After Freshwater Fish by David Alderton. 1996, Sterling Publishing Company, New York, NY.

Marine Aquarium Keeping, 2nd ed., by Stephen H. Spotte. 1993, John Wiley & Sons, New York, NY.

Periodicals and Publications

Aquarium Fish Magazine: A magazine on aquariums, tropical fish, ponds, and pond fish: $24.97 per year, 12 issues. Call (800) 365-4421 to order.

Tetra Press
3001 Commerce St.
Blacksburg, VA 24060
Tetra Press publishes many fish and aquarium care guides. See your local pet store or write for catalog.

Additional Business Ideas

"Pondscaping;" ornamental pond installation and/or maintenance services for homeowners and businesses. Contact landscapers. (See "Still More Green Business Ideas.")

◢ 2 ◣

"FOR THE BIRDS"

This business is for a true bird watcher or lover of wild birds. It is estimated by *WildBird* magazine that some 66 million people feed, photograph, or watch wild birds. As more of our country's land is developed, people miss the contact with nature. Many travel to parks or wildlife sanctuaries to see birds and animals that once were in our backyards.

Since Rachel Carson's book, *Silent Spring*, was published, people have become more aware of our vanishing wildlife and natural resources. Public and cable television wildlife documentaries over the past three decades have also helped to educate and interest people in wildlife. Programs like the "Backyard Habitat Program" sponsored by the National Wildlife Federation have encouraged people to set up "mini-habitats" so they can observe wildlife on their own property.

A wild bird store gives people the opportunity to purchase quality products to make their yards more "wildlife friendly."

Start-Up Costs
$20,000 to $55,000

Pricing Guidelines
Retail businesses generally operate on a narrow profit margin; 5 percent is the norm, but you must continually monitor sales revenue, operating expenses, and profit. (See "Small Shops" and "General Resources"). With a hobby such as birding, many people are willing to pay for good-quality products that will last.

Essential Equipment
❖ Inventory: bird equipment, feeders, seed, birding optics, houses, books, magazines, etc.
❖ Computer for inventory, billing, customer listings.
❖ Cash register, bags, other standard retail equipment.

Marketing and Advertising Methods and Tips

✤ Word of mouth.

✤ Sponsor bird talks and/or workshops.

✤ Give local tours.

✤ Put flyers in local penny-saver papers.

✤ Have tables at mall shows.

✤ Place flyers at local nature centers, parks, and garden centers.

✤ Take out classified and display ads.

✤ Send out an informative newsletter based on your customer mailing list; it will help establish you as an authority, and promote your business.

Recommended Training, Experience, or Skills

It helps to have a basic background in birding, especially covering those common to your area. Read birding books, subscribe to birding magazines. Enroll in ornithology courses at a local community college. Join any local birding groups.

Income Potential

Depends on the demand. Potential $25,000 to $50,000 per year.

Best Customers

Well-educated, married, owners of single-family homes, ages 30 and up.

Helpful Tips

Sell quality products at reasonable prices. Be knowledgeable about feeds, feeders, which are best for each species. Have handy tips for both new and experienced birders.

Franchises

Wild Bird Centers of America, Inc.
7687 MacArthur Blvd.
Cabin John, MD 20818

Start-up costs range from $75,000 to $131,000, including the franchise license fee.

For More Information

Associations
American Birding Association
P.O. Box 6599
Colorado Springs, CO 80934-6599
For membership information, call (800) 850-2473; for whole-sale and retail catalogs, call (800) 634-7736.

Periodicals and Publications
Bird Watcher's Digest
P.O. Box 110
Marietta, OH 45750-9962
$18.95 per year, 6 issues.

WildBird
P.O. Box 52897
Boulder, CO 80323-2898
$23.97 per year, 12 issues

Books
Birdhouses: Unique Woodworking Projects for Houses and Feeders by Mark Ramirez. 1996, Storey Communications, Pownal, VT.
Backyard Birdfeeding by John F. Gardner. 1996, Stackpole Books, Mechanicsburg, PA.

Backyard Habitat Information
The National Wildlife Federation
310 Tyson Dr.
Winchester, VA 22603
Write to request the price of the backyard habitat packet.

Additional Business Ideas
❖ Sell your designed birdhouses and feeders to nature and bird stores, feed centers, farm centers, and nursery and garden centers, and at flea markets,.
❖ Have a mail-order catalog of bird and nature supplies (see "Mail Order," in "General Resources").

⚐ 3 ⚑

CAT BOARDING AND GROOMING

Pets Are Inn franchise says: "54 million American households own a pet, with 78 percent of those taking vacations annually." *Cats Magazine* reports that research by the American Pet Products Manufacturer's Association shows that there are 59.4 million cats in the U.S., with 28.3 million households owning an average of two cats. Cats have special needs, and you can offer overnight care as well as grooming services. You can also sell various cat products to the owners.

Start-Up Costs
+ $250 to $2,000 if you board and groom them in your home.
+ $10,000 to $20,000 and up if you have a separate building or shop.

Pricing Guidelines
Follow association guidelines; compare going rates of other kennels and groomers in your area.

Essential Equipment
Scissors, brushes, combs, grooming tables, hair products, crates, assorted food dishes, beds, scratching posts, etc. (See catalog listed below.)

Marketing and Advertising Methods and Tips
+ Classified or display ads.
+ Tables at pet and cat shows.
+ Flyers in veterinarians' offices and pet supply stores.
+ Word-of-mouth referrals from satisfied cat owners.

Recommended Training, Experience, or Skills
A love of cats and experience in handling them as your own pets or working in a veterinarian's office, animal shelter, or

grooming facility, or preparing cats for shows. You must have a thorough understanding of cat behavior.

Income Potential
$17,000 to $30,000 for a sole owner. $35,000 and up with an assistant.

Best Customers
Cat owners, especially owners of cats with special grooming needs.

Helpful Tips
❖ Keep your facilities sanitary and odor-free.
❖ Have a veterinarian on call for any emergencies. Know what immunizations are needed before a cat can be boarded.
❖ Have any necessary licenses from local and state agencies.
❖ Check with your insurance agent and lawyer for the proper insurance and liability coverage.
❖ Pamper the pets in your care and treat them with special care.

Franchises
Pets Are Inn
7723 Tanglewood Ct., Suite 150
Minneapolis, MN 55439
Pets are cared for in carefully screened "Host Families." 90 percent of the pets are dogs, 9 percent are cats, 1 percent others. Write for more information.

For More Information
Associations
(Send SASE for more information)
American Boarding Kennels Association
4575 Galley Rd., Suite #400-A
Colorado Springs, CO 80915
Nonprofit trade association. Sponsors animal boarding education programs. Offers accreditation and a publication on designing and operating kennels. $155 per year dues.

American Cat Fanciers Association
P.O. Box 203
Point Lookout, MO 65726
Sets competition standards; members receive bulletin; $30 per year dues. Send SASE for more information.

Books
The American Animal Hospital Associations Encyclopedia of Cat Health & Care by Les Sussman. 1994, Hearst Books, New York, NY.
The Complete Book of Cat Care by Jan Olivi. 1994, Book Sales, Inc., Edison, NJ.
Complete Cat Book: Expert Advice on Every Phase of Cat Ownership by Gebhardt. 1995, Howell Book House, Inc., New York, NY.
Kennels and Kenneling by Joel M. McMains. 1994, Howell Book House, Inc., New York, NY.

Business Guide
"Pet Sitting & Grooming"; $39.95 + $5 for shipping and handling; (800) 947-7724.

Periodicals and Publications
Cat Fancy, $25.97 per year, 12 issues; Call (800) 365-4421 to order.

Cats Magazine
P.O. Box 290037
Port Orange, FL 32129
$21.97 per year, 12 issues.

Additional Business Ideas
Care and boarding of birds, reptiles, and/or other exotic pets.

⚞ 4 ⚟

FARRIER

The United States Department of Agriculture has estimated that there are nearly 10 million horses in the U.S. today. Farriers (blacksmiths, horseshoers, and platers) are responsible for the care and treatment of these horses' feet and lower legs. While this is still a male-dominated career, there are women farriers all over the country who love their craft and the horses they shoe.

Start-Up Costs
Though some farriers still have a blacksmith shop where horses are brought for work, most farriers travel to their customers' barns to do the shoeing, so a van, pickup truck, or trailer is fitted as a mobile blacksmith shop.

* $1,000 to $5,000 and up for basic equipment.
* Cost of schooling.
* Cost of a vehicle to be equipped with the necessary equipment.

Pricing Guidelines
The American Farrier's Association (AFA) says rates may range from $5 for simple trimming, to $26–$48 for normal shoeing, to $35–$75 for gaited horses, to even more for handmade and special work.

Essential Equipment
A wide variety of hand and mechanized tools such as: a small furnace for heating metal; a pyrometer (measures temperature); tongs, hardy, pritchel, measuring devices, swedge block, forepunch, acetylene torch, rasps, files, hoof ointments, grinder, leather apron, goggles, steel-tipped shoes, and other tools as needed for the trade.

Marketing and Advertising Methods and Tips
* Word-of-mouth advertising from satisfied customers.
* Referrals from other farriers, including those you have assisted.

✤ Referrals from veterinarians.
✤ Ads in local classified and free newspapers and the Yellow Pages.
✤ A booth at a local horse show.
✤ Direct mail to local riding clubs and stables.

Recommended Training, Experience, or Skills
✤ Attendance at a farrier school or 2-year or 4-year college program.
✤ After completion of study, a new farrier should apprentice with an established farrier and assist local veterinarians before going out on her own.
✤ Personal qualifications: must be physically fit and strong, and have good eyesight and hand-eye coordination, agility, and a good sense of balance. Must have an understanding of the nature of horses and a "knack" for handling them.

Income Potential
$10,000 per year. part-time; $30,000–$40,000 per year. full-time. A farrier typically shoes 6 to 10 horses per day.

Best Customers
Owners of backyard pleasure horses are the most likely customers, with owners of show horses making up the next greatest number of customers. Farriers may also work at boarding stables, breeding farms, training stables, race tracks, farms, and ranches.

Helpful Tips
✤ Must know (and love) horses.
✤ Be willing to work under extreme conditions and with recalcitrant horses. There is always the danger of being injured by a horse because of their size, weight, and varying temperaments.
✤ Must be knowledgeable as a self-employed sole proprietor of a business.

✦ Should attend clinics and stay current with the latest developments.

✦ Accompany farriers and observe farrier schools to get an idea of what this demanding career requires.

For More Information
Associations
The American Farrier's Association (AFA)
4059 Iron Works Pike
Lexington, KY 40511
Will send membership information, including a listing of North American Farrier Schools, for SASE with $.55 postage; $75 per year annual membership fee includes a subscription to *American Farriers Journal,* a bimonthly newsletter, an AFA directory, and optional group insurance rates.

Books
The Farrier and His Craft by Leslie Price. 1990, State Mutual Book & Periodical Services, Ltd., New York, NY.
Farrier Science: Study Guide & Workbook by Doug Butler. 1994, Butler Publishing & Tools, LaPorte, CO.
The Principles of Horseshoeing II: An Illustrated Textbook of Farrier Science and Craftsmanship by Doug Butler. 1985, Butler Publishing and Tools, LaPorte, CO.

Periodicals and Publications
American Farriers Journal
P.O. Box 624
Brookfield, WI 53008-0624
$42.95 per year.

Anvil Magazine
P.O. Box 1810
Georgetown, CA 95634-1810

Online
Contact Baron Taylor of Farrier's Choice, in Denver, PA: (717) 336-3696 for a Web site featuring farriery and hoof care.

Additional Business Ideas
Blacksmithing in related metalworking careers or in decorative art, jewelry, or sculpture.

≥ 5 ≤
SPECIALTY ANIMAL RAISING

With the search for low-cost meat, plus the interest in exotic pets from miniature horses to pot-bellied pigs, raising unusual or specialty animals is a fast-growing business across the country. Raising and caring for any animal is a required commitment for success. If you love animals, though, it can be a rewarding business.

Start-Up Costs
Llamas
$10,000 to $100,000 for quality stock; their popularity has increased because of their use for pulling carts for hikers and trekkers, their wool, and just for the fun of owning and exhibiting them in shows.

Emus
$20,000 to $50,000 for breeding stock; they have become popular for their low-cholesterol meat, for their hide (used for apparel and accessories like handbags and boots), and for their oil (used in skin-care, hair, perfume, and suntan products, and even in the treatment of burns).

Cage Birds
$1,000; they have always been popular pets because they can be kept and raised anywhere.

Pricing Guidelines
Check with the local trade associations, other breeders, trade manuals, and publications for price recommendations. Prices

will vary with the demand. Exhibiting at breed shows will help to establish your stock as quality animals.

* Llamas: $4,000 to $5,000 each, with quality show stock going much higher.
* Emus: $5,000 each; chicks less.
* Cage birds: $20 to $800 apiece, depending on the species.

Essential Equipment
* Llamas: need land (approximately 15 to 20 acres for a small herd) for grazing; barns or sheds for shelters; grooming tools, harness, leads; feed; trailer for transporting them.
* Emus: can be raised on two or more acres; feed, watering cans, shelter from extreme weather.
* Cage birds: cages, breeding boxes, perches, etc.

Marketing and Advertising Methods and Tips
* Classified ads in newspapers; display and classified ads in trade journals, pet magazines, pet newspapers.
* Flyers at pet and feed stores.
* Exhibiting at breed shows helps to establish you as having quality breeding stock.

Recommended Training, Experience, or Skills
It helps to work or spend some time with breeders of the specialty animal or bird which interests you.

Income Potential
* Llamas: $19,000 to $36,000 a year with a herd of at least 45 to 50 females.
* Emus: $20 per pound of meat; approximately 25 pounds of meat are produced by an adult bird.
* Cage birds: $35 to $75 for small birds, and $400 to $800 each for larger birds.

Best Customers
* Llamas: other llama owners; llamas are herd animals, so owners need at least two.

❖ Emus: other people who want to raise these birds; outlets for organic foods, since their meat is chemical-free.

❖ Cage Birds: pet stores, individuals.

Helpful Tips

❖ As mentioned in the previous chapter, raising any animal or bird is a commitment of time and money. It becomes a way of living because the animals require daily care. Make sure that you are ready to work every day to keep your stock healthy and to improve its quality.

❖ The more personal attention these animals receive—especially the llamas and cage birds—the nicer their personalities will be. This will increase your sales from word-of-mouth referrals.

❖ For cage birds, attend local bird club meetings, attend seminars, read books, talk to owners of birds that interest you. Join national associations of specific bird breeders.

For More Information
Llamas

International Llama Association
2755 Locust St., Suite 114
Denver, CO 80222
Send SASE.

Llama Banner
P.O. Box 1968
Manhattan, KS 66502
$24 per year, 6 issues (add $12 per year for Canada and Mexico; $20 per year for overseas); $5 sample issue.

Llamas for Love and Money, 2nd ed., by Rosana Hart. 1994, Juniper Ridge Press, Olympia, WA.

Come On LET'S PLAY
Packer's Haven Camelid & Art Co.
P.O. Box 79A
Cornell, WI 54732

A fun and informative guide for the general public about raising llamas; $5.50 + $3.50 for shipping and handling (Wisconsin residents add sales tax).

Emus
American Emu Association
P.O. Box 8174
Dallas, TX 75205
Send SASE and ask about their information packet; $100 per year membership.

The Emu Farmer's Handbook by Phillip and Maria Minnaar. 1992, Nyoni Publishing Company, Groveton, TX.
Emu Today & Tomorrow, Box 7, Nardin, OK 74646; $25 per year, 12 issues.

Cage Birds
Avicultural Society of America
P.O. Box 5516
Riverside, CA 92517
Cannot give individual advice, but will send a sample monthly bulletin for $1 and SASE.

Breeding Exotic Birds: A Beginner's Guide by Fran Gonzalez. 1993, Neon Pet Products, Inc., Cypress, CA.
Looking After Cage Birds by David Alderton. 1996, Sterling Publishing Co., Inc.

Additional Business Ideas
❖ Raising ostriches:
   U.S. Ostrich Information Center
   65 E. Palantine Rd.
   Prospect Heights, IL 60070
   Write for cost of Ostrich Industry Overview Manual.
❖ Raising rabbits, game birds:
   Lessiter Publications
   P.O. Box 624
   Brookfield, WI 53008-0624
   Write for a listing of publications.

❖ Raising goats, sheep, pigs, and other animals:
  Storey Communications
  Schoolhouse Rd.
  Pownal, VT 05261
  Write for a "How-To Books for Country Living" catalog.

  Animal Breeding: An Introduction by Rodney B. Harrington. 1995, Interstate Publishers, Inc., Danville, IL.
  Keeping and Breeding Snakes by Chris Mattison. 1996, Sterling Publishing Co., Inc., New York, NY.
  Hamsters: The Complete Guide to Keeping, Breeding & Showing by Jimmy McKay. 1996, Sterling Publishing Co., Inc., New York, NY.

  Tetra Press
  30001 Commerce St.
  Blacksburg, VA 24060
  Write for a listing of cat, dog, small animal, and reptile publications.

≈ 6 ≈
WOOL PRODUCTS

Many people who love animals prefer raising breeds from which they can profit other than by selling them for meat or hides. Wool-producing animals such as angora rabbits, llamas, long-haired goats, and sheep can produce wool that can be turned into a small or part-time business. The wool can be sold by itself, and/or used to produce unique handcrafted items.

Start-Up Costs
❖ The price of land if you do not own any.
❖ For sheep-raising: about $20,000 for set-up.

Pricing Guidelines
Check with members of local breed clubs and fiber associations for the current price of wool, usually by the ounce or pound; you can charge more if you have spun that wool.

Essential Equipment

Breeding pens, cages; shears, related animal-care products; feeding and watering equipment; shipping crates, trailers, or a truck for hauling; specific breed supplements for maintaining health.

Marketing and Advertising Methods and Tips

+ Place classified ads in local papers and trade publications.
+ Get word-of-mouth referrals from breed or fiber associations.
+ Exhibit your animals at breed shows.
+ Give workshops or demonstrations at local farm centers and folk festivals.

Recommended Training, Experience, or Skills

+ Attend specific breed and club meetings.
+ Talk and spend time with animal owners.
+ Do your own research in books and trade publications.

Income Potential

+ $6,000 to $12,000 with a small herd of sheep; more with a larger herd.
+ Part-time income with smaller breeds of animals.

Best Customers

Hobbyists; handcrafters who make and sell special fiber arts; handcraft shops; folk and/or craft fair attendees; catalog houses. You can also sell your products by mail order (see "General Resources").

Helpful Tips

+ Diversify your product: sell unspun wool, finished products, animal-related supplies, spinning wheels.
+ Teach continuing education classes and give private lessons on spinning.
+ This is more likely to be a part-time than a full-time business, especially at the start.
+ If financially necessary, start slowly by buying a few breeding pairs at a time.
+ Treat this as any other business start-up, with a good business plan and management system.

For More Information

Associations

❖ Check with local breeders in your area for chapters you can attend and join. Also check the *Encyclopedia of Associations* (Gale Research, Detroit, MI) for a listing of national and regional associations.

❖ Check your local and state crafts guilds for members who work in fiber.

❖ Check with your local County Extension Agent (see "Government" in "General Resources").

Books

Interweave Press
201 E. Fourth St.
Loveland, CO 80537-5655

Publishes a number of books on wool products and spinning; write for a current catalog. Some of their books are:

In Sheep's Clothing: A Handspinner's Guide to Wool by Nola & Jane Fournier, 1995.

Angora by Erica Lynn, 1992.

Spinning Wheel Primer, 2nd ed., by Alden Amos, 1990.

Storey's "How-to Catalog" (See "Specialty Animal Raising")
Turning Wool into a Cottage Industry by Paula Simmons, 1991.

Raising Sheep the Modern Way by Paula Simmons, 1989.

Wool and Mohair: Producing Better Natural Fibers, 2nd ed., by Thomas Harmsworth and Graham Day. 1990, Inkata Press, Ltd., Portland, OR.

Weaving Profits by James Dillehay. 1992, Warm Snow Publishers, Torreon, NM. This book is out of print, but check your local library or The Front Room Publishers, Dept. Catalog B12/95, P.O. Box 1541, Clifton, NJ 07015-1541.

Additional Business Ideas

See "Helpful Tips" above.

≈ 7 ≈

AQUACULTURE

Aquaculture is the cultivation of aquatic plants and animals for recreational or commercial purposes. It has been practiced for over a century in the U.S., and is the fastest growing component of U.S. agriculture. Due to the U.S. and worldwide demand for seafood, the Office of Aquaculture (USDA/CSRS) predicts that aquaculture production will have to increase seven-fold—to 77 million metric tons—by the year 2025.

This billion-dollar-a-year industry farms nearly 100 aquatic species for food. Farm-raised aquatic species include trout, shellfish, catfish, baitfish, carp, and ornamental fish, including aquarium species for home hobbyists.

If you like fish and being outdoors, this is a good business for you.

Start-Up Costs
* $12,000 to $50,000 and up. The investment needed ranges from $2,000 to $4,000 per surface acre, depending on what type of fish you will be raising. Underground water from wells and springs is preferred because it is free of wild fish and parasites.
* Aquaculture centers recommend that you start with small, simple systems that are both practical and relatively inexpensive but will give you valuable experience.

Pricing Guidelines
Depends what the going rate is for your species. The average farm prices run approximately 79 cents/lb.

Essential Equipment
* Levee and watershed ponds; spring-fed ponds; cages, tanks, nets, shipping containers; aerators, pumps, hauling vehicle, etc.
* Most essential is the quality of water, and the amount of water.

Marketing and Advertising Methods and Tips
Ideas for developing markets are contained in the SRAC Publication No. 350, "Small-Scale Marketing of Aquaculture." See your County Extension Office or write the Aquaculture Information Center listed in "For More Information," below.

Recommended Training, Experience, or Skills
❖ Have experience raising and working with commercial aquatic fish.
❖ Take courses in aquaculture and attend local workshops; see your County Extension Agent to see if courses are offered.
❖ Join local and national trade clubs and associations for networking information and support.
❖ Be ready to work long hours under adverse conditions.

Income Potential
❖ Depends on the markets you develop. You will have to wait 6 to 18 months for income until your first crop attains marketable size and can be sold.
❖ Can range from a few thousand dollars a year to millions. It all depends on the size of your operation.

Best Customers
Wholesale fish markets; garden centers for sale of ornamental fish and grass-eating carp; other fish farms.

Helpful Tips
❖ Visit and/or work for a time with established aquatic farms.
❖ Make sure you have done a thorough business plan to see if you can economically handle such an operation.
❖ Beginners should consider starting with small, simple systems. As you gain experience raising some fish in an existing pond or with a small shellfish plot, you can then decide if you want to try a larger, more complex operation.

For More Information

Association

National Aquaculture Association: One Industry, One Voice
111 West Washington St., Suite 1
Charles Town, WV 25414-1529
Write for membership information.

Books

Catfish and the Delta by Richard Schweid. 1995, Ten Speed Press, Berkeley, CA.

Farming in Ponds and Dams by Nick Romanowski. 1995, Lothian Publishing Co., Cincinnati, OH.

How to Start and Manage a Fish Farming Business by Jerre G. Lewis and Leslie D. Renn. 1995, Lewis & Renn Assocs., Interlochen, MI.

Freshwater Fish Pond Culture & Management: Appropriate Technologies for Development by Marilyn Chakroff. 1994, Diane Publishing Co., Upland, PA.

Storey's "How-To" Books for Country Living, Schoolhouse Rd., Pownal, VT 05261

Other Publications

Aquaculture Information Center
National Agricultural Library
10301 Baltimore Blvd.
Beltsville, MD 20705-2351
Send SASE for a list of publications on aquaculture, including "Is Aquatic Farming for You?"

Government

Office of Agriculture, USDA/CSRS
Ag Box 2260
Washington, DC 20250-2260

Local County Extension Office agents can supply you with some of the SRAC publications on aquaculture. There may be a local agent knowledgeable about aquaculture.

County Soil Conservation Service Offices offer free pond planning and layout services which can help insure that ponds get built the right way.

Periodicals and Publications

Aquaculture Magazine
Box 2329
Asheville, NC 28802
$19 per year, 6 issues. Special issue: Buyer's Guide, Industry Directory in December of each year.

Additional Business Ideas
Raising grass-eating carp for ponds and baitfish for local fishermen.

➴ ● ➶

MISCELLANEOUS
ANIMAL-RELATED BUSINESSES

❖ Pony rides for parties.
❖ Puppy-training classes.
❖ Personalized pet Christmas ornaments.
❖ Animal Behavior Specialist: give talks and demonstrations; solve owners problems with their pets.
❖ Animal walking, exercise, and yard clean-up.

Miscellaneous Books

Career Success with Pets: How to Get Started, Get Going, Get Ahead by Kim Barber. 1996, Macmillan Publishing Company, Inc., New York, NY.

277 Secrets Your Dog Wants You to Know by Paulette Cooper and Paul Noble. 1995, Ten Speed Press, Berkeley, CA.

Business Services

Currently, many businesses are either downsizing or cannot afford to hire full-time employees. This gives the new entrepreneur the opportunity to offer services that these businesses still need.

If you have business expertise, you may want to market yourself as a business services consultant. Business services consultants are hired for many tasks: planning new marketing strategies, training employees, helping with company programs or specific projects, and so on. You have to have solid experience behind you with some good referrals to get your first clients.

≈ 8 ≈
ADVERTISING SPECIALTIES

In this business, you sell advertising for your customers using unique products to carry their names and/or slogans. You either put the printing and designs on the products yourself or you have distributors or subcontractors supply them for you. Promotional products are powerful advertising tools, and this is a $7 billion industry according to the Advertising Specialty Institute in Langhorne, Pennsylvania.

Start-Up Costs
$6,000-$13,000

Pricing Guidelines
❖ Depends on the products chosen, how intricate the design, and the quantity ordered.
❖ Profit margin: 30 percent to 50 percent.

Marketing and Advertising Methods and Tips
❖ Personal calls and visits to small businesses and local sports teams.
❖ Classified ads in publications catering to sports such as tennis, horsemanship, golf.
❖ Flyers, brochures, business cards to hand out.
❖ Friends and family giving out your business name on specialty products or wearing it on T-shirts, etc.
❖ Word-of-mouth referrals.

Essential Equipment
Answering device, fax, computer with design programs.

Recommended Training, Experience, or Skills
❖ Sales and marketing experience and ability.
❖ Good communication skills.
❖ Artistic and writing talent helpful in creating designs and slogans.

Income Potential
❖ $200 to $650 per month at the start, with the potential to double or triple as your business grows.
❖ $30,000 per year and up.

Best Customers
❖ Sports teams
❖ School-related teams and organizations
❖ Small and home-based businesses
❖ Church youth groups

Helpful Tips

❖ Unless you want to produce the products yourself, search for good, dependable suppliers and ones that will deal in small quantities.

❖ Carry samples of everything you sell, especially those of former customers in the same community as a prospective customer. People prefer to hold a sample instead of seeing it in a catalog.

❖ Keep current with the latest advertising specialties.

❖ Get referrals from satisfied customers, friends, family, networking colleagues.

❖ Have the promotional product tie in with the business, team, or organization as closely as possible.

Franchises
Adventures in Advertising
2353 130th Ave. NE, Suite 100
Bellevue, WA 98005
(206) 885-9900
Producing unique and fun promotional products. Write or call for more information.

For More Information
Business Guide
Entrepreneur's Start-Up Guide, "Advertising Specialties." (800) 421-2300; $69.50 plus shipping.

Additional Business Ideas
Screen printing: State-of-the-art equipment makes it easier and more affordable to do your own screen printing of T-shirts, aprons, jackets, tote bags, hats, etc. from a garage or basement.

Book
Screen Printing Production Management by Richard C. Webb. 1989, S.T. Publications, Inc., Cincinnati, OH.

Supplies
Dick Blick Art Materials Catalog
P.O. Box 1267
Galesburg, IL 61402-1267

◄ 9 ►
APARTMENT/HOME PREPARATION SERVICE

This service, usually for rental or real estate agencies, combines the skills of decorating, cleaning, and repairing. You prepare apartments and new housing for occupancy. If you are handy, you can do the work yourself, or you can subcontract jobs like repairing electricity or plumbing for which you may not be qualified.

Start-Up Costs
$5,500 to $12,000

Pricing Guidelines
$50 to $100 per day or $25 to $30 per hour, depending what has to be cleaned, painted, and/or repaired.

Marketing and Advertising Methods and Tips
❖ Flyers, brochures to real estate agencies, builders, landlords.
❖ Auction agencies: mature adults moving to extended care homes often will have their items sold at an auction. They can often refer you to people who may need your service.
❖ Classified ads in free home-sales and apartment-listing newspapers.

Essential Equipment
❖ Standard tools: hammer, screwdrivers, pliers, an assortment of paint brushes, pans.
❖ Cleaning supplies: heavy-duty vacuum cleaner, rug shampooer, rags, buckets, small stepladder.

Recommended Training, Experience, or Skills
❖ Work part-time for a professional cleaner and/or painter to earn money for your business and pick up some tips of the trade.
❖ You must be handy at fixing household problems. Study home repair manuals or carry one with you.

❖ Volunteer with such organizations as "Habitat for Humanity" and other local agencies that help the disadvantaged fix up homes or apartments.

❖ Attend hardware and home-supply store seminars on home maintenance.

❖ Enroll in courses at your local vocational-technical schools to learn basic home-maintenance skills or to expand your skills.

Income Potential
$25,000 to $40,000 per year for a sole proprietor.

Best Customers
Real estate agents, builders, leasing services, landlords.

Helpful Tips
❖ Be thorough and pay attention to detail.
❖ Be knowledgeable about getting stains out.

For More Information
Rehabilitating Apartments: A Recycling Process by Robert A. Cagann. 1993, Institute of Real Estate Management, Chicago, IL.

Additional Business Ideas
Be an apartment manager.

How to Become an Apartment Manager (Fast) and Live Rent Free edited by Robert Stuart. 1994, Pro-Guides, Professional Publishing, Davis, CA.

Managing Rental Properties for Maximum Profit by Greg Perry. 1994, Prima Publishing, Rocklin, CA.

Managing Rental Properties Like a Pro: How to Keep Your Buildings & Your Pockets Full by Susan J. Underhill and Ken Upshall. 1992, Probus Publishing Co. Inc., Burr Ridge, IL.

≫ 10 ≪

BUSINESS COST REDUCTION SERVICE

This business combines the skills of an auditor, the knowledge of an operations research analyst and business manager, and the background of a human resource expert to help businesses, organizations, and institutions to operate more efficiently, thus saving money. Your business service can evaluate work patterns of employees and all the purchasing decisions, and monitor the utility, telephone, and shipping bills. Your purpose is *not* to eliminate jobs, but to help the company increase profits by reducing overhead costs.

Start-Up Costs
$2,000 to $8,000

Pricing Guidelines
* Charge a percentage (40 percent to 50 percent) on costs saved or a fee for a complete analysis.
* You can charge for a one-time overall review and subsequent periodic (annual) reviews.

Marketing and Advertising Methods and Tips
* Directly solicit businesses in your area.
* Offer free, on-site first consultation.
* Place ads in trade publications.
* Get referrals from other businesses and/or professionals (lawyers, accountants, bookkeepers, etc.).
* Network with others in local business associations.

Essential Equipment
* Office equipment: computer, business software, telephone with voice mail or answering service, promotional materials.

Recommended Training, Experience, or Skills
* You will need to have some business education, experience, and training in each of the services you offer. Get

referrals from previous businesspersons with whom you
have worked.

✤ Be able to communicate competently with people at all
positions in a company.

✤ You will need good math and analytical skills.

✤ Be skilled at problem-solving, and have good attention to detail.

✤ Be familiar with laws and taxes.

Income Potential

People with established businesses average between $20,000
per year and $50,000 per year or more, depending on how
many clients they have and the size of the businesses that
use their services.

Best Customers

✤ Start with businesses where you have a contact who will
give you referrals to others.

✤ New businesses may use your service for recommendations as to how to save money.

Helpful Tips

✤ You may have to educate businesses of the need for your
services. You can do this through talks at local business
groups and associations meetings and by publishing articles about business savings in business publications.

✤ Send a monthly tip sheet or short newsletter to clients and
potential new customers.

✤ Offer workshops and seminars at business fairs and conventions.

Franchises

General Business Services (see "Other Business Services," p. 126).

For More Information

Books

Project Management: Planning and Control by Rory Burke. 1994,
John Wiley & Sons, Inc., New York, NY.

The Total Business Manual: A Step-by-Step Guide to Planning, Operating, and Evaluating Your Business by E. James Burton and W. Blan McBride. 1991, John Wiley & Sons, Inc., New York, NY.

Start-Up Guides
"Utility & Telephone Bill Auditing." ($69.50) Entrepreneur's Small Business Development Catalog, (800) 421-2300.

Additional Business Ideas
Develop new cost-saving software for specific trade businesses.

⚜ **11** ⚜
CLIPPING/INFORMATION RETRIEVAL SERVICE

This service involves surveillance and gathering of written, electronic, and other sources of data to specifically fit individuals' and business clients' information needs. You can offer your services for one-time projects or on an ongoing basis. Using your computer, modem, and specific software, you can put together and publish an electronic newspaper that you can print out. This information will help your clients in the areas of market research, reports on the competition, patent searches, and anything that will help increase business.

Start-Up Costs
$5,000 to $20,000

Pricing Guidelines
$20 to $100 per hour or by the project. Cost for online databases and printed copies are charged as additional expenses.

Marketing and Advertising Methods and Tips
❖ You may want to specialize in one or more information topics that relate to your experience and/or training.

❖ Determine which trades or professions will want your specific information, and reach them via ads in trade journals, articles, and talks.

❖ Network with other businesspeople and contacts in your field. Word-of-mouth referrals are an important method of getting business.

❖ Offer seminars and workshops at conventions.

❖ Do a direct mailing to businesses and professionals that would be interested in your information.

❖ Advertise specific search services to consumers on medical topics and other areas of personal concern.

Essential Equipment
❖ Standard business equipment, including fax machine, copier, and one or two telephone lines.
❖ A computer with a hard drive and a high-speed modem.
❖ Specialized software.
❖ Online databases and services.
❖ Subscriptions to trade journals and publications.

Recommended Training, Experience, or Skills
❖ Training in research and information accessing.
❖ Computer and software training to use the information software.
❖ Strong writing and editing skills.

Income Potential
$20,000 to $80,000 per year.

Best Customers
Businesses and individuals needing information in your field of expertise.

Helpful Tips
❖ Prompt and personalized attention to your customers will enable you to compete against the bigger online services.

❖ Establish yourself as an expert in your field.
❖ Publish a regular newsletter or tip sheet to those on your customer mailing list. Offer a free issue to potential customers and as a promotional tool when you contact prospective clients.

For More Information
Association
Association of Independent Information Professionals
245 Fifth Ave., Suite 2103
New York, NY 10016
$85 per year association membership; no start-up information available.

Databases
❖ CompuServe (800) 848-8199; purchase the "Journalist" basic package.
❖ Dow Jones News/Retrieval (800) 552-3567; set-up fee, then charges per 1,000 characters.
❖ Individual Inc. (800) 414-1000; inquire about "Heads Up" package.

See other online resources in "Internet Sources" and "Online Services," in "General Resources" at the back of this book.

Books
The Complete Idiot's Guide to Modems & Online Services by Sherry Kinkaph. 1994, Alpha Books, Indianapolis, IN.
Find It Online! By Robert I. Berkman. 1994, TAB Books, Blue Ridge Summit, PA.
Information Broker's Handbook, 2nd ed., by Sue Rugge and Alfred Glossbrenner. 1995, The McGraw-Hill Companies, New York, NY.
Making Money on the Internet by Alfred Glossbrenner. 1995, TAB Books, Blue Ridge Summit, PA.
Researching on the Internet by Robin Rowland and Dave Kinnaman. 1995, Prima Publishing, Rocklin, CA.

Researching on the Worldwide Web: Complete Guide to Organizing, Searching, and Qualifying by Prima Development Staff. 1996, Prima Publishing, Rocklin, CA.
Start Your Own Information Broker Service. 1995, Pfeiffer & Co., San Diego, CA.

Periodicals and Publications
Information Today. Learned Information, 143 Old Marlton Pike, Nedford, NJ 08055. $43.95 for 11 issues.

Also see "Fact Finder" and "Online Services," in "General Resources," at the end of this book.

Additional Business Ideas
Start your own online information service. See "Online Services," in "General Resources" at the end of this book.

◁ 12 ▷

COLLECTION SERVICE

With the popular use of credit cards, charge accounts, and installment loans, many consumers overextend themselves and are unable to pay back the debts they have built up. Your service works with the credit provider to help secure payment of those debts. Another aspect of this business service is the collection of debts from companies that have not paid for products or services already delivered.

Start-Up Costs
$10,000 to $50,000. The American Collections Association, Inc., recommends that you have enough collection business secured to carry you for the first six months.

Pricing Guidelines
Commissions average 25 percent to 50 percent when court cases are involved; about 15 percent for collection of child-support payments.

Marketing and Advertising Methods and Tips
Get known by as many potential clients as possible: direct mail, classified newspaper ads, Yellow Pages ads, membership in local business groups and associations, word-of-mouth referrals from satisfied clients.

Essential Equipment
Office equipment: desk, files, chairs, adequate telephone system; fax machine, computer, and trade software; attractive business stationery and cards.

Recommended Training, Experience, or Skills
* To be successful, it is imperative that you have had previous experience in credit and collections.
* Read about and study the trade.
* Be ready to work long and sometimes unusual hours.
* As a service business, good service and communication with your clients is a must!
* *You must be familiar with the federal laws governing collections: the Fair Debt Collection Practices Act (FDCPA) as well as your state laws and any licensing requirements.*
* Have good communication skills, act professionally under stress, and be persistent but politely firm.
* A knowledge of psychology is helpful.

Income Potential
$30,000 to $60,000 per year

Best Customers
Any business that bills it customers, day-care centers, health-care providers.

Helpful Tips
Do market research to determine whether your community has an adequate economy and diversity to support a collection service.

Franchises
ACCT Corporation International
7414 NE Hazel Dell Ave., Suite 209
Vancouver, WA 98665.
Send a self-addressed envelope with two first-class stamps.

For More Information
Association
American Collectors Association
P.O. Box 39106
Minneapolis, MN 55439-0106
$10 (paid in advance, or MasterCard or Visa) for Information
Pack (includes *Starting and Managing a Collection Service*).

Book
*Start Your Own Collection Agency: Million Dollar Collection Agency
Business Start-Up Manual*, 2nd ed., by Ralph Thomas. 1990,
Thomas Publications, Austin, TX.

Periodical
The Collector (published by the American Collectors Association; see above).

Start-Up Guides
"Collection Agency" ($69.50); Entrepreneur's Business Guide
(800) 421-2300.
"Collection Agency" ($39.95); National Business Library (800)
947-7724.

Additional Business Ideas
"Skip Tracing": this is the name given to collection services or
agencies that track down missing delinquent parents.

≥ 13 ≥

COURT SERVICES

In court services, you work as an independent court reporter or "scopist" (also called a "note reader"), or you can have an agency that supplies these court transcriptionists. Court reporters use computer-based writing machines that record their stenographic notes onto floppy disks. After the day's proceedings have been recorded, it is up to the scopist to transform the CAT (computer-assisted transcription) into edited notes. A scopist must also be able to read the steno-typed notes if she cannot understand a portion of the text.

Start-Up Costs
$6,000 to $16,000

Pricing Guidelines
60 cents to a dollar per page; a scopist can do 120–150 pages a day or more.

Marketing and Advertising Methods and Tips
❖ Court reporting services: contact your local or national court reporters' association for referrals. Contact local courts.
❖ Scoping: Contact court reporters or court reporting agencies in your area.

Essential Equipment
Office supplies and equipment: computer system with hard drive and modem; fax machine, printer, CAT software; business stationery and cards.

Recommended Training, Experience, or Skills
❖ Court reporter: check with the National Court Reporters Association (listed below) for schools that offer training, which can take up to two years.
❖ Scopist: must attend an accredited notereader/scopist program.

❖ Both a court reporter and scopist must have excellent typing skills, as well as good grammar, spelling, and punctuation; you should know the terminology that you are proofreading.

Income Potential
$21,000 to 40,000 per year

Best Customers
❖ Court reporter: Local courts, court reporting agencies.
❖ Scopist: court reporters, court reporting agencies.

Helpful Tips
❖ Be proficient in your skills and strive to keep them up to date.
❖ Be professional, and develop a reputation for fast, accurate work.

For More Information

Association
National Court Reporters Association
8224 Old Courthouse Rd.
Vienna, VA 22182
For both court reporters and scopists. Offers a publication, seminars, and referrals. Also ask if there is a court reporter association in your state.

Books
Computer-Aided Transcription: Scoping and Editing by Jean Gonzalez and Margaret Cline. 1992, Middleton Wasley, Huntington Beach, CA.
Legal & Paralegal Businesses on Your Home-Based PC by Kathryn Sheehy Hussey and Rick Benzel. 1994, Windcrest/McGraw Hill, Blue Ridge Summit, PA.
Stenotype Theory for the Professional Scopist by Jacqueline A. Nash and Joann Kincaid. 1995, Stenotype Educational Products, Inc., Melrose, FL.

Distance Education Learning (Correspondence Schools)
At-Home Professions
2001 Lowe St.
Fort Collins, CO 80525
Legal transcription.

Stenotype Institute of Jacksonville, Inc.
500 9th Avenue North
P.O. Box 50009
Jacksonville Beach, FL 32250
Course in court reporting using stenotype machine shorthand.

Online
CompuServe "Court Reporters' Forum" has a special section for scopists. Call (800) 872-4768 for information.

Schools
There are over 400 different court reporting schools (see "Association" for details).

Court Reporting Institute of Orleans Technical Institute
1845 Walnut St., 7th Floor
Philadelphia, PA 19103-4707
Court reporting and scopist programs of study.

Additional Business Ideas
Information service tailored to legal firms or paralegal services.

≤ 14 ≥

CUSTOMER SERVICE

With companies either too big to give personal attention to all their customers, or too small to have a customer service department, you can offer these businesses a number of customer services: customer service consulting and evaluations; handling customer service for the companies, offering 24-hour automated and/or personal response; being a secret shopper; promoting products for companies.

One of the fastest-growing customer services is having a secret or mystery shopping service. With this service (featured in this section), a secret or silent shopper checks out the following: how employees are handling customers and sales; if employee training is being followed through; if there is employee theft; if security systems and checks are working properly; and how competitors' services compare.

Start-Up Costs
$1,000 to $8,000 for basic office equipment, business stationery and cards, and promotional materials.

Pricing Guidelines
An average of $20 to $40 per hour; $60 to $100 per visit.

Marketing and Advertising Methods and Tips
Trade shows; ads in Yellow Pages; direct mail and follow-up calls and visits to targeted companies; word-of-mouth referrals from satisfied clients; do a free-of-charge shopping evaluation and then contact the company with your findings.

Essential Equipment
Office equipment: computer and related software, fax machine, telephone system, promotional materials.

Recommended Training, Experience, or Skills
* Licensing: some states require you to be licensed like a private investigator.
* It is recommended that you have worked in customer service departments; it is also recommended that your client companies be in an industry in which you have knowledge, background, and experience.

❖ Be observant, yet unobtrusive, so that you will look and act like a typical shopper.

Income Potential
❖ You can offer packages to your customers that include investigating a given number of businesses per year at an hourly rate, or $20 to $100 per visit, depending on how extensive the evaluation (written reports, recommendations, etc.).
❖ As an independent contractor (secret shopper), you can work part time and earn $100 to $500 a month.
❖ If you own a secret shopper service and have independent contractors working for you, you can earn $25,000 per year part-time and $50,000 per year full-time. (See "Workshops," in "For More Information.")

Best Customers
Those in your field of expertise.

Helpful Tips
Your business success will depend on how effective an evaluation you do for your clients. If you can help your clients improve their customer response and reduce profit loss from theft and poor service, you will see an increase in your own business.

For More Information
Books
Customer Driven Growth by Whiteley. 1996, Addison-Wesley Publishing Company, Inc., Reading, MA.
Customer Satisfaction Measurement & Management: Using the Voice of the Customer by Naumann. 1995, South-Western Publishing Company, Cincinnati, OH.
Talking with Your Customers: What They Will Tell You About Your Business When You Ask the Right Question by Michael J. Wing. 1996, Upstart Publishing Company, Dover, NH.

Winning at Customer Retention by JoAnna Brandi. 1995, Lakewood Publications, 50 South 9th Street, Minneapolis, MN 55402; $14.95.

Video
"The Basics of Profitable Customer Service"
Lakewood Publications
50 South 9th Street
Minneapolis, MN 55402
$99.95 for videotape and workbook by Jeff Blackman.

Workshops, Materials
Judith Rappold, President
Business Resources
2222 Western Trails, Suite 107
Austin, TX 78745
Offers 3-day workshop on a secret shopping service; cost of workshop, including workbook and all materials, is $4,999; For the materials alone, the cost is $599 + $10 shipping and handling; Texas residents add 7.25 percent sales tax.

Additional Business Ideas
Doing in-store demonstrations of products for companies. Much of your business as an independent agent is carried out in grocery stores for food manufacturers.

⚞ 15 ⚟
COMPUTER DATA BACKUP SERVICES PROVIDER

This business offers remote backup service. Backing up clients' files is handled via modems and computers. You and your client have a contract for the business service you provide. At an agreed-upon time, the specialized software on your client's unit automatically transfers the data to your host computer. These data are then transferred to a tape drive which you will store at another location, such as a bank safe-deposit box. This should be a growing business service as companies look for a low-cost and secure way to back up their files.

Start-Up Costs
$5,000 to $10,000, including lawyer's fee for setting up contracts.

Pricing Guidelines
$35 to $40 per month

Marketing and Advertising Methods and Tips
* Direct mail followed up by personal visits.
* Talks at business association meetings, conventions.
* Referrals from computer repair services.

Essential Equipment
* Computer hardware: a 386-, 486-series, or higher, computer with at least a 250 megabyte hard drive and at least 16 megabytes of RAM; a 28.8 baud modem or faster; tape backup system; specialized remote backup software; tapes (in sizes that fit your backup systems).
* A dedicated telephone line.
* Fax machine, copier.
* Contracts, promotional brochures.

Recommended Training, Experience, or Skills
* Must be knowledgeable about computers, modems, hard drives, and operating systems, and how to install them.
* Previous business experience and contacts are important for referrals and growth.

Income Potential
$12,000 to $30,000 per year, and more if combined with other computer services.

Best Customers
Any business for which loss of files could be a catastrophe, such as a law office, accounting firm, or bookkeeping firm.

Helpful Tips

❖ You must have the necessary computer skills to run this type of business, or have access to an on-call computer consultant.

❖ Have clients use backup encryption software that ensures security by making data unreadable to anyone without a password.

❖ Offer free consultations which will educate your potential client about the practicality of your business service.

For More Information
Precision Data Corp., Inc. (PDC)
1720 Harbor Ave.
Memphis, TN 38113
PDC offers *The RBS Book* by Robert Cosgrove ($499 with software), and *The RBS Demo Kit* ($25); write or call (901) 947-6306, ext. 230.

Additional Business Ideas
Computer referral/brokerage business: you provide everything a company needs to computerize its business—installation, consulting, software, technicians, engineers, trainers, etc.

Also see "Computer-Related Businesses."

≈ 16 ≈
DATABASE CONSULTANT

This is another business for the computer entrepreneur. The database consultant writes and maintains custom databases for individual companies.

Start-Up Costs
$12,000 to $35,000 (costs less if started from your home).

Pricing Guidelines
$65 to $90 per hour, depending on the complexity of the project.

Marketing and Advertising Methods and Tips
* Use an agency that specializes in placing database consultants.
* Get a booth at a business trade show.
* Advertise in trade publications.
* Network and get referrals from business clients.

Essential Equipment
* Office equipment: computer with at least 16 megabytes of RAM; possibly a laptop computer; laser printer, telephone system, fax machine, copier.
* Promotional materials.

Recommended Training, Experience, or Skills
* A degree or training in computer programming.
* Experience in setting up databases.

Income Potential
$25,000 to $100,000 per year and up.

Best Customers
Businesses in your community that are growing; check with your local Chamber of Commerce.

Helpful Tips
* Offer a free evaluation to potential clients.
* Become an expert by specializing in one or more industries.
* Pay attention to customer needs, offer training, and provide technical support to retain clients and get good recommendations and referrals.
* Network with other independent computer experts and keep current with the latest in software, etc.

For More Information
Association
Independent Computer Consultants Association
933 Gardenview Office Parkway
St. Louis, MO 63141
Send SASE for membership information.

Book
Introduction to Database Management by Kathi Davis. 1996, Addison-Wesley Publishing Company, Inc., Reading, MA.

Periodical
Data Based Advisor, P.O. Box 469013, Escondido, CA 92046-9964; $39 per year, 12 issues.

⚓ 17 ⚓
IMPORT/EXPORT BUSINESS

According to the Office of Economic Research of the U.S. Small Business Administration, 20 percent of American exporters have fewer than 500 employees whose businesses account for one-third of the nation's exports. Improved technology and communications has made it easier and more affordable for businesses to export their products. The U.S. Department of Commerce expects the number of exports to increase over the years because of recent trade agreements, with more to come because of possible future trade agreements.

In this business, a product is bought in one country and sold in another. A person can profit by buying from manufacturers and selling directly to retailers or through mail order. Others sell products to wholesalers in another country.

Start-Up Costs
$7,000 to $29,000

Pricing Guidelines
Depends on the product line and the profit margin. Tariffs on certain items may make it unprofitable to import or export them. You must research the markets thoroughly to make a profit.

Marketing and Advertising Methods and Tips
Direct letters to U.S. manufacturers, and letters and faxes to your contacts in other countries.

Essential Equipment

❖ Telephone system; a fax machine is essential for receiving incoming faxes 24 hours a day.

❖ Computer with modem.

❖ Subscription to one of the online services for contacts.

Recommended Training, Experience, or Skills

❖ It is helpful to have some experience in sales, business management, and trade, and to be familiar with international trade laws.

❖ Experience in sales and marketing will be an asset in finding new customers and identifying your market.

Income Potential

$35,000 to $150,000 per year or more.

Best Customers

Companies that want to buy something from a company in another country—computers and accessories to ski equipment to clothing. Contact foreign embassies and ask for leads.

Helpful Tips

❖ Assess your strengths and background to help you decide in what areas to specialize.

❖ Do your research into the industry; read trade publications, attend trade shows.

❖ Find out if there is an import/export advisory board in your community to help you.

❖ Have good people or organizations working for you who can move your products: custom brokers, freight forwarders who will be able to handle the tasks of preparing documentation, using the right shipping method, and getting your products to your overseas buyers.

❖ Contact the Department of Commerce's International Trade Administration (see below); they provide counseling and seminars on this business.

For More Information

Association

American Association of Importers and Exporters
11 W. 42nd St.
New York, NY 10036
Send SASE for membership information.

Books

Doing Business in Asia: A Small Business Guide to Success in the World's Most Dynamic Market by David L. James. 1993, Betterway Books, Cincinnati, OH.

The Entrepreneur Guide to Starting an Import-Export Business, by Entrepreneur Magazine Staff. 1995, John Wiley & Sons, Inc., New York, NY.

Export-Import: Everything You & Your Company Need to Know to Compete in World Markets (revised edition) by Joseph A. Zodl. 1995, Betterway Books, Cincinnati, OH.

How to Start & Operate Your Own Export-Import Business at Home. Gordon Press Publishers, New York, NY.

How to Be an Importer & Pay for Your World Travel by Mary Green and Stanley Gillmar. 1993, Ten Speed Press, Berkeley, CA.

Import Export: How to Get Started in International Trade, 2nd ed., by Carl A. Nelson. 1995, The McGraw-Hill Companies, New York, NY.

Government

International Trade Administration
The U.S. Department of Commerce
Herbert C. Hoover Bldg.
14th Street and Constitution Ave. NW
Washington, DC 20230
(202) 482-2000

Offers export counseling, overseas market research, export financing information, and advice on licenses and controls.

The National Trade Databank ((800) USA-TRADE) maintains data from 17 government agencies that can help you identify markets.

Exporter's Guide to Federal Resources for Small Business, 1992
($4.75; stock number: 045-000-00263-2) describes the
major federal programs designed to assist small business
owners in exporting their goods and services. Order from
Superintendent of Documents, P.O. Box 371954, Pittsburgh, PA 15250-7954.
The Export Opportunity Hotline: (800) 243-7232. Answers
questions on overseas trade.

Business Guides
"Import/Export Business Guide," $69.50 from Entrepreneur's
Small Business Development Catalog; (800) 421-2300 to
order or for a copy of the catalog.
"Import/Export Business," $39.95 from National Business
Library, (800) 947-7724.

Periodical
The Journal of Commerce, World Trade Center, New York, NY
10048; $365 per year, daily.

Online
CompuServe's "International Trade Forum" (800) 848-8199.
SBA's internet site at *http://www.sba.gov*; from there, a person
can link to the home page for the Office of International
Trade for information about countries with the strongest
demand for a given product, the top import and export
markets for a given product, and the top import and
export products for a selected country; same info available by faxing 202-244-7311.

Additional Business Ideas
Foreign buying service: buying items in foreign countries
where you speak the language for customers who want specific items from those countries.

⚞ 18 ⚟

MAILING LIST SERVICES

In this business service, computers and software are used to compile and maintain mailing lists. Added services include executing bulk mailings and periodically updating the mailing lists.

Start-Up Costs
$5,000 to $10,000

Pricing Guidelines
❖ 7 to 10 cents per name to add names to a mailing list.
❖ 15 to 50 cents a name for a periodic updating of lists.

Marketing and Advertising Methods and Tips
❖ Direct mail to businesses, organizations, churches with follow-up calls and visits. Give them a free consultation.
❖ Networking at association or chamber meetings; word-of-mouth referrals.
❖ Ads in the Yellow Pages, Women's Yellow Pages, regional business newspapers and publications.

Essential Equipment
❖ Office: computer with hard drive and CD-ROM.
❖ Related software: database, mailing list, bar-coding, etc.
❖ Telephone system, business stationery, cards, promotional materials, etc.

Recommended Training, Experience, or Skills
❖ Working as an employee for a similar service—even at minimum wage or part-time—will acquaint you with the business; if it is a local business, however, you may have to sign a statement saying that you will not start a competing business, then start one in a noncompeting region (but check with an attorney first).
❖ Call the larger postal centers to find out if they are holding any seminars or workshops to explain the latest regulations.

Income Potential
$30,000 to $90,000 per year.

Best Customers
* Stores that have people sign mailing lists.
* Small businesses.
* Community organizations.

Helpful Tips
* Know your mailing regulations.
* Try for community recognition with business supplements.

Franchises
Val-Pak Direct Marketing System Inc.
8650 Largo Lakes Dr.
Largo, FL 34643
Co-op direct mail advertising. Write for more information.

For More Information
Association
Direct Marketing Association Inc.
1120 Avenue of the Americas
New York, NY 10036
Guidelines, publications on mailings; mail order business; conferences and seminars.

Books
Making Money with a Mailing List Service at Home. Write to Here's How, P.O. Box 5091, Santa Monica, CA 90409.
Mailing List Services on Your Home-Based PC by Linda Rohrbough. 1994, TAB/McGraw Hill, Blue Ridge Summit, PA.

Software
"Mailer's + 4," is a mailing list program with quarterly postal updates. It is produced by Mailer's Software for $249. Call

for information on this and other programs: (714) 492-
7000.

Periodical
Business Mailers Review
Pasha Publications, Inc.
P.O. Box 9188
Arlington, VA 22219-9900
Monitors the Postal Service, private carriers, and suppliers;
$279 for 25 issues.

Additional Business Ideas
* Cooperative advertising services: provide bulk mailing of
  retailers' and professionals' promotional materials together
  in one envelope to area residents. The owner of this service
  either prepares the envelopes for mailing or provides the
  entire service.
* Create your own mailing lists and sell or rent them to
  interested companies.
* Be a mailing list broker: compile lists from groups and find
  a buyer for them.

⚞ 19 ⚟

MANUFACTURER'S AGENT

A manufacturer's agent or representative is a self-employed
salesperson who represents one or more manufacturers on a
commission basis. Many small- to medium-sized manufacturing companies sell most of their products through manufacturer's agents. Agents may specialize in selling compatible
lines of products, but not competitor's lines.

   An agent takes the products to wholesalers, retailers, government agencies, institutions, etc. and markets these products via demonstrations that stress the best points of the
product. Besides having a thorough understanding and technical knowledge of the products, the agent must handle the

business aspects of quoting prices and setting credit terms, delivery dates, and shipping procedures. How well the agent makes these product presentations determines the sales of the products.

Start-Up Costs
$3,000 to $10,000

Pricing Guidelines
❖ Manufacturer's agents or "reps" (representatives), are paid on commission, which can range from 3 percent to 15 percent.
❖ Some industries' products bring a higher-percentage commission than other lines of products.

Marketing and Advertising Methods and Tips
❖ Thoroughly research your prospective clients and their needs so you can bring them the product they will want (see Thomas Register of Manufacturers, below).
❖ Know your product line from your own experience, background, training, and/or education.
❖ Immerse yourself in the industry you are representing: attend trade shows and conventions; make as many direct contacts as you can from networking, cold-calling, etc.

Essential Equipment
❖ Computer: standard, or a laptop to use when traveling.
❖ Fax machine, copier, printer.
❖ Cellular phone for travel, date book, and other assorted business supplies.
❖ Promotional materials.

Recommended Training, Experience, or Skills
❖ Background, education, and training in sales, marketing, merchandising, math, and business.
❖ Technical education if planning on selling technical products.
❖ You must be good with people and communication and have confidence in yourself.

Income Potential
❖ The first year, you may only earn $10,000 to $12,000.
❖ Average net income is $56,000 annually; it can go much higher, but traveling expenses can cut into your earnings.

Best Customers
Wholesalers, retailers, government agencies, institutions; those in need of a certain product or service.

Helpful Tips
Decide early in your career which products you can sell the best and to whom.

For More Information
Association

> Manufacturers' Agents National Association (MANA)
> 23016 Mill Creek Rd.
> P.O. Box 3467
> Laguna Hills, CA 92654-3467
> Send SASE for membership information.

Books

> *The Complete Guide for the Manufacturer's Rep: How to Get & Hold Key Accounts* by Louis H. Clark. 1975, The McGraw-Hill Companies, New York, NY.
>
> *Making $70,000 a Year as a Self-Employed Manufacturer's Representative* by Leigh and Sureleigh Silliphant. 1988, Ten Speed Press, P.O. Box 7123, Berkeley, CA.
>
> *Thomas Register of American Manufacturers,* Thomas Publishing Co., New York. Published annually. Check your local library's reference section.

Periodical

> *Agency Sales*
> 230 Mill Creek Rd.
> P.O. Box 3467
> Laguna Hills, CA 92654-3467

Magazine published by Manufacturers' Agents National Association.

Additional Business Ideas

Manufacturer's displays: set up displays of products for manufacturers in stores.

⚞ 20 ⚟
MARKET RESEARCH ANALYST/CONSULTANT

Marketing research and consulting covers a number of aspects of helping businesses attract customers. It includes advertising, promotions and sales, analyzing customer buying patterns, public relations, direct mailings, and commercials. Marketing analysts are consultants who are experts in one or more industries. They help companies analyze past customer responses to products and services and create marketing plans to acquire new business.

Start-Up Costs
$4,000 to $10,000

Pricing Guidelines
* Consultants charge by the hour or by the project, or by the seminar/workshop, or they may be contracted on a regular basis.
* Rates and fees are based on one's experience and reputation for getting results; they range from $40 per hour to $100 per hour and more.

Marketing and Advertising Methods and Tips
* Direct mail with follow-up calls and visits.
* Networking, word-of-mouth referrals.
* Specific trade shows; making talks, holding seminars.
* Advertisements, articles in trade publications.

Essential Equipment

* Office equipment: computer (including a laptop) with hard drive, modem, and business and marketing software.
* Cellular phone; telephone and communications system.
* Business promotional materials, including self-published manual, marketing portfolio.

Recommended Training, Experience, or Skills

Education (college courses recommended), training, and employment experience in your field of marketing expertise.

Income Potential

$30,000 to $100,000 per year; more if you have employees or handle larger clients.

Best Customers

* Those that fit into your business "niche" and expertise.
* Companies that are downsizing.
* Smaller companies that cannot afford a full-time advertising or marketing department.
* Home-based businesses that are isolated from networking opportunities (their phenomenal growth offers a growing potential for new customers).
* Women entrepreneurs (research the problems women have in starting businesses so that you can help advise them).

Helpful Tips

* Get work experience in one or more companies' marketing divisions.
* Before you start your own company, learn all you can about the current trends in your industry.
* Attend trade seminars and workshops for your own education and to see how they are conducted.
* Take courses and training on starting and running a consulting business.

For More Information

Association

Market Research Association
2189 Silas Deane Highway, Suite 5
Rocky Hill, CT 06067-0230

A source of information about careers in marketing and opinion research; offers a brief *Career Guide* for $2; also offers a wide array of publications and membership information. A publications catalog and membership information may be obtained by calling them at (860) 257-4008 from 9:00 a.m. to 5:00 p.m. (EST).

Books

The Consultant's Manual: A Complete Guide to Building a Successful Consulting Practice by Thomas L. Greenbaum. 1990, John Wiley & Sons, Inc., New York, NY.

The Marketer's Guide to Public Relations: How Today's Top Companies Are Using PR to Gain a Competitive Edge by Thomas L. Harris. 1991, John Wiley & Sons, Inc., New York, NY.

Marketing Research, 5th ed., by David A. Aaker and George S. Day. 1995, John Wiley & Sons, Inc., New York, NY.

Target Marketing for the Small Business, 2nd ed., by Linda Pinson and Jerry Jinnett. 1996, Upstart Publishing, Dover, NH.

Periodical

Journal of Marketing Research
American Marketing Association
250 S. Wacker Dr., Suite #200
Chicago, IL 60606

Members $40 per year, 4 issues; nonmembers $75 per year; membership dues $100 per year.

Correspondence Schools

ICS Learning Systems
925 Oak St.
Scranton, PA 18515

Business courses, etc.; write for brochure.

Additional Business Ideas

Market consultant referral business: match up market specialists with specific companies' needs.

⚮ 21 ⚮

ONLINE SERVICES

As the use of the Web and Internet grows every day, more and more businesses, consultants, professionals, and consumers want to get online to do business, make contacts, and gain information. This task is overwhelming to many newcomers. Your business as a Web-page designer and/or online consultant is to design a home page—a site on the World Wide Web—for your clients' businesses.

Start-Up Costs

$8,000 to $10,000

Pricing Guidelines

Depending on your skills and experience, average hourly rates for design work range from $50 to $150. A basic Web site containing three to five pages of information can cost between $500 and $1,500 to design.

Marketing and Advertising Methods and Tips

* Take out display ads in local and trade business publications.
* Encourage word-of-mouth referrals from satisfied customers.
* Write articles about online advertising.
* Advertise online.

Essential Equipment

* Office equipment: computer, telephone systems and individual lines, access to the Internet and Web; business and online software; fax machine.
* Promotional materials.

Recommended Training, Experience, or Skills
✤ Computer technology knowledge and training; some programming skills.
✤ Advertising background helpful.
✤ Knowledge of graphic design helpful.
✤ Observe pages online to see how effective they are.

Income Potential
$25,000 to $50,000 per year

Best Customers
Businesses with products; new businesses; writers; for-profit associations.

Helpful Tips
✤ Provide a free consulting session so that you can interview your clients as to what they hope a Web page will do for their business. Ask what their objectives are.
✤ Encourage your clients to use their home page in conjunction with their other promotional materials.
✤ In designing a Web page, strike a balance between illustrations and text. Too many graphics may take too long to download, and a potential customer may leave.
✤ Design an interactive home page where the prospective customer is requested to take action, such as ordering, leaving a note, requesting more information, etc.

For More Information
Books
101 Businesses You Can Start on the Internet by Daniel S. Janel. 1996, Van Nostrand, Reinhold Publishing, New York, NY.
The New Internet Business Book by Jill H. Ellsworth. 1996, John Wiley & Sons, Inc., New York, NY.

Additional Business Ideas
✤ Train companies about e-mail and navigating the Internet.
✤ Personal online shopper.
✤ Computer programming consultant.

⚜ 22 ⚜

BUILDER'S CLEANUP

This is a nontraditional job for women, but one that fills a need. Builders, roofers, and homeowners who are doing remodeling jobs need someone to pick up the debris left over from construction, building, roofing, remodeling, etc. It is a physically demanding job, but one that is very much needed. Homeowners are often working and do not have the time to clean up after remodeling or re-roofing.

You may branch out to do other cleaning services such as yard clean-up in the spring, cleaning out garages and/or attics, and removal of small sheds; trash pick-up for communities after a carnival may also be included. You will have to contact your community's trash service for fees to dump any of the picked-up items. Often there is good wood and other materials you can recycle and sell for additional profits.

Start-Up Costs
$5,000 plus the cost of a truck for hauling.

Pricing Guidelines
Price by the hour, the day, or (more likely) the project; $100 to $200 per day for construction clean-up.

Marketing and Advertising Methods and Tips
❖ Direct mail to builders, remodelers, and local government officials, followed by calls and visits.
❖ Offer a free estimate of the project.
❖ For homeowners, put up flyers on community bulletin boards and at local hardware stores and building supply centers; take out ads in classified-ad papers.
❖ Get referrals from satisfied customers.
❖ Send out ads in co-op advertising.

Essential Equipment
❖ Telephone system.
❖ Promotional materials; start with good cards and brochures.

❖ Truck and/or trailer for light hauling.
❖ Gloves, protective eyewear, a commercial magnet for picking up nails, a wheelbarrow, assorted tools.

Recommended Training, Experience, or Skills
❖ As this is primarily a physical job, you can do this with little preparation or training.
❖ You should enjoy physical work and get satisfaction from completing a job for which you have contracted.

Income Potential
$6,000 to $8,000 per year part-time; $20,000 to $40,000 per year and up full-time. This is a good job to start part-time or on weekends.

Best Customers
Builders, roofers, public parks, homeowners.

Helpful Tips
Even in the nineties, you may face discrimination because you are a woman, so be professional and let your company's performance speak for itself.

Additional Business Ideas
Clean windows in new housing developments where there is blowing dust.

≤ 23 ≥
SEMINAR LEADER

Giving seminars, workshops, and/or speeches is a fast-growing field. Attendees like these events because they get a concentrated amount of information in a shorter time period than if they took a 6- to 10-week course at a school. Companies like them because they can be held in-house and for a large number of employees.

In addition to setting up and speaking at your own workshops, you can speak at trade shows, conventions, business meetings, etc. You can also sell your own manuals and materials. People love to learn, especially if they can improve their finances, their personal relationships, their careers, or their lives in general. If you also make your presentation interesting, active, and fun for your attendees, you will be a success.

Start-Up Costs
$4,000 to $13,000 at the low end; $30,000 to $45,000 at the high end.

Pricing Guidelines
$60 to $180 per day to $7,000 for several days ($2,000 per day for business seminars).

Marketing and Advertising Methods and Tips
* Send promotional materials to Chambers of Commerce, professional and trade associations, colleges, and schools.
* Take a booth at trade shows.
* Advertising: online; display ads in business and trade publications.
* Write articles in business and trade publications about your seminar topics.
* Write a book on the topic; self-publish it or approach publishers with proposals.

Essential Equipment
* Office equipment: computer with desktop publishing software; modem, fax machine, copier, telephone system.
* Seminar-related materials: workbooks, manuals, audiovisual aids to enhance your talks.
* Promotional materials: brochures, business cards, posters, professional photos.

Recommended Training, Experience, or Skills
* Take some public speaking courses at local colleges or schools.

❖ Observe and attend various seminars and workshops to see what you like and do not like about them.

❖ Know your material; you have to talk intelligently and with confidence.

Income Potential
$25,000 to $100,000 per year and up

Best Customers
Those in your profession or trade who want to gain insight into improving themselves or their finances.

Helpful Tips
❖ Start out offering free or low-cost speeches or one-night courses at schools, colleges, and continuing education programs. Have your students evaluate you and your information.

❖ Decide whether you are speaking to make a profit or to promote your business, your book, etc.

❖ Let your information sell you or your product. Do not make your seminar an all-day "infomercial."

❖ Be prepared for follow-up responses to your seminar. Have order forms and extra materials to buy (set yourself up to take checks and credit cards). If you are promoting your business, have your name and contact information printed in your workshop or follow-up materials.

❖ Be enthusiastic and knowledgeable about your subject, and sincere and honest with your attendees. Make your attendees feel that your seminar was worth the money they spent. They *are* your customers, so try to give them the information you promised you would give them!

For More Information
Books
How to Make It Big in the Seminar Business by Paul Karasik. 1992, McGraw-Hill, Inc., New York, NY.

Seminars Directory, Gale Research, Inc. Detroit, MI; a reference book that lists seminars.

How to Run Seminars and Workshops: Presentation Skills for Consultants, Trainers, & Teachers by Robert Jolles. 1993, John Wiley & Sons, Inc., New York, NY.

Business Guides
"Seminar Promoting," $69.50, Entrepreneur's Small Business Development Catalog; call (800) 421-2300 to order or for the catalog.

"Seminar Promoting," National Business Library's Start-Up Guides; call (800) 947-7724 to order or for the catalog.

Periodical
Marketing Seminars and Conferences, $95 per year, LERN (Learning Resources Network) Co., 1550 Hayes Dr., Manhattan, KS 66502, (913) 539-5376; other membership plans available; write or call for additional information.

Additional Business Ideas
❖ Public speaker

Scared Speechless: Public Speaking Step-by-Step by Rebecca McDaniel.

Speak and Grow Rich, 2nd ed., by Dottie Walters. 1996, Prentice-Hall, Englewood Cliffs, NJ.

Speaking with Confidence by Wand Vassallo. 1990, Betterway Books, Cincinnati, OH.

❖ Multimedia service: Help speakers and seminar leaders to create impressive presentations using multimedia technology.

"Multimedia Services," Entrepreneur's Start-Up Business Guide, (800)421-2300. $69.50 plus shipping.

The Business Week Guide to Multimedia Presentations by Robert L. Lindstrom. 1996, Lakewood Publications, Minneapolis, MN.

⚘ 24 ⚘
OTHER BUSINESS SERVICES

Business Referral Services
You create a database of consultants, trainers, experts, and professionals who market their services to businesses, then match up businesses with people who can fill their needs.

Resource
"Referral Service," Entrepreneur's Small Business Development Catalog; call (800) 421-2300 to order, or for the catalog.

Business and Financial Services:
Skills trainer/corporate trainer: teach skills in your area of expertise to businesses' employees and executives.

Resource
Lakewood Publications
50 S. Ninth St.
Minneapolis, MN 55402
Many publications; write for catalog.

Cleaning:
Graffiti removal, window cleaning.

Business Consultant:
Additional Tips and Sources
   If you have specific knowledge and experience in an area of business, you can make from $40 to $260 per hour or more as a consultant, depending on the knowledge you have and who your clients are. You have to market yourself constantly and promote yourself through articles, books, seminars, and/or success stories from businesses that benefited from your expertise.

Start-Up Costs
$4,000 to $18,000

Income Potential
$20,000 to $100,000 per year

Franchises
General Business Services (GBS)
1020 N. University Parks Dr.
P.O. Box 3146
Waco, TX 76707
Offers its clients business, tax, financial, and management counseling as well as accounting services, products, and personnel services. Write, or call (817) 745-2525 or (800) 583-6181 to be matched with the nearest GBS counselor.

Association
Association of Professional Consultants
National Bureau of Professional Consultants
3577 Fourth Ave.
San Diego, CA 92103

Books
Become a Successful Consultant: Manage and Market Your Skills Effectively by Raymond Hebson. 1995, Atrium Publishers Group, Santa Rosa, CA.

The Complete Guide to Consulting Success by Howard L. Shenson and Ted Nicholas. 1995, Upstart Publishing, Dover, NH.

The Computer Consultant's Workbook by Janet Ruhll. 1995, Technion Books, Rhul Computer Services, Leverett, MA.

The Consultant's Handbook by Stephan Schiffman. 1988, Bob Schiffman, Bob Adams, Inc., Boston, MA.

How to Start and Run a Successful Consulting Business by Gregory Kishel and Patricia Kishel. 1996, John Wiley & Sons, Inc., New York, NY.

The Ten Hottest Consulting Practices: What They Are, How to Get into Them by Ron Tepper. 1995, John Wiley & Sons, Inc., New York, NY.

The following books are written by Herman Holtz and published by John Wiley & Sons, Inc., New York, NY:

The Business Plan Guide for Independent Consultants, 1994.
How to Succeed As an Independent Consultant, 3rd ed., 1993.
The Independent Consultant's Brochure and Letter Book, 1995.

Government Contract Specialist:
Help businesses learn about federal, state, and local contracts and help them through the process of qualification and application. There are SBA offices to help people for free, but this specialist can help locate the contracts that are available at all levels of government and match them up with the appropriate businesses.

There is a special need for new women business owners to have someone help them through the steps of bidding for a contract. Of course, you should have had experience in business and be familiar with completing government forms.

Books
Government Contract Negotiations: A Practical Guide for Small Business by David C. Moore. 1996, John Wiley & Sons, Inc., New York, NY.
Government Giveaways for Entrepreneurs II by Matthew Lesko. 1994, Information USA.

Periodicals and Publications
Government Contracts & Leads Directory (1996, $89.50) and *Government Prime Contracts Monthly* ($8 per month). Order from Government Data Publications, Inc., (Dept. 38-12) 1155 Connecticut Ave. NW, Washington, DC 20036.

Commerce Business Daily
P.O. Box 37194
Pittsburgh, PA 15250-7954
Subscription: $324 per year or $162.50 for six months for first class; $275 per year or $137.50 for six months second class; or check to see if your local library has a copy.

Video
"Your Guide to SBA Loans and Programs"
IWS, Inc.
24 Canterbury Road
Rockville Centre, NY 11570
$49.95 (plus $4 shipping and handling).

Outplacement Service:
Help executives and other professionals who have lost jobs
due to downsizing to re-evaluate their careers and guide
them to new ventures or jobs.

Business Guide
"Outplacement Service" Entrepreneur's Guide, $69.50; call
(800) 421-2300.

Children's Services

Research has shown that Americans spend billions of dollars every year on their children—not just for products, but for specialized services as well. Market experts predict that this trend will increase the demand for such services as day care, fitness, special events, tutoring and learning centers, transportation, safety, dance and sports, and products such as educational toys and materials, clothing, and books.

If you enjoy children, a child-related business may be right for you. Research the kinds of products, services, franchises, etc. that exist in your community to serve children or their parents, and see if there is a need for a business that you would enjoy starting. Here are a few possibilities to give you an idea for a business niche.

⊴ 25 ⊵
CHILDREN'S FITNESS CENTER

Despite all the sports and activities in which our children are involved, the National Center for Health Statistics states that "4.7 million youth (11%) ages 6 to 17 are severely overweight—more than twice the number observed in the 1960s." The center blames "fast foods, TV sets, and video games." The U.S. Department of Health and Human Services and the Centers for Disease Control and Prevention state that "ninety-eight percent of all American school children may already have at least one heart-disease risk factor, with obesity being a serious health problem for American children resulting in 1 in 5 preteens being overweight."

If you have sports and fitness training and/or experience, and enjoy working with children, you can offer individualized, specialized classes at YMCAs, local youth recreation centers, church halls, etc. If you get a good response to your course, you can start your business by renting rooms or halls in your community and eventually open your own fitness center. You may specialize in one activity or offer a variety of fitness courses. Just remember to make it fun for the children, or they will not want to come back!

Start-Up Costs
$15,000 starting out of a rented hall; $125,000 for setting up your own facility.

Pricing Guidelines
❖ Charge $45 to $90 for a 6- to 8-week course.
❖ Or charge a monthly fee per student for a given number of classes.

Essential Equipment
❖ Mats, sports equipment, first aid kit, assorted-sized playground balls, parachute, assorted-length jump ropes, orange play cones, sponge or yarn balls.
❖ Other equipment appropriate to the physical activities being taught.
❖ Look for good used equipment at school auctions.

Marketing and Advertising Methods and Tips
❖ An ad in the Yellow Pages; ads in local newspapers.
❖ Flyers to parents at day-care centers and schools.

❖ Press releases; have a special event to announce your opening.
❖ Talks to parent groups.
❖ A column (some newspapers offer this) in the local newspaper answering questions about children's fitness and sports.
❖ Sponsor a children's athletic team.
❖ Direct mail (ad coupons).
❖ Direct calls.
❖ Get involved in charity runs and events.

Recommended Training, Experience, or Skills
❖ Classes at colleges in fitness, children's psychology, elementary physical education.
❖ Red Cross certification: swimming, CPR, first aid.
❖ Work or volunteer in children activities at school or in clubs to see if this is something you enjoy and want to do for a living.

Income Potential
❖ Part time: $40 to $60 per hour.
❖ Owning a center with other instructors: $15,000 to $100,000 per year and up.

Best Customers
❖ Parents of upper-middle-class to upper-class income levels.
❖ Schools, centers for children with special needs.

Helpful Tips
❖ Know the mental and physical capabilities and limitations of the children at your center.
❖ Find out what licenses and teaching certificates you may need to teach children.
❖ Be sure to have adequate insurance coverage.
❖ Make it fun for your students, parents, and employees.

Franchises

Pee Wee Workout
34976 Aspenwood Lane
Willoughby, OH 44094
Aerobic fitness for children.

For More Information

Books

Fitness for Children by Curt Hinson. 1995, Human Kinetics Publishers, Champaign, IL.

The Cooperative Indoor & Outdoor Game Book by Priscilla Y. Huff. 1992, Scholastic Professional Books, New York, N Y.

Business Guides

"Children's Fitness Centers," Entrepreneur's Small Business Development Catalog. Call to order or for a catalog: (800)421-2300.

Additional Business Ideas

❖ Mobile fitness van: Travel to day-care centers and schools with your fitness and game equipment to present regular classes, special game-day events, etc. Also offer adapted fitness activities and games for centers with children who have physical and mental disabilities.

❖ Athletic trainer: If you have a degree in athletic training, you can offer your services and those of other trainers and EMTs (emergency medical technicians) to community children's sports teams. Very few have any trained personnel present during games and events.

❧ 26 ❧
CHILDPROOFING

Too many children are seriously injured or die from household accidents. As a baby/childproofing expert, it is your business to inspect the homes of new parents for hazards and to make safety recommendations. Then you can offer the parents the option of having safety devices installed by you or do it yourself.

Start-Up Costs
$6,000 to $9,000

Pricing Guidelines
* Average charges: 3 percent to 4 percent of the square footage of the area being evaluated; about $75 to $80 and up per house.
* Approximately $800 to have a house child-proofed.

Essential Equipment
* Office: computer with fax/modem; printer; desktop publishing program; reference books on safety.
* High-quality safety products.

Marketing and Advertising Methods and Tips
* Ads to new parents in local parents' newspapers.
* Write a regular safety column (paid ad) for your local papers.
* Flyers in pediatrician's offices; referral from pediatricians, EMTs and/or emergency room staff.
* Talks to parents-to-be at local health-care institutions, safety classes.
* Referrals from satisfied clients.
* Talks at senior citizen centers about keeping homes safe for grandchildren.
* Flyers at children's furniture stores; offer a free seminar.

Recommended Training, Experience, or Skills
✤ Take safety courses sponsored by local parenting and health-care institutions.
✤ Read and do research about home hazards.
✤ Take first aid courses and child CPR for your own knowledge and information.
✤ Spend time with toddlers and children and observe their behavior and what attracts them.
✤ Be a good communicator and teacher, as you are educating people about preventive measures for safety.

Income Potential
$25,000 to $50,000 per year.

Best Customers
New parents, grandparents, guardians, child-care workers.

Helpful Tips
✤ Learn all you can about baby and child safety, and keep up to date on the latest developments and products in the safety industry.
✤ Take classes on safety and preventive measures.
✤ Discuss your business liability with your insurance agent and lawyer.

Franchises
Safe-T-Child Inc.
401 Friday Mountain Rd.
Austin, TX 78737
Child security and identification program; write for information. $12,900 to get started.

For More Information
Books
Child Safety from Preschool to Adolescence edited by Bill Gilham and James Thompson. 1995, Routledge, New York, NY.

The Childwise Catalog, 3rd ed., by Jack Gillis and Mary Ellen R.
Fise. 1993, Harper Perennial, New York, NY.
The Complete Guide to Making Your Home Safe by David Heberle
and Richard M. Scutella. 1995, Betterway Books, Cincinnati, OH.
Home Safety Desk Reference by Dr. Ted Ferry. 1994, Career Press,
Franklin Lakes, NJ.
*Keeping Your Baby Safe: A Guidebook for You to Protect Your
Child* by Jane Dyche. 1994, Tri-Oak Education, Murfreesboro, TN.

School
Pediatrics Trauma Prevention School, Dr. Baby Proofer, Inc.;
Thomas Golden, owner. $7,500 for five-day course on
how to start your own business in this field. Not a franchise. For more information, write to P.O. Box 595834,
Dallas, TX 75359-5834.

Additional Business Ideas
❖ Mail-order catalog of children's safety devices.
❖ Invent/design a safety device for kids.
❖ Offer to evaluate and/or research children's products and
toys for their safety, for a fee.

27
CREATIVE LEARNING CENTER

Working parents and parents concerned with the cutbacks in
educational spending across the nation are looking for ways
to supplement their children's education and to foster their
creativity. Much of the time available would be for after
school and on the weekends. You could offer a transportation
service: you could work out arrangements with a children's
taxi service or use your own employees to provide transportation from schools to your center.

You could offer daytime courses for preschoolers, and enrichment courses and tutoring for schoolchildren in the afternoons, evenings, and weekends. Your center could specialize in dance, acting, or art, or offer other enrichment courses such as creative writing, poetry, music, foreign languages, and computer skills. Tutoring in all academic areas, helping to establish good study habits, college preparation, and even counseling could also be offered. Children could also come just to relax and read or do their homework. A creativity center like this can be a valuable asset to your community.

If successful, you could also offer scholarships and/or sliding fees for disadvantaged children. All children are creative and should be given the opportunity to express their creativity and learn!

Start-Up Costs
$15,000 low start-up if in your home; $100,000 high start-up if you use rented facilities.

Pricing Guidelines
* $25 to $200 per child per course, depending on the days, materials, instructors' fees, etc.
* Monthly fees that allow the student to take a certain number of courses or just come to study.

Marketing and Advertising Methods and Tips
Local parents' newspapers; Yellow Pages; brochures to school parent groups; talks to community groups; referrals from satisfied parents.

Essential Equipment
* Home-based: desks, reference books, art supplies, computer with modem and printer; ideally, a separate room with a separate entrance from the rest of the house.
* Your own facility: look for a good location, convenient to the community and transportation. You can start by renting religious buildings' rooms or halls, or space above

CHILDREN'S SERVICES   137

office buildings. Depending on the growth and demand of your center, you can build or remodel a building to fit your center's needs.

Recommended Training, Experience, or Skills
+ If possible, work at one or more enrichment centers as an instructor and familiarize yourself with the organizational duties of the program director.
+ Have a background in education and/or the arts.
+ Hire qualified people and those who are creative in their teaching skills.
+ Check on zoning, licensing, and regulations before you open.
+ Make a good business plan and do your market research to see if there are parents who want a center in their community.

Income Potential
$15,000 per year if home-based or by yourself; $75,000 to $100,000 per year with instructors, etc.

Best Customers
Children from the neighborhood and nearby private or public schools.

Helpful Tips
+ Investigate creative and enrichment centers in non-competing areas to see how they are run, what they offer, who their customers are, what they charge, and how many children they serve. Then evaluate your own background, finances, possible instructors, and facilities.
+ With many of our public schools in a crisis, you may have more business than you can handle!

Franchises
Computertots
10132 Colvin Run Rd.
Great Falls, VA 22066

Imagine Tomorrow
P.O. Box 200
Park Ridge, NJ 07656

Little Scientists Franchise Corp.
497 Main St.
Ansonia, CT 06401

Tutor Time Learning Centers
1 Park Place, 621 Northwest 53rd St.
Boca Raton, FL 33487

For More Information
Books
Creative Activities and Seatwork!! 845 Enchanting ABC Books & Activities: From Preschool to High School by Cathie H. Cooper. 1995, Scarecrow Press, Inc., Lanham, MD.

Additional Business Ideas
✦ Offer enrichment courses, home-schooling advising, etc. during the day for the growing number of home-schooled children across our country.
✦ Offer family nights, birthday parties, educational field trips.

≈ 28 ≈
SUMMER CAMP INFORMATION
AND REFERRAL SERVICE

With this service, you supply information on summer camps to parents. Parents fill out a questionnaire and you provide them with a listing of camps that best meet their child's interests and their criteria.

Start-Up Costs
$5,000 to $10,000 (office equipment and advertisements).

Essential Equipment

❖ Office: computer with CD-ROM, fax/modem; telephone and answering system; copier, separate fax machine; mailing list software.

❖ Other: the American Camping Association's guide, including a copy on disk; ACA camp brochures.

❖ Promotional materials for your referral business.

Pricing Guidelines

Charge a flat fee for listing: $60 for one report for one child; $110 for two children; $150 for three children.

Marketing and Advertising Methods and Tips

❖ Display ads in local parents' newspapers; classified ads in parents' magazines; small display ads in Sunday editions of major city newspapers.

❖ Articles in newspapers and magazines about camping and children: how to choose a camp; how to pack; dealing with homesickness, etc.

Recommended Training, Experience, or Skills

❖ Spend some time as a camp counselor at both day and residential camps.

❖ Talk to parents of campers and survey what they did or did not like about their children's camps.

❖ Visit some of the camps where your customers send their children.

❖ Have good response time to customer inquiries and requests.

Income Potential

$8,000 per year at the start; $25,000 to $30,000 per year and up as your business and reputation grow.

Best Customers

Parents of campers.

Helpful Tips

✤ Take some time to work in and research the camping industry.

✤ Follow up your customers' requests with evaluations of the camps where they sent their children.

For More Information

Association

American Camping Association
5000 State Rd, 67 North
Martinsville, IN 41651-7902

Offers guide to camps that it has accredited (see "Resource Guide," below).

Resource Guide

Guide to Accredited Camps, 1996-1997 by American Camping Association Staff. 1996, American Camping Association, Martinsville, IN. $16.95 for the guide; $19.95 for the guide on disk. The guide also offers information on how to choose a camp for your child and information on camps for children with special needs.

Additional Business Ideas

Hold your own day camp with specific themes: sports, reading and writing, creativity, etc.

"Child Services," $69.50, Entrepreneur's Small Business Development Catalog. Call (800) 421-2300 to order or for catalog. This business guide gives an overview of five of the most popular child services today, including how to start your own children's camp.

≍ 29 ≍

TOY INVENTOR/DESIGNER

With toys, you create a business for children. Someone once said, "Play is a child's work." Your work, then, is to make child's play. You can come up with your own ideas, which you can patent or sell to a toy company. Other ideas include selling at craft shows, in small shops, through catalogs, or via your own mail-order business. You are only limited by your imagination and what interests a child.

Start-Up Costs
$1,000 to come up with the idea and a prototype; $250,000 to manufacture and distribute it yourself.

Pricing Guidelines
Research the kind of toys out there and compare your price to theirs.

Essential Equipment
Your tools and craft supplies, drafting tools and drawing implements to sketch your idea(s).

Marketing and Advertising Methods and Tips
✤ Write directly to toy companies first to learn about their policy on being approached with new toy ideas. Then write for their application procedures.
✤ Exhibit your toys at toy trade shows.
✤ Have order forms, business cards, and brochures with you at arts and crafts shows and wholesale shows.

Recommended Training, Experience, or Skills
✤ Knowledge of the industry's best-selling products.
✤ Knowledge of children and their stages of development— what toys appeal to a certain age level and what children can do physically at various ages.
✤ Think like a child!
✤ Consult with inventor groups for advice and feedback.

Income Potential
Market-driven; depends on the sales and the demand. $1,000 to $2,000 per year at local craft shows; $10,000 to $100,000 if picked by national company.

Best Customers
Parents, grandparents, and other relatives attending craft shows.

Helpful Tips
✤ It's difficult to get your toy idea reviewed by toy manufacturers, but if you thoroughly research what toys are popular and why, you will have a better chance of selling your idea.

✤ Protect your ideas by keeping a notebook and illustrating it. Then have two witnesses sign your notebook, which can then be notarized.

✤ Watch out for scams involving invention-development companies.

✤ Look for smaller markets: small manufacturers, small shops.

For More Information
See "Inventor" in the "Creative Businesses" section.

Associations
Toy Inventors of America
5813 McCart Ave.
Fort Worth, TX 76133
Send SASE for information.

Toy Manufacturers Association of America
200 Fifth Ave., Suite 740
New York, NY 10010
Send SASE for information about their trade show (but the show is not for consumers) and "Toy Inventors' Guide."

Books
The Toy and Game Inventor's Guide: For Selling Products into the Toy & Game Industry by Gregory J. Battersby and Charles W. Grimes. 1996, Kent Communications, Ltd., P.O. Box 1169, Stamford, CT 06904-1169.; $34.95 plus $3.95 for shipping/handling; CT residents add sales tax.

Toy Making on a Budget by Nancy E. Carlberg. 1993, Carlberg Press, Anaheim, CA.

Toys to Build by the Editors of *Workbench*. 1996, AKC Publishing (can order from Chilton Book Company, Radnor, PA).

"200 Catalog House Labels ($15)," "Catalog House Directory ($7)," and "Selling To Catalog Houses ($7)," available from Success Publications, 3419 Dunham, Box 263, Warsaw, NY 14569.

Periodicals
PlayThings Magazine
51 Madison Ave.
New York, NY 10010
Publishes *The PlayThings Toy Guide* annually, which contains a listing of toy manufacturers, suppliers, and designers and is included with a subscription; $29 per year, 12 issues.

Crafts Report
P.O. Box 1992
Wilmington, DE 19899-1992
See the July, 1996, issue of this crafts marketing magazine features an in-depth look at toys by today's toymakers, traditional and contemporary, including doll marketing.

Additional Business Ideas
❖ Toy company:
   "Toy Company" business plan from *Business Plan Handbook, 1st ed.,* edited by Kristin Kohrs. 1995, Gale Research, Inc., Detroit, MI.
❖ Game inventor:
   The Game Inventor's Handbook, 2nd ed., by Stephen Peek. 1993, Betterway Books, Cincinnati, OH.
❖ Used toy store:
   Toy Traders
   4334 Leland Street
   Chevy Chase, MD 20815
   Secondhand toy store franchise.

✤ Toy kits (puzzles) for children
✤ Piñatas for children's parties
✤ Rocking horses:
   Rocking Horses: Woodworking Projects by Margaret Spencer.
   1991, Trafalgar Square, North Pomfret, VT.
✤ Mail order: specialty toy catalog (see "Mail Order" in "General Resources").

≈ ● ≈

MISCELLANEOUS CHILD-RELATED
BUSINESSES AND SOURCES

✤ Children's transportation
✤ Family, child, or family travel newsletter
✤ Swimming school for infants and children
✤ Dance and motor development instructor
✤ Sports photos
✤ Children's used clothing and toy consignment shop (see "Consignment Shop," in the "Small Shops" section of this book)
✤ Rentals of children's products
✤ Educational materials and supplies
✤ Toy bags for children—sell to professionals for their waiting rooms
✤ 900 telephone number for parenting tips
✤ Baby support: childbirth classes, nanny services, designing and furnishing nurseries, postpartum services (see "Medical Businesses")
✤ Design a special line of children's clothing
✤ Day-care supplies on wheels
✤ Cleaning toys in hospital and professionals' waiting rooms
✤ See also, in *101 Best Home-Based Businesses for Women* (1995, Prima Publishing, Rocklin, CA): Child Care, Costumes, Children's Parties, School Programs and Assemblies

Children Entrepreneurs

Books

101 Marvelous Money-Making Ideas for Kids by Heather Wood. 1995, Tor Books, New York, NY.

The Totally Awesome Business Book for Kids by Arthur Berg Bochner and Adrienne G. Berg. 1994, Random House, 400 Hahn Rd., Westminster, MD 21157; $13 includes postage and handling.

Computer Services

⚞ 30 ⚟
COMPUTER BUSINESSES

Almost every business, large or small, has or will have a computer. The same with consumer households. The cost of computers has come down in recent years; stores now offer good used computers as people upgrade, and more companies are offering computers by mail order. If you are thinking of buying a computer, do you want it for business and/or personal use? What software will you need? Will you need support services? Researching your business ideas will help you determine what kind of hardware and software you will need.

If you are knowledgeable about computers, you may want to start a business that shares your expertise with others. The following is basic start-up information on computer-related businesses (see also "Clipping Service," "Database Consultant," "Mailing-List Service," "Graphic Designer," "Typesetting," "Independent Publishing," and "Fact Finder" for other computer-related businesses).

Computer Consultant

Provide computer education, trouble-shooting, and computer hardware and software installation.

❖ Start-up costs: $5,000 to $13,000.
❖ Potential income: $40 to $80 per hour; $35,000 to $75,000 per year; more if your area of expertise is in demand.
❖ Training/background: A degree in computer technology; overall knowledge of the most popular hardware and software used by businesses and consumers.

Resources

"Computer Consulting," $69.50, Entrepreneur's Small Business Development Catalog; call (800) 421-2300 to order or for catalog.

The Computer Consultant's Guide: Real-Life Strategies for Building a Successful Consulting Career by Janet Ruhl. 1993, John Wiley & Sons, Inc., New York, NY.

CompuServe's "Computer Consultant's Forum," (800) 848-8990.

Multimedia Service

Produce multimedia presentations for corporations, small and home-based businesses, organizations, seminar promoters, public speakers, and consumers.

❖ Start-up costs: $10,000 to $15,000.
❖ Potential income: $25,000 per year to as high as $200,000 per year.
❖ Training/background: video, computer, and marketing education and experience.

Books

The Business Week Guide to Multimedia Presentations by Robert L. Linstrom. 1995, Lakewood Publications, 50 S. 9th St., Minneapolis, MN 55402; $39.95.

Making Money with Multimedia by David Rosen. 1994, Addison-Wesley Publishing Co., Inc., Reading, MA.

Business Guide

"Multimedia Service," $69.50, Entrepreneur's Small Business Development Catalog; call (800) 421-2300 to order or for catalog.

Software Designer/Publisher

❖ Start-up costs: $2,500 to $5,000.

❖ Potential income: $50,000 to $100,000 per year and up.

Association

Software Publishers Association
1730 M Street NW, Suite 700
Washington, DC 20036-4510
Internet: *http://www.spa.org.* This is the principal trade association serving the software industry. Membership includes conferences, market research and support, business management guides, publication catalog, etc.

Books

Building a Successful Software Business by David Radin. 1994, O'Reilly & Assocs., Inc., Cambridge, MA.

How to Develop a Sound Software Business, prepared by the Stein Software Corp. 1994. Order from the Software Publishers Association (see "Association," above).

The Software Developer's Complete Legal Companion by Thorne D. Harris, III. 1994, Prima Publishing, Rocklin, CA.

Software Development: A Legal Guide by Stephen Fishman. 1994, Nolo Press, Berkeley, CA.

Business Plans Handbook, 1st ed., Gale Research, Inc., Detroit, MI. A library reference book with sample business plans for different businesses, including a "Software Developer."

General Computer Business Resources

Association

Independent Computer Consultants Association
933 Gardenview Office Parkway
St. Louis, MO 63141

"Supporting the success of computer consultants in providing professional services to their services." Send SASE for membership information and the closest chapter.

Books

Launching A Business with Your PC by Mike Griffin. 1993, New Business Enterprises, a division of Macmillan Computer Publishing, Indianapolis, IN.

Making Money with Your PC! by Lynn Walford. Ten Speed Press, Berkeley, CA.

Making Money with Your Computer at Home by Paul and Sarah Edwards. 1993, Jeremy P. Tarcher/Putnam Book, G.P. Putnam's Sons, New York, NY.

Schools

Graduate School, USDA Correspondence Program
Ag Box 9911, Room 1112, South Agriculture Building
14th Ave. SW
Washington, DC 20250-9971

ICS Learning Systems
925 Oak St.
Scranton, PA 18540-9889

NRI Schools
4401 Connecticut Ave. NW
Washington, DC 20078-3543

Other Computer Business Ideas

❖ Computer cleaning services
❖ Computer game development
❖ Computer rental or leasing
❖ Data entry services
❖ Tabulating services
❖ Optical scanning data services

Creative Businesses

According to the American Crafts Council, there are some 500,000 men and women in the U.S. who earn a part- or full-time income with their art or handcrafts. Arts and handcrafts—as a hobby and profession—have created a $2.5 billion a year industry! Although many people consider their crafts to be hobbies, many others are professional artisans and handcrafters, turning their skills into successful businesses.

This section of the book will begin with helpful resources for those wishing to earn money with their art and/or handcraft.

Arts and Handcrafts Businesses: General Resources
Associations
American Craft Council (ACC)
72 Spring St.
New York, NY 10012
$40 per year membership include a subscription to *American Craft* magazine, free admission to juried craft fairs, access to library, discounts, etc.

American Craft Association
21 South Eltings Corner Rd.
Highland, NY 12528

A division of the ACC gives its members access to health benefits, a credit card program, discounts, etc. Membership includes a subscription to the newsletter, "The Voice."

Books

The Arts and Handcrafts Sourcebook: How to Learn and Earn Money with Your Creative Skills by Priscilla Y. Huff; not yet available. Write to P. Y. Huff, Box 286, Sellersville, PA 18960 for publication date.

The Basic Guide to Selling Arts and Crafts by James Dillehay. 1995, Warm Snow Publishers, P.O. Box 75, Torreon, NM 87061; $18.45 (includes postage and handling).

Crafting As a Business by Wendy Rosen. 1994, Chilton Book Company, Radnor, PA.

How to Sell What You Make: The Business of Marketing Crafts, revised and updated, by Paul Gerhards. 1996, Stackpole Books, Mechanicsburg, PA.

Marketing Your Arts & Crafts by Janice West; order from Chester Book Co. (See "Book Clubs," below.)

Book Clubs and Mail-Order Catalogs

Better Homes & Gardens Crafts Club
P.O. Box 8824
Camp Hill, PA 17012-8824
Many selections each month. Write for information about membership.

Chester Book Company
4 Maple St.
Chester, CT 06412
Books by fine and creative artists and handcrafters. Write for catalog.

Dover Publications, Inc.
31 East 2nd St.
Mineola, NY 11501
A wide selection of books in all fields including art and crafts, and books with copyright-free designs. Write for catalog (takes 3 to 4 weeks to arrive).

Success Publications
3419 Dunham Rd., Box 263
Warsaw, NY 14569
Several publications on selling arts and crafts; send SASE for a current list.

TCR (The Crafts Report) Book Club
Box 1992
Wilmington, DE 19899-1992
Offers the following books:

Directory of Wholesale Reps for Craft Professionals by Sharon Olson.
In Search of Arts and Crafts on the Internet by Kathleen McMahon.
The Law (in Plain English) for Craftspeople by Leonard DuBoff.
Photographing Your Artwork by Steve Meltzer.
Working with Wholesale Giftware Reps:, A Beginner's Handbook by Jill Poulsen Ford.

The Front Room Publishers
P.O. Box 1541
Clifton, NJ 07015-1541
Write for a copy of the "Learning Extension Catalog," which carries many directories and books on crafts marketing; World Wide Web: *http://www.intac.com/~ rjp.*

Success Publications
The Success Group
3419 Dunham, Box 263
Warsaw, NY 14569
They sell numerous directories and guides for making money with arts and crafts. Write for a free copy of their listings and a copy of their newsletter.

Business Guides
Entrepreneur's Start-Up Guide, "Craft Business." (800) 421-2300; $69.50 plus shipping.
National Business Library's Start-Up Guide, "Make $ with Your Crafts." (800) 947-7724; $39.95.

Directory

The Directory of Artists, Crafters, Artisans by Patricia Nay, 1935
D Waters Edge, Fort Collins, CO 80526; for a fee, you can
be listed in this directory that gives shop owners access to
crafters all over the country. Write for more information.

Online Information

CompuServe, "The Crafts Forum" (within CompuServe, type
GO CRAFTS); (800) 848-8990.
Also see *The Crafts Report*, below.

Periodicals and Publications

The Crafts Report: The Business Journal for the Crafts Industry
P.O. Box, 1992
Wilmington, DE 19899
$29 per year, 12 issues; on the Web: *http://www.craftsreport.com*

Crafting for Profit
Better Homes & Gardens
1912 Grand Ave.
Des Moines, IA 50309
Newsletter for arts and crafts professionals; $60 per year.

Show Guides

Arts 'n Crafts Showguide
A.C.N. Publications
P.O. Box 104628-Q
Jefferson City, MO 65110-4628

A Step Ahead, Ltd.
Ronay Guides
2950 Pangborn Rd.
P.O. Box 33462
Decatur, GA 30033
Lists more than 2,800 arts and crafts shows, fairs, festivals,
competitions, and exhibits for GA, FL, AL, TN, NC, SC, and
VA. Write (include SASE) for current price. Each state guide is
sold separately.

Software
  Silver Lining
  1320 Standiford, Suite 170
  Modesto, CA 95350
Business accounting software for IBM compatibles; software for artists, craftspeople, and retail operations.

  Mailer's Software
  970 Calle Negocio
  San Clemente, CA 92673-6201
Direct mail software; a PC-based mailing list management program for small-volume mailers. Call (714) 492-7000 for catalog.

Supplies
The Crafts Supply Sourcebook: A Comprehensive Shop-by-Mail Guide, 3rd ed., by Margaret Boyd. 1994, Betterway Books, Cincinnati, OH.

Catalog of Art Materials
Dick Blick Art Materials
P.O. Box 1267
Galesburg, IL 61402-1267
To order or for catalog, call (800) 447-8192.

≈ 31 ≈

CARTOONIST/CARICATURIST

In this freelance artistic business, you draw cartoons and/or caricatures for your clients to illustrate their magazine articles or stories; create logos, characters, and designs/clip art for software; and fill other requests for illustration. You can also create your own special character that you use in a comic strip and cartoons. If successful, you can market your designs on products such as jewelry, T-shirts, and other items.

Lauren R. Rabinowitz, a.k.a. "Lauren the Cartoon Goddess," is one such humorous illustrator, cartoonist, and animator. She holds a master's degree from Parsons School of Design. In addition to her illustrations and cartoons, Rabinowitz has done typesetting, desktop publishing, and logos. Her clients include environmental groups, cafés, magazines, theaters, and others. She produces pins, earrings, T-shirts, and items featuring "Lauren the Cartoon Goddess."

Start-Up Costs
$5,000 to $12,000 for equipment, supplies, and promotional materials.

Pricing Guidelines
The Graphic Artists Guild Handbook (see "Books," below) gives good instruction on how to determine your prices. It also has a good sample contract you can follow; you should have a signed contract for every job.

Essential Equipment
Art supplies, sketchbooks.

Marketing and Advertising Methods and Tips
✦ Network with other artists for information.
✦ Attend art shows, association meetings, seminars, and writer/illustrator conferences.
✦ Send samples to publishers, editors, public relations departments, etc. Follow up with appointments to show your other work.
✦ Join your trade association and local chapters to stay aware of the market trends and of who is hiring.
✦ Join a local business association.

Recommended Training, Experience, or Skills
✦ Training in art, design, computer technology.
✦ Should have some natural artistic ability and a sense of humor.
✦ It helps to work as a commercial artist to get the background in paste-up, etc.

Income Potential
$20,000 to $30,000 per year as a freelance business; cartoonists say that income is extremely variable, ranging from $10,000 to $40,000 per year.

Best Customers
* Businesses: logos, illustrations for ad campaigns, marketing projects, etc.
* Restaurants and cafés, for their menus.
* Magazine editors, book publishers.

Helpful Tips
These tips come from Lauren R. Rabinowitz:

* "You have to be out there selling your work. Between marketing yourself and doing your work, it is hard to have a family or relationship."
* It helps to have formal art training in techniques.
* Keep a sketchbook handy and draw often and everywhere.
* "Wear your art" for people to see. Get T-shirts and hats printed with your illustrations and cartoons.
* You have to be really dedicated to this career to succeed.
* This can be a challenging business, financially, but the rewards of creativity and satisfaction are gratifying.

For More Information
Associations
Graphic Artists Guild
11 West 20 St., Eighth Floor
New York, NY 10011-3704

"The Graphic Artists Guild is a national labor organization dedicated to advancing the economic and social interests of professional graphic artists." Its membership consists of freelance and staff artists of all disciplines—graphic design, illustration, cartooning, surface/textile design, etc. Membership benefits include a pricing and ethical guidelines handbook, national and chapter publications, group health insurance, etc. Publishes "Cartoonists' Directory." You can order trade books and publications through its Guild Book Shelf. Write for more information.

Friends of Lulu
Jackie Estrada
4657 Cajon Way
San Diego, CA 92115
A nonprofit organization encouraging women cartoonists and public support of them. Send SASE for membership information.

Books

Artist's & Graphic Designer's Market, North Light Books/Writer's Digest Books (F&W Publications), Cincinnati, OH.; annual market guide for artists and graphic designers.

The Graphic Artists Guild Handbook: Pricing & Ethical Guidelines, 8th ed., $24.95 from Graphic Artists Guild, attn: Publications (see above).

Books published by North Light Books, Cincinnati, OH:

The Complete Book of Caricature by Bob Staake. 1991.

The Complete Book of Humorous Art by Bob Staake. 1996.

Getting Started Drawing & Selling Cartoons by Randy Glasbergen. 1993.

How to Be a Successful Cartoonist by Randy Glasbergen, 1996.

How to Draw & Sell Cartoons by Ross Thomson and Bill Hewison. 1985.

Additional Business Ideas
✤ Medical illustrator
✤ Greeting card designer (see *101 Best Home-Based Businesses for Women*)

Book
The Complete Guide to Greeting Card Design & Illustration by Eva Szela. 1994, North Light Books, Cincinnati, OH.

≈ 32 ≈

WOOD CARVER

According to Edward F. Gallenstein, editor of *Chip Chats*, the trade publication of the National Wood Carvers Association, "... there are a goodly number of women among their 56,000 members, world wide." He says there are several who work full-time at carving.

Wood carving is sculpting wood through the use of gouges, chisels, and knives. There are two main kinds of carving: relief carving (chip and incision) and carving in round.

This is an art that will take training and practice from which you can profit. You will have to study the art—on your own or at a carving school—and develop your own style and recognition. Joining this association and taking courses will help you determine if this is a career for you.

Start-Up Costs
$5,000 for basic tools and books; money for courses.

Pricing Guidelines
Varies according to your ability and reputation as a carver, and the wood you use. One carver, who specializes in birds, sells his small pieces for $15 to $20 each; his unique bird trees start at $40 apiece and go up from there.

Essential Equipment
Carving knives, chisels, gouges, straps, compounds (for sharpening), combination rasp, mallets, wood files, rifflers, clamps, carpenter's vise, bench clips, thumb and bench screws.

Marketing and Advertising Methods and Tips
+ Exhibit at juried wood and/or craft shows.
+ Sell unique pieces to specialty gift catalogs.
+ Develop your own mailing list collected at shows, and send flyers of new pieces.

✤ Exhibit at local libraries, banks, galleries, and other places that offer public showings.
✤ Give out a brochure with each piece sold, or free at shows, describing your experience, specialty, etc.
✤ Keep and display a photo file of your carvings.

Recommended Training, Experience, or Skills

✤ Take basic wood-carving courses at continuing education schools, craft centers, or specific wood-carving schools (look for ads in trade publications).
✤ Join a local wood-carving club for networking information and opportunities.
✤ Gain a basic knowledge of woods and their properties.

Income Potential

$5,000 to $10,000 per year at shows, selling by mail order, or through catalogs.

Best Customers

Individual collectors, art galleries, gift stores.

Helpful Tips

✤ Develop a carving specialty.
✤ If possible, work with a master to keep from forming bad habits.
✤ Look for ways to get your name known for your carvings: send out press releases, teach courses, write articles, etc.

For More Information

Association
National Wood Carvers Association
P.O. Box 43218
Cincinnati, OH 45243
For amateur and professional wood carvers; $11 per year membership includes subscription to *Chip Chats*.

Books

Woodcarving Basics by Alan and Gill Bridgewater. 1996, Sterling Publishing Company, Inc., New York, NY.

Woodworker's Guide to Pricing Your Work by Dam Ramsey. 1995, Betterway Books, Cincinnati, OH.

Woodworker's Source Book, 2nd ed., by Charles Self. 1995, Betterway Books, Cincinnati, OH.

Stackpole Books
5067 Ritter Rd.
Mechanicsburg, PA 17055-6921

Stackpole publishes a number of wood-carving books, including:

Woodcarving Step by Step by Rick Butz.

Woodcarving Illustrated and *Woodcarving Illustrated Book 2* by Roger Schroeder and Paul McCarthy.

Tools and Supplies

Lee Valley Tools, Ltd.
P.O. Box 1780
Ogdensburg, NY 13669-0490

Write for copy of their catalog.

Additional Business Ideas

❖ Woodcutting: if you have artistic talent, you can make one-of-a-kind woodcuts and make prints from them.

Woodcut: Step-by-Step Lessons in Designing, Cutting, & Printing the Woodblock by David L. Oravery. 1992, Watson-Guptill Publications, Inc., New York, NY.

❖ Wood turning

❖ Pyrography (wood burning)

The Complete Pyrography by Stephen Poole. 1996, Sterling Publishing Company, Inc., New York, NY.

☆ 33 ☆
GRAPHIC ARTIST/DESIGNER

This is a businesses using technology such as computers to create designs, illustrations, etc. Graphic artists and designers specialize in designing furniture, textiles, packaging, museum exhibits, stained glass, ornamental metalwork, and more.

Start-Up Costs
$5,000 to $10,000, and possibly up to $30,000, depending on your specialty and necessary equipment.

Pricing Guidelines
❖ Go by the industry standards (see *Graphic Artists' & Designer's Handbook of Pricing and Ethical Guidelines* from the Graphic Artists Guild information which follows)
❖ Compare your prices with those of other graphic designers in your area.

Essential Equipment
❖ Office: a computer with enough memory to run software such as QuarkXPress and Photoshop; scanner, large-screen monitor; fax/modem; a separate fax machine; laser printer (preferably color); telephone system; filing and bookkeeping software; and related tools for your specialty
❖ Other: promotional materials; samples and portfolio of your past work; graphic arts reference books, guides, etc.

Marketing and Advertising Methods and Tips
❖ Take out ads in local newspapers and business publications; have a home page on the World Wide Web.
❖ Research companies that would best fit your style and send direct mailings, with follow-up calls and visits.
❖ Join the national trade association for updates on the industry and opportunities.
❖ Join local business groups and home-based business associations for local networking and contacts with potential clients.

Recommended Training, Experience, or Skills
* Training and education in graphic design and computer technology.
* Work experience in a design firm.
* Business courses to gain management skills.
* Good communication skills to understand what your clients want.

Income Potential
$26,000 to $55,000 per year

Best Customers
Advertising agencies, businesses, art departments of corporations, publishers of newsletters and illustrated publications, clip-art services, design studios, manufacturers, museums, department and furniture stores.

For More Information
Association

The Graphic Artists Guild
11 West 20th St., Eighth Floor
New York, NY 10011

"The Graphic Artists Guild is a national labor organization dedicated to advancing the economic and social interests of professional graphic artists." Its membership consists of freelance and staff artists of all disciplines: graphic design, ilustration, cartooning, surface/textile design, etc. Membership benefits include a pricing and ethical guidelines handbook, national and chapter publications, group health insurance, etc. As a member of the guild, you can order trade books and publications through its Guild Book Shelf. They carry graphic design business books, such as *Career by Design: Electronic Design & Publishing Practices*. Write for more information.

Books

Artist's & Graphic Designer's Market, North Light Books/Writer's Digest Books (F&W Publications), Cincinnati, OH; annual market guide for artists and graphic designers.

The Graphic Artists Guild Handbook: Pricing & Ethical Guidelines,
8th ed., $24.95 from Graphic Artists Guild, ATTN: Publi-
cations (see above).

Books published by North Light Books, Cincinnati, OH (call
(800) 289-0963 to order or to request a complete catalog):

Graphic Design Basics Series (how-to books on layouts, creat-
ing brochures, booklets, logos, etc.)
The Graphic Designer's Sourcebook by Poppy Evans. 1996.
Marketing and Promoting Your Work by Maria Piscopo. 1995.
Starting Your Small Graphic Design Studio by Michael Fleish-
man. 1993.

Business Guides
Entrepreneur's Start-Up Guide, "Graphic Design," $69.50
plus shipping. (800) 421-2300 to order or for catalog.

Distance Education/Correspondence Course
"Desktop Publishing & Design"
ICS Learning Systems
925 Oak St.
Scranton, PA 18540-9888
Write for information.

Additional Business Ideas
Sell your illustrations and designs to clip-art software publishers or start your own clip-art service.

34

PORTRAIT OR SKETCH ARTIST

Painting has been done for thousands of years, and talented
artists can be found exhibiting their paintings in community
shows, galleries, and fairs across the country. Selling one's
paintings or art is another matter. If you want to earn money
with your art, you have to approach it like any other business.

If you have the artistic skills and the right markets, you can earn money with your work.

All artists (and writers, sculptors, artisans, etc.) have to find a style and medium that makes them stand out. You can do custom paintings or sketches of clients, or you can create what you want to on canvas and try to find a market.

Some ideas for earning money with your art are: doing landscapes, still-lifes, and portraits of people or pets from sittings or photographs; doing pencil sketches of houses or buildings; and so on.

Start-Up Costs
$1,000 to $3,000 for art supplies and courses (more if you go to art school).

Pricing Guidelines
* Depends on your market, your reputation, your expertise, etc.
* Commissioned paintings: $125 and up.
* Portrait, single subject, framed, ready to hang: $150 and up.
* On-the-spot caricatures at shows and fairs: $12 to $27.

Essential Equipment
* Oils: brushes (flat-bristle, bright-bristle, round and long sable, etc.); oil colors, oil cups, painting knife, palette knife.
* Watercolors: brushes (wide flat, narrow flat, oval, small round, large round); paints in tubes watercolor set.
* Display: tables, frames, easels; display set-up with tent to protect from weather.
* Promotional materials.

Marketing and Advertising Methods and Tips
* Brochures, business cards (with a sample of your painting on them).
* Attend and exhibit at art shows.
* Community exhibitions at banks, libraries.
* Teach courses.

❖ Create your own line of greeting cards, stationery products, etc.

❖ Send press releases to local newspapers when you are exhibiting or receiving an award.

Recommended Training, Experience, or Skills
❖ Artistic ability—art schools, private instruction, community courses, books, videos.
❖ Practice and perfect your skills and style.
❖ Read and study all you can on the subject.

Income Potential
❖ $1,500 at a weekend art show.
❖ $100 to $1,000 for book illustrations.

Best Customers
❖ Individual collectors.
❖ Families for portraits.
❖ Pet owners for pet portraits.
❖ Patrons of galleries, attendees of art shows.
❖ Publishers of books, calendars, greeting cards.

Helpful Tips
❖ You must be good in your area, but it is an individual's preference as to whether he or she likes your work or not.
❖ There is no substitute for hard work.
❖ Invest in a few lessons to see if you have the talent and desire to go for further education and/or training.
❖ Observe and study all you can about your art.

For More Information
Association
American Society Of Artists
P.O. Box 1326
Palatine, IL 60078
The group's purpose is to help professional artists and craftspeople in their work. Maintains an art referral and information

exchange service. Special Arts Services for persons with disabilities. Send SASE for information; to receive appropriate materials, specify the medium in which you work.

Books

Art Marketing Sourcebook for the Fine Artist, 2nd ed. (updated every two years), 1995, ArtNetwork, 18757 Wildflower Dr., Penn Valley, CA 95946; $21.95 + $4 shipping; CA residents add sales tax; (916) 432-7630 for credit-card orders.

The Art of Selling Art: Between Production and Livelihood by Bill Richie, Jr. 1996, Richie's Perfect Press, Seattle WA.

Artist's & Graphic Designer's Market (annual listing of markets for artists and designers). North Light Books, Cincinnati, OH.

Artist's Resource Handbook by Daniel Grant. 1994, Allworth Press, NY.

The Business of Being an Artist by Daniel Grant. 1991, Allworth Press, NY.

Drawing: A Step-by-Step Guide to Drawing Techniques by Angela Gair. 1996, Sterling Publishing Co., Inc., New York, NY.

On Becoming an Artist by Daniel Grant. 1993, Allworth Press, NY.

North Light Books offers numerous books on painting techniques. Call (800) 289-0963 to order a catalog.

Publication

The Artist's Magazine
F&W Publications, Inc.
1507 Dana Ave.
Cincinnati, OH 45207-1005
$24 per year; call (800) 333-0444 to order or check your newsstand for a copy.

Distance Education/Correspondence Course

Art Instruction Schools
500 S. Fourth St.
Minneapolis, MN 55415
Art advertising courses. Write for information.

Supplies
Dick Blick Art Materials
P.O. Box 1267
Galesburg, IL 61402-1267
To order or for catalog call (800) 447-8192.

Videos
Bob Ross Company
P.O. Box 946
Sterling, VA 20167
How-to videotapes on painting techniques; write for a free brochure.

Art Video Library
P.O. Box 68
Ukiah, OR 97880
For a membership fee, members can rent art videos on oil, acrylics, watercolor, pastel, airbrush techniques, etc. Write for free brochure, include a business-size envelope with $.55 postage.

Additional Business Ideas
❖ Decorative hand-painted chests and other furniture.
❖ Tole painting on old or new objects: furniture, saws, driftwood, etc.
❖ Sign painting.
❖ Restoration and repair of paintings for museums, galleries, and individuals.
❖ Illustrator of children's books.
   Children's Writer's & Illustrator's Market edited by Alice P. Buening. 1996, Writer's Digest Books, Cincinnati, OH. Published annually.
❖ Hold painting seminars: $400 to $500 for a five-day seminar.
❖ Teach painting: $7 to $15 per hour.

⚞ 35 ⚟

JEWELER

Go to any flea market, craft show, or fine arts show and you will probably see more displays of jewelry and woodcrafts than any other items. Yes, jewelry making is a competitive art and craft, but if you look closely, no two jewelry exhibits are alike. There are many styles and materials from which jewelry is made: traditional metals, polymer clays, fabric, glass, ceramics, wood, leather, recycled items, and plastic.

Thus, if jewelry-making interests you, you should study the basics, experiment to find the materials that you enjoy working with the most, develop your own style or signature, then work on finding your market "niche" in this fascinating craft.

Start-Up Costs
$1,500 to $6,000

Pricing Guidelines
❖ $10 to $20 for smaller pieces; more for more complex pieces or pieces that require expensive materials.
❖ Costs depend on materials, the time required, complexity of design, the demand for your line, your customers, and where you are selling your jewelry (a juried show versus a small craft show, for example).

Essential Equipment
Tools depend on the jewelry you are making. Clasps, fasteners, string, wire, pins, earring bases, and specific supplies for your style of jewelry.

Marketing and Advertising Methods and Tips
❖ Packaging is important in showing off your pieces and projecting a professional image.
❖ Do your own market research: visit shows, fairs, shops, galleries, etc. to see if your line is on the same level as those being exhibited. Note, too, what is popular among

customers. Talk to some of the craftspersons and ask them what are their best-selling shows.

❖ Exhibit in community showcases.

❖ Take samples to shops and galleries.

❖ Wear your own jewelry and have your friends and family wear it to be seen.

❖ Invest in color brochures (with price lists) that tell about you and the story behind your jewelry.

❖ Have booths at trade shows.

❖ Send regular mailings of new pieces and what your show schedule will be to those on a mailing list you have developed at past shows.

Recommended Training, Experience, or Skills

❖ Take courses in jewelry making and design.

❖ If possible, apprentice with a jewelry craftsperson.

❖ Study books and videos, and experiment with design and style.

❖ Read trade publications.

❖ Artistic ability and creative design are essential in this craft.

Income Potential

$500 to $1,000/wk; $20,000 per year and up depending on the demand for your jewelry and where you sell it.

Best Customers

Craft and jewelry trade show attendees, artisan shops, craft malls, tourists, previous customers, gift shops, gift catalogs, cable shopping channels, boutiques.

Helpful Tips

❖ If you decide to sell your jewelry wholesale, be sure you can meet the possible demand.

❖ Invest in having a catalog sheet and price list that includes ordering information, terms, etc. that you can give to potential buyers at both consumer and trade shows.

❖ Never stop looking for other markets or ways to expand your line of jewelry.

For More Information
Books
Jewelry & Accessories: Beautiful Designs to Make and Wear by Juliet Bawden. 1995, North Light Books, Cincinnati, OH.

Make Your Own Jewelry: Creative Designs to Make & Wear by Wendy Milne. 1994, Storey Communications, Pownal, VT.

The Design and Creation of Jewelry, 3rd ed., by Robert von Neuman. 1982, Chilton Book Company, Radnor, PA.

Introduction to Lapidary by Pansy D. Kraus. 1987, Chilton Book Company, Radnor, PA.

Books through the Mail
Chilton Book Company
One Chilton Way
Radnor, PA 19089-0230

Write for a listing of books on enameling, silversmithing, and modeling in wax.

Chester Book Co.
4 Maple St.
Chester, CT 06412

Write for a catalog from which you can order the following books and others on jewelry-making techniques:

The Encyclopedia of Jewelry-Making Techniques by Jinks McGrath. 1995, Running Press

Jewelry Making by David Rider. 1994. (For the beginning jeweler.)

Periodical
Jewelry Crafts Magazine
5000 Eagle Rock Blvd. #105
Los Angeles, CA 90041

$12 per year, 6 issues; sample copy $3.50.

Distance Education/Correspondence Course
Gemological Institute of America
1660 Stewart St.
Santa Monica, CA 90404-4088

Write for information.

Supplies

Alpha Supply
P.O. Box 2133
Bremerton, WA 98310
Thousands of supplies, items for jewelry making, faceting, and lapidary needs. Also offers a large selection of books on jewelry making. Catalog costs $7, but contains a $10 coupon toward a purchase.

Additional Business Ideas

✤ Jewelry from recycled materials:
Joyce Chambers
Paper Art Originals
2526 Lamar Ave., Suite 231
Paris, TX 75460
Kits and information for making jewelry from recycled paper. Send SASE.

✤ Jewelry from polymer clay:
"Mastering the New Clay" is a series of video tapes with Tory Hughes; $40 each + $2.50 shipping ($3.50 in CA); send SASE for information to:
GAMEPLAN, ARTRANCH
2233 McKinley
Berkeley, CA 94703

✤ "Soft" jewelry:
How to Make Soft Jewelry by Jackie Dodson. 1991, Chilton Book Company, Radnor, PA.

✤ Jewelry from beads:
The Complete Bead Resource Book: An Essential Guide to the Bead Business from The Complete Resource Book, 4432 Sandburg Way, Irvine, CA 92715; $29.99 + $3.50 shipping (CA add 7 3/4% sales tax).

✤ Jewelry from buttons:
The Button Craft Book by Dawn Cusick. 1994. Order from Chester Book Co., 4 Maple St., Chester, CT 06412.

✤ Combine old pieces of jewelry into one-of-a-kind pins for women's suits and dresses.

✤ Jewelry repair.

≈ 36 ≈

STAINED GLASS ARTIST

Stained glass was first used in houses and buildings in England in the mid-19th century. The movement soon spread to the U.S., and many old homes still have stained glass windows, doors, transoms, and panels. Stained glass is a popular hobby and is becoming a profitable business, with many artisans starting from their home studios doing custom work, lamps, ornaments, sculptures, mirrors, and other items.

Start-Up Costs
$1,000 for basic supplies; $150 to $250 for instructional workshops.

Pricing Guidelines
$75 to $100 per square foot

Essential Equipment
Glass cutters, grousing tools, grinder, patterns (commercial, then design your own), pliers, lead, glass, soldering iron, jewelry supplies, other tools as your skill increases.

Marketing and Advertising Methods and Tips
* Take courses; develop your line and your specialties.
* Visit shows and other stained glass studios.
* Stay current with the news on stained glass.
* Attend glass shows.
* Carry a variety of items with prices everyone can afford plus some special, one-of-a-kind pieces.
* Attend workshops at least once a year to learn new techniques and what is popular.
* Decide who your customers are and create for that market.
* Exhibit at community art shows.
* Invest in good-quality brochures providing price lists and ordering information, and showing where you will be exhibiting; send them to builders and architects.
* Advertise in local newspaper real estate sections.

Recommended Training, Experience, or Skills
* Take evening courses.
* Attend workshops.
* Work in a stained glass or craft shop or studio.
* Study and read about crafts and art marketing; attend seminars about crafts business.
* It helps to have artistic "eye" for patterns.

Income Potential
$20,000 to $80,000 per year

Best Customers
Craft and art show attendees, galleries, retail stained glass markets, architects, interior designers, builders, home-owners.

Helpful Tips
* Wall hangings, sun catchers, lamps, windows, and mirrors are all popular items.
* Find your niche (what you do well).
* Offer a variety of affordable items such as sun catchers, mirrors, and jewelry.

For More Information
Association
Stained Glass Association of America (SGAA)
P.O. Box 22642
Kansas City, MO 64113
Educational and art-oriented—not start-up—information. Send SASE for membership information.

Books
How to Work in Stained Glass, 2nd ed., by Anita and Seymour Isenberg. 1983, Chilton Book Company, Radnor, PA.
Stained Glass Basics by Chris Rich with Martha Mitchell and Rachel Ward. 1996, Sterling Publishing Co., Inc., New York, NY.

Business Guide
"Getting Started in Stained Glass," from the editors of *Income Opportunities* magazine. Workbook and video package $19.95 + $5 shipping. To order call (800) 338-7531.

Exposition
Annual Glass Craft Expo sponsored by *Income Opportunities* magazine and Las Vegas Management, held March/April each year. Write to:

Las Vegas Management
2408 Chapman Dr.
Las Vegas, NV 89104-3455.

Periodicals and Publications
The Glass Craftsman Magazine (formerly *Glass Artist*)
P.O. Box 678
Richboro, PA 18954
E-mail: gcmagazine@aol.com
Covers all types of creative glass including stained glass, fusing, sandblasting, beadwork, lampmaking, paintings, etc. Columns on the business of glasswork. $25 per year, 6 issues; $3 sample copy.

Glass Art: The Magazine for Stained and Decorative Glass
P.O. Box 260377
Highlands Ranch, CO 80163
Four-color publication featuring technical articles on techniques, industry news, features on successful artists, etc.; $24 per year, 6 issues.

"Craftsmanship Guide," a stained glass newsletter, includes how-to articles and tips; order from Vic's Crafts at (800) 332-VICS.

Supplies
Vic's Crafts (Vicki Payne)
P.O. Box 241713
Charlotte, NC 28224

Catalogue carrying tools, videos, books, glass, bevels, bead making supplies, jewelry supplies, kits, etc. Write or call for catalogue at (800) 332-VICS.

Additional Business Ideas

❖ If you have the skills, you could offer to repair and restore old windows and other stained glass pieces.

❖ Glass etching:
   Professional Glass Consultants
   2442 Cerrillos Rd., Suite 350
   Santa Fe, NM 87505
   Write for brochure containing glass-etching seminars, information, books, videos, by experts Norm and Ruth Dobbins.

⚞ 37 ⚟

BROOM-MAKER

In early America, most farm families grew broomcorn to make brooms for their own use. It was a pleasurable task, often done by the light of a fire on early fall nights or on rainy days. Our man-made fibers have substituted for the broomcorn, and most brooms are made in factories. However, there are still people who enjoy this nature craft for fun and profit. Handmade brooms do as good a job—if not better—of sweeping up dust and litter, but most are used as decorative accents in colonial homes. This is not a difficult craft to learn, and it is not seen at many craft shows today.

You can raise your own broomcorn if you have enough space. It is very easy to grow and harvest, but you will need a few acres to raise enough for your demand, or you can order it by the pound from the sources below. If you like taking raw materials and turning them into a finished product, then this American craft might be for you.

Start-Up Costs
$500 to $1,000 for basic supplies, broomcorn, and promotional materials.

Pricing Guidelines
Handmade brooms run from $12 to $80 each, or more for intricately carved handles.

Essential Equipment
Broomcorn, various woods for handles (oak, birch, willow, sassafras, etc.), twine, currycomb for combing seeds off corn, sharp knife, colorful yarn, hemp for tying up handle, nails, tying block, carving tools for handles (optional).

Marketing and Advertising Methods and Tips
Craft shows, display ads in folk and craft magazines, folk festivals, brochures, join a local craft co-op, offer demonstrations at folk festivals, school demonstrations.

Recommended Training, Experience, or Skills
❖ Make a broom from a kit to find out if this is a craft you would like to do.
❖ Practice until you perfect the skill and can begin to make your own variations.
❖ You must enjoy working with your hands and have good manual coordination.

Income Potential
$1,500 to $2,000 a show

Best Customers
Craft shops, craft show and festival attendees, interior decorators, country shops.

Helpful Tips
❖ Practice until you feel that your brooms look handmade with skill.

❖ Add your own variations such as unique handles or braided handles.

❖ Add different kinds and sizes of brooms to your line, such as whisk brooms and sapling brooms; make brooms from yellow birch or other soft woods.

For More Information

Books

The Complete Book of Nature Crafts by Eric Carlson, Dawn Cusick, and Carol Taylor. 1992, Rodale Press, Emmaus, PA. Page 122 gives instructions for making a "Hickory Scrub Broom."

Buy a Broom Besom: The Story of a Broom by William Henry Young. Includes instructions on broom-making. Send a check for $9 to: Thomas Monahan Co., P.O. Box 250, Arcola, IL 61910.

Kits

Ralph Gates
8 Willow Creek Rd.
Leicester, NC 28748
Finished brooms are $10 to $70, kits are $10 to $45. Send SASE for a complete price list.

Seeds

George W. Park Seed Co., Inc.
Cokesbury Rd.
Greenwood, SC 29647-0001
Request catalog; order "Broom Corn, Mixed Colors."

Supplies

R.E. Caddy & Co., Inc.
P.O. Box 14634
Greensboro, NC 27415
Broomcorn, twine, and a selection of handles. Send SASE for a listing of current prices. Ten pounds of broomcorn will

make at least 6 to 8 sweepers or hearth brooms. Introductory special for novice broom-makers: 10 pounds of raw corn for $25 including shipping ($30 if west of the Mississippi); check or money order.

Additional Business Ideas
✤ Other folk art:
   Folk Art: Style & Design by Stewart and Sally Walton. 1996, Sterling Publishing Co., Inc., New York, NY.
✤ Sell corn-husk dolls—angels made of dried corn husks that you grow or order from a craft supply store.

≈ 38 ≈
TALENT/ENTERTAINMENT BOOKING AGENT

If you want to start a full-fledged talent agency, in many states you will have to follow certain regulations and apply for a license. An easier way to start a business is to be a booking agent for local clowns, magicians, entertainers, speakers, historical impersonators, school assembly performers, storytellers, puppeteers, science and animal educational programs, etc.

Start-Up Costs
$1,000 to $5,000

Pricing Guidelines
Charge a percentage (5 percent for TV bookings, 10 percent for clubs, 20 percent for colleges) of the performer's fee to schedule them. You may or may not charge them a basic sign-up fee.

Essential Equipment
A computer with mailing list software, fax machine, copier, standard contracts.

Marketing and Advertising Methods and Tips

❖ Direct mail brochures featuring your services and the entertainers you represent to schools, businesses, churches, institutions, and nursing homes.

❖ Advertise for both your entertainers and your business: classified ads in local papers, Yellow Pages, ads on local cable television, classified ads in parents' newspapers.

❖ Word-of-mouth referrals.

Recommended Training, Experience, or Skills

❖ You should have experience as an entertainer or speaker.

❖ You must be able to evaluate performers and match them with the appropriate place to perform.

Income Potential

$10,000 part-time to $20,000 and up full-time. Up to $100,000 for successful, experienced agents.

Best Customers

Schools, institutions, parents of young children for birthday entertainment, associations who need speakers, scouting groups and sports teams for their annual banquets, nursing homes for periodic entertainment, businesses for special promotions.

Helpful Tips

❖ Hand out your business cards to both entertainers and consumers.

❖ Check with a lawyer as to the wording of contracts, etc.

❖ Check with your insurance agent as to what coverage you will need for your business.

❖ Have your entertainers and speakers regularly hand out mail-in evaluation sheets to their audiences to measure the quality of your service.

Additional Business Ideas

❖ Instead of being a booking agent, compile a directory of entertainers, etc. Charge them to be listed in the directory.

Then sell or distribute it free to your customers and let them schedule the entertainers directly.

✤ Be an historical impersonator and speak at schools, folk festivals, museum programs.

✤ Be a clown (see "Clowning" in *101 Best Home-Based Businesses for Women*).

✤ Be an actor or model.

✤ Start your own community theater group.

Peter Glenn Publications, Ltd.
42 West 38th St., Suite 802
New York, NY 10018
Send SASE for a book list, which includes:

The International Directory of Model & Talent Agencies & Schools ($29.95 + $5 shipping).

Madison Avenue Handbook: The Image Makers Source, a directory for the film, tape, music, and print production industries; $59.95 + $6 shipping.

﹅ 39 ﹅
DOLLMAKER/REPAIRS

Dolls will always be popular among little girls and women who collect dolls for nostalgia and as a hobby. Dolls are made of many materials, but two of the most common methods are the traditional cloth dolls and the new sculpted dolls.

Start-Up Costs

✤ $5,000 to $7,000 for sculpted dolls, including equipment, lessons, and materials.

✤ $500 for cloth dolls, for a sewing machine and notions.

✤ $200 start-up for the repair of cloth dolls.

Pricing Guidelines

✤ Custom-sculpted dolls can sell for as much as $200 to $450 and up for ornately decorated dolls.

✤ Cloth dolls: $10 to $30.

✤ Repairs: $30 to $150 for clothing and body replacements and repairs.

Essential Equipment

✤ Sculpted dolls: kiln, molds, special paints, clays, doll accessories, and parts.

✤ Cloth dolls: sewing notions, fabric, sewing machine (industrial if doing heavy sewing).

✤ Repairs: sewing notions, sewing machine, dollmaker's eye tool kit, fabrics.

Marketing and Advertising Methods and Tips

✤ Sculpted dolls: attend toy and doll trade shows; have color brochures made up.

✤ Cloth dolls: attend craft shows, fairs, and carnivals; give dolls as gifts or as prizes at a charity function.

✤ Repair: distribute cards and flyers at doll shows.

✤ Take out ads in the Yellow Pages and in local parents' newspapers.

✤ See *The Crafts Report* "Toy" issue (July, 1996) for tips on doll marketing.

Recommended Training, Experience, or Skills

✤ Sculpted dolls: attend workshops and special courses; study videos and books.

✤ Cloth dolls: be talented with a needle. First make one from a kit, then try patterns from dollmaking books, then design and create your own.

✤ Repairs: practice on old dolls; take sewing classes at your local sewing center.

Income Potential

✤ Sculpted dolls: $5,000 to $10,000 per year part-time, $30,000 full-time, or more if you are known and your dolls are originals.

❖ Cloth dolls: $5,000 to $10,000 per year. More if you are able to sell in a catalog.

❖ Repairs: $250 to $600 a week, especially if you have a good reputation.

Best Customers

❖ Sculpted dolls: collectors, parents who buy the dolls to mark a special occasion, gift shops, mail order, doll show attendees.

❖ Cloth dolls: attendees at craft shows and doll shows.

❖ Repairs: doll collectors, consumers who have a favorite doll they want restored, antique collectors, store owners.

Helpful Tips

❖ Sculpted dolls: develop your own line of dolls; practice until you perfect your techniques.

❖ Cloth dolls: look for new lines or ideas to come up with your own niche.

❖ Repairs: become adept at doing all kinds of repairs; do an excellent job for future referrals; check with a lawyer about liability when you are asked to repair an expensive doll.

For More Information

Books

The Art of Making and Marketing Art Dolls by Jack L. Johnston, edited by Kathleen Ryan and Barbara Campbell. 1994, Scott Publications, Livonia, MI.

Creating & Crafting Dolls: Patterns, Techniques, & Inspirations for Making Cloth Dolls by Eloise Piper and Mary Dilligan. 1994, Chilton Book Company, Radnor, PA.

The Doll by Contemporary Artists by Krystyan Poray Goddu and Wendy Lavitt. Features 100 doll artists, their dolls, and the techniques they used to create them. Order from Chester Book Co., 4 Maple St., Chester, CT 06412. Write for catalog.

Teach Yourself Cloth Dollmaking by Jodie Davis. 1995, Michael Friedman Publishing Group, New York, NY.

Periodical
Dollmaking—Crafts & Designs
P.O. Box 5000
Iola, WI 54945
$19.95 per year, 18 issues.

Supplies
+ See the back of doll and craft magazines.
+ The Crafts Supply Sourcebook by Margaret Boyd (see "Arts and Handcrafts Businesses: General Resources").

Videos
Dollfather Videos
22930 SW Schmeltzer Rd.
Sherwood, OR 97140
Seven step-by-step videos by Lewis Goldstein. $49.95 each + $3 postage and handling. Call (503) 628-2098 or write for list.

Course
Lewis Goldstein also offers a one-year doll-sculpting course for $2,000; includes monthly lessons with videos, instructions, etc. See Dollfather Videos, above, for address.

Association
The National Institute of Doll Artist (NIADA)
690 Trinity Court
Longwood, FL 32750
For doll artists and patrons. Contact Nancy Walters for information. Send SASE.

Additional Business Ideas
+ Make apple dolls, the early-American craft of creating dolls from carved dried apples.
+ Make personalized life-size dolls on order for special gifts.

≥ 40 ≤

WOOD CRAFTS WHOLESALER

When Sharon Apichella quit teaching ten years ago to be with her children, she looked for a way to supplement her husband's teaching salary. Her interest in wood crafts began when she made a wooden toy as a gift for her son. Sharon and a friend made more wood items and sold them at craft shows. When her friend decided to go back to a regular job, Sharon kept making items to sell at shows, but the weekend shows kept her away from her family.

That's when Sharon attended a wholesale show and decided to sell her items at a show near her home. As a result, she came home with $5,000 worth of orders. She now shows at only four to five wholesale shows a year, and makes over $30,000 a year. Her products are sold to over 300 shops in the U.S. and several countries.

Woodworking is no longer just a man's hobby. Go to any woodworking trade show, and at least a third of the attendees are women, asking questions and trying out tools. Women have successful businesses making children's furniture, wooden toys, clocks, woodturning objects, and other items. Of course wholesaling means that you have to be able to make items that can be sold at wholesale prices and still make a profit. And you have to have a production method that allows you to fill $5,000 worth of orders!

Start-Up Costs
* $600 to $1,500 and up for tools and equipment.
* Show fees: $15 to $1,500 for craft and/or wholesale trade shows.

Pricing Guidelines
Estimate what it will cost to make each item. Then add your profit. Then double that price (the shops that buy your items will add 50 percent to 100 percent to your price). Then test-market the items at their retail prices at a craft show or compare them with similar items in stores to see if it is a reasonable price for a consumer to pay.

Essential Equipment

❖ Woodworking equipment: new or secondhand band saw, radial-arm saw, drill press, floor sander, wood stains, paints, rags.

❖ Office equipment: computer with mailing and billing software, fax/modem, hang tags, boxes for shipping.

❖ Promotional materials: a sheet with descriptions and/or photos of the items you supply, with prices and ordering terms and information.

Marketing and Advertising Methods and Tips

❖ Test-market new products at craft shows.

❖ Display items at trade shows.

❖ Get color brochures and business cards.

Recommended Training, Experience, or Skills

❖ Take courses in woodworking at local vo-tech schools.

❖ You must be well organized and keep good business records and mailing and shipping records.

❖ Be able to fill your orders. You will have periods of working many-hour days.

❖ Develop good safety habits.

❖ Keep up with buyer trends

Income Potential

$15,000 to $37,000 per year

Best Customers

Retailers who sell items similar to those that you make.

Helpful Tips

❖ Develop your own line; try to stay ahead of the competition with new items, but do not sacrifice the quality of your wood crafts.

❖ Be professional in the way you conduct your business: taking and fulfilling orders, quality control, and giving your customers the best product you can make.

❖ Learn how to operate your tools and equipment properly, proficiently, and safely.

❖ Keep good business records for customers and follow-ups, for taxes, and to see if you are making a profit.

❖ Buy supplies in bulk with other craftspeople.

For More Information
Books

The Complete Woodworker by Bernard E. Jones. 1993, Ten Speed Press, Berkeley, CA.

Creating Your Own Woodshop by Charles Self. 1994, Betterway Books, Cincinnati, OH.

Make Your Woodworking Pay for Itself, revised edition, by Jack Neff. 1996, Betterway Books, Cincinnati, OH.

Pocket Guide to Wood Finishes by Nigel Lofthouse. 1993, Betterway Books, Cincinnati, OH.

The Stanley Book of Woodworking Tools, Techniques, and Projects by Mark Finney. 1995, Betterway Books, Cincinnati, OH.

Woodworker's Guide to Pricing Your Work by Dam Ramsey. 1995, Betterway Books, Cincinnati, OH.

Periodicals and Publications

American Woodworker
Rodale Press
P.O. Box 7579
Red Oak, IA 51591-0579

Fine Woodworking
63 South Main Street
P.O. Box 5506
Newtown, CT 06470-9971
$29 per year, 6 issues.

Plans, Projects, Books, Videos

The New Yankee Workshop Library
P.O. Box 9345
South Burlington, VT 05407-9345
Send SASE for catalog.

Supplies

Woodworker's Source Book, 2nd ed., by Charles Self. 1995, Betterway Books, Cincinnati, OH.

Additional Business Ideas

❖ Sell woodturning pieces (bowls, egg cups, wood art, etc.): *Basic Woodturning Techniques* by David Regester. 1993, Betterway Books, Cincinnati, OH.

❖ Make wooden clocks:
Clockmaking: 18 Designs for the Woodworker by John A. Nelson. 1995, Stackpole Books, Mechanicsburg, PA.
How to Build 35 Great Clocks by Joseph Daniele. 1988, Stackpole Books, Mechanicsburg, PA.

❖ Make children's furniture:
Children's Furniture You Can Make by Paul Gerhards. 1993, Stackpole Books, Mechanicsburg, PA.

❖ Make wooden toys for children and collectors.

≈ **41** ≈

CRAFT SHOP/CRAFT CO-OP

If you want to investigate other ways of selling your art and handcrafts, you may want to think about having a craft shop or starting a craft co-op. In a craft shop, you own or rent the shop and sell your crafts and/or the crafts of other craftspersons. You can do this by consignment, by renting shelf space to craftspersons, or by buying crafts wholesale and selling them retail from your store.

A craft co-op, on the other hand, is a group of craftspersons who come together to form a crafts association with the purpose of selling the individual members' crafts, and also sponsoring group projects, such as workshops and seminars. The benefit of having such a group is that you can incorporate if you wish, get a state sales tax number as a group, order wholesale supplies together, hold workshops and seminars, and operate craft shows or a retail shop to sell the group's items.

Start-Up Costs
$2,000 for first month's rent and other craft shop start-up expenses.

Pricing Guidelines
Retail businesses generally operate on a narrow profit margin (5 percent is the average). However, pricing approaches vary depending on location, competition, and the market. Here are some craft pricing tips:

* Pricing is an ongoing dilemma—one that a shop owner must concentrate on. Keep careful records of profits and losses.
* Keep your prices appropriate for the current market.
* Pricing formulas may be different for high- and low-priced items.
* Some owners add 10 percent to 20 percent to the wholesale price to cover higher shipping costs of some items, or a small charge to cover extra packaging.

Essential Equipment
Counters, display racks, shelves, cash register, an assortment of tags; a computer is helpful to keep track of inventory, track sales, maintain mailing lists, do bookkeeping, etc.

Marketing and Advertising Methods and Tips
* Flyers at craft shows.
* Display ads.
* Press releases for special events and sales.
* Referrals from regular customers.
* Have a special event at least once a year (a contest, special sale, seminar, free lesson on a craft, etc.).

Recommended Training, Experience, or Skills
* Work in a craft shop or small retail store.
* Take business management and business start-up courses.
* Work up a good business plan.
* Have a knack for knowing what your customers prefer.

Income Potential
$20,000 to $100,000 per year, depending on the location of your shop and the customers who patronize your store.

Best Customers
✣ Those who have purchased something from you before.
✣ Hobbyists

Helpful Tips
❖ Do market research to assure yourself that you will have customers for your items.
❖ If you take items on consignment, make sure you have signed contracts.

For More Information
How to Start a Retail Craft Business
Success Publications
3419 Dunham
Box 263
Warsaw, NY 14569
Send SASE for information on this publication and others on craft and sewing businesses.

How to Start & Run a Successful Handcraft Co-op by Catherine Jokelson Gilleland. 1995, The Front Room Publishers ($8.95). See "Additional Business Ideas," below, for address.

Also contact your County Extension Agent to see what booklets may be available on forming craft co-ops. Call your county's administrative office for the number of the extension office in your county.

Additional Business Ideas
❖ Be a craft sales representative.
❖ Ideas from Success Publications, 3419 Dunham Rd., Box 263, Warsaw, NY 14569 (send SASE for a complete list and ordering information):
Selling Arts & Crafts by Mail Order ($7).

How to Run a Home Craft Boutique ($7).
How to Sell Your Homemade Creations ($16.50).
❖ Ideas from The Front Room Publishers' Learning Extension Catalog, P.O. Box 1541, Clifton, NJ 07015-1541 (write for a copy of the catalog):
Directory of Craft Shops/Galleries ($12.95).
Selling To Catalog Houses ($11.95).
Start and Run a Profitable Retail Business, $14.95.

42

INVENTOR

"Inventor" was put into this chapter because inventing a new design, system, variation, or anything else is a creative process that starts with an idea and (one hopes) ends with a new, workable product. However, an invention may or may not turn into a business. Like any other entrepreneurial endeavor, you have to research, research, and then do more research to find out if there is a market for your product—is there anything else out there like it?

As one member of a reputable inventor's networking group put it, "... anything involving invention can be a high-risk gamble, even when it is a worthy endeavor." However, more than a few women have done very well with their inventions.

If you have an idea for an invention, and you have the money and the time (lots of it!) to research the idea-to-product process, then you may be able to profit from your ingenuity.

Start-Up Costs
$7,000 to $20,000 or more for the entire process; less if you are willing to do much of the legwork yourself.

Pricing Guidelines
The financial agreement you work out with your manufacturer will depend on production expenses and how much research they have to do.

Essential Equipment
An idea—and then whatever tools it takes for you (or someone else) to make a prototype.

Marketing and Advertising Methods and Tips
❖ First, do extensive research to see whether your idea is truly unique and therefore patentable. Invest the money to do a patent search before you spend money manufacturing your product.
❖ If your idea is unique, and you want to start the patent application process, develop an extensive business plan. Begin your marketing strategy by targeting a specific group first, then expand to others as your product sells.
❖ In addition to consulting a patent attorney, consult an insurance agent and product liability attorney to see if the insurance rates will drive up the costs of your product too far to be cost-effective to manufacture.

Recommended Training, Experience, or Skills
Before you even begin the process, read literature, go to inventor support groups, and talk with inventors who have gone through the entire patent procedure to see if it is worth all the trouble and expense.

Income Potential
❖ $20,000 or more, depending on demand for your invention.
❖ If you are not careful, you could lose money to unscrupulous marketing firms that ask for up-front fees!
❖ If you are successful, you could be guaranteed a steady income over the life of the patent (17 years).

Best Customers
Depends on the purpose of your invention; you will determine who your market is through thorough market research.

Helpful Tips
If you are considering working with a prototype-development assistance provider or invention-marketing firm:

❖ Check out the organization's credentials.

❖ Get references or referrals from other inventors/entrepreneurs.

❖ *Do not fall victim to high-pressure tactics or promises of riches!*

For More Information

Associations

The American Society of Inventors
P.O. Box 58426
Philadelphia, PA 19102

An all-volunteer group offering some helpful tips for aspiring inventors, and networking information amongst the membership. $35 per year membership fee. Send SASE for information.

Inventors Awareness Group, Inc.
1533 East Mountain Rd., Suite B
Westfield, MA 01085-1458

This is an "all-volunteer consumer group formed in 1992 to serve and protect the dreams and aspirations of the independent inventor." $25 per year membership. Send SASE for information. Their booklet, "Invention ...Truth or Consequences," ($5) is *highly recommended* for anyone with an invention idea.

Books

Girls & Young Women Inventing: 20 True Stories about Inventors PLUS How You Can BE One Yourself by Frances A. Karnes, Ph.D. and Suzanne M. Bean, Ph.D. For ages 11 and up. $12.95; order from Free Spirit Publishing, Inc., 400 First Ave. N, Suite 616, Minneapolis, MN 55401-1730.

How to Be an Inventor by Murray Suid. 1993, Monday Morning Books, Inc., Palo Alto, CA.

Inventor's Desktop Companion by Richard C. Levy. 1995, Gale Research, Detroit, MI.

The Inventor's Handbook, 2nd ed., by Robert Park. 1990, Betterway Books, Cincinnati, OH.

Marketing Your Invention by Thomas Mosley. 1992, Upstart Publishing Co., Dover, NH.

Patent It Yourself, 4th ed., by attorney David Pressman. Order from Nolo Press, 950 Parker St., Berkeley, CA 94710; also available on CD-ROM.

CD-ROM
"The Idea Machine," ($59.95) an interactive CD-ROM designed to help the home-based, independent inventor protect ideas and develop and market new products. Based on the 1994 book, *EUREKA! The Entrepreneurial Inventor's Guide to Developing, Protecting, & Profiting from Your Ideas* by Robert Gold, Prentice-Hall, New York, NY. Order from Cyber Knight International Corporation, P.O. Box 64, Spicewood, TX 78669.

Government
U.S. Patent and Trade Office
Washington, DC 20231
Write or call the office's introductory switchboard at (703)-308-HELP.

Government Contact for Invention Fraud
Federal Trade Commission (FTC), Boston Office
101 Merrimac St., Suite 810
Boston, MA 02114-4719

Pamphlet
Facts for Consumers: Invention Promotion Firms, a free Federal Trade Commission (FTC) publication about invention-marketing fraud. To order, call (202) 326-3650, or write to: FTC, Public Reference Branch, Washington, DC 20580.

Additional Business Ideas
License your product to others. Consult an attorney familiar with licensing agreements.
How to License Your Million Dollar Idea: Everything You Need to Know to Make Money from Your New Product Idea by Harvey Reese. 1993, John Wiley & Sons, Inc., New York, NY.

43
⚞ SONGWRITER ⚟

Like inventing, songwriting is not a guaranteed business idea, and it is difficult to make money at it. But if it is a talent that you feel you possess, why not investigate the process of getting your songs published?

One young woman who writes and produces her own songs gives concerts at community centers, churches, and schools, and has opened for groups like the Nitty Gritty Dirt Band. Overcoming blindness caused by a degenerative eye disease, this young woman and her guide dog were often seen in Suburban Street Station in Philadelphia, where she would sing a repertoire of her songs to help support herself. Today she has recorded three albums and performs her contemporary folk and country music regularly. She has not yet made the Top 10, but she never stops singing, writing, and performing.

Start-Up Costs
✤ $1,000 and up for promotional materials.
✤ Costs of renting a studio for making a "demo" tape.

Pricing Guidelines
Based on royalty agreements. See *Song Writer's Market*, listed below, for pricing guidelines.

Marketing and Advertising Methods and Tips
✤ Flyers to schools and churches.
✤ Hire an agent.
✤ Send demo tapes to song-publishing companies (see "Books," below).

Recommended Training, Experience, or Skills
✤ Musical talent and training.
✤ It helps to sing with a band.
✤ Work in the music industry to observe how successful songwriters have made it.

Income Potential
❖ $5,000 to $8,000 per year singing at schools, churches, etc.
❖ As a songwriter, income is variable and depends on the demand for your songs.

Best Customers
❖ For entertainment: local schools, churches, clubs, and cafés; local and state fairs.
❖ For songs: music publishers, recording companies, and advertising firms.

Helpful Tips
❖ Songwriting is highly competitive. Study the market, see what songs are out there in your specialty and who is singing them.
❖ Read contracts carefully and have them looked at by an attorney in the music industry. Research companies before signing or giving money in advance.
❖ Develop a unique style.

For More Information
Books
Writer's Digest Books publishes several interesting titles (call (800) 289-0963 for credit card orders):
Beginning Songwriter's Answer Book by Paul Zollo. 1993.
The Craft and Business of Song Writing by John Braheny, 1995.
Make Money Making Music (No Matter Where You Live) by James Dearing. 1990.
Selling Songs Successfully by Henry Boyce. 1994, Lifetime Books, Inc., Hollywood, FL.
Song Writer's Market: Where and How to Market Your Songs. 1996, F&W Publications, Cincinnati, OH; annual market guide for songwriters.
You Can Write A Song by Amy Appleby and Music Sales Staff. 1995, Music Sales Corporation, New York, NY.

Additional Business Ideas
❖ Home recording studio:
  Hot Tips for the Home Recording Studio by Hank Linderman.
  1994, Writer's Digest Books, Cincinnati, OH.
❖ Performer:
  The Performer's Guide to Theater Songs: The Best Solo Songs for Study, Auditions, and Revues by Brian Hall. 1994, Rovey Research in Performing Arts, Scottsdale, AZ.

⊿ 44 ⊾
NEON CRAFTER

Neon sign-making, artwork, and lighting almost vanished in the 1970s, but is regaining popularity for use in unique signs, decorative accents for homes and businesses, and as artwork. One neon sign-maker says that women who work in neon are generally more into the artwork than into producing commercial signs. He said that there are good opportunities in lampwork for the scientific field, and also in glass bead-making. If this craft appeals to you, talk to neon craftspersons, visit a school, and do some market surveys and research in the area where you plan to do business.

Start-Up Costs
$20,000 to $26,000 for your studio set-up, equipment, office, and promotional supplies.

Pricing Guidelines
$100 to $200 per sign

Essential Equipment
Burners, torches, hoses and connections, tubing, tools.

Marketing and Advertising Methods and Tips
❖ Yellow Pages ad, referrals.

❖ Send a color brochure to businesses.
❖ Exhibit at art shows and craft festivals.
❖ Have some in homeowners' or business owners' windows at high-traffic intersections or roads.

Recommended Training, Experience, or Skills
❖ Attend a good school.
❖ If possible, work as an apprentice or work part-time for another neon craftsperson.
❖ It takes persistence and practice to perfect your skill and speed.

Income Potential
$15 to $20 per hour working part-time or as an apprentice. $500 to $700 a week; $40,000 to $50,000 per year and up with your own studio.

Best Customers
Businesses; homeowners who like unusual decorating effects.

Helpful Tips
Perfect your skills and develop your own style.

For More Information
Books
Glass Casting & Moldmaking: Glass Fusing by Boyce Lundstrom. 1989, Vitreous Publications, Colton, OR.
Neon Principles: The Art of Shaping Light with Neon by Randall L. Caba. 1992, Neon Press, Gresham, OR.
Neon Principles Workbook: A Guide to Shaping Light with Neon by Randall L. Caba. 1993, Neon Press, Gresham, OR.

School
Bristol School of Neon
1534 Euclid Ave.
Bristol, VA 24201
They offer a six-week course. Write for information.

Supplies
M-Tech Industries
P.O. Box 1358
Cedar Ridge, CA 95924
Glass-blowing, lampworking, laboratory supplies, books, and videos. Write, or call (800) 260-2137, for quotes or for catalog information.

Additional Business Ideas
Vinyl sign-maker: Investment $30,000 to $50,000.

Franchise
Fastsigns
2550 Midway Rd., #150
Carrollton, TX 75006.

Resource
Entrepreneur's Business Guide, "Instant Sign Store." (800) 421-2300; $69.50 + shipping.

❖ Magnetic sign-maker: signs sell for an average of $200 a set (one for each side of a vehicle).
❖ Lawn signs: earn an average of $110 a day.

⚹ 45 ⚹
RUBBER STAMPS

Rubber stamping is a popular hobby and decorative craft. People love to collect them and use them in various creative projects. You can use your creative or artistic talent to create your own rubber stamps to sell at craft shows, fairs, via mail order, or by custom order.

Start-Up Costs
$5,000 to $10,000 for equipment, office supplies, and ads.

Pricing Guidelines
Retail, 4 to 6 times your cost to make them.

Essential Equipment
Books of public-domain art (see "For More Information," below), handles for rubber stamps, designing knives.

Marketing and Advertising Methods and Tips
+ Ads in craft magazines.
+ Brochures.
+ Direct mailings to customer lists you garner from craft shows and fairs.
+ Sell in a kiosk cart in malls.
+ Mail-order catalog.
+ Promotional newsletter to regular customers.

Recommended Training, Experience, or Skills
Take courses at adult evening schools or craft centers.

Income Potential
+ $15,000 per year part-time.
+ $50,000 per year and up full-time with an established client list.

Best Customers
Rubber stamp collectors, people from your mailing list, catalogs, craft stores, gift shops.

Helpful Tips
+ Develop your own style, patterns, themes.
+ Add complementary items to sell.

For More Information
Books
Stamp Magic by Stewart and Sally Walton. 1995, Anness Publishing, Ltd., New York, NY.
Stamping Made Easy by Nancy Ward. 1995, Chilton Book Company, Radnor, PA.
Terrific Stencils & Stamps by Jo'Anne Kelly. 1996, Sterling Publishing Co., Inc., New York, NY.

Dover Publications
31 East Second St.
Mineola, NY 11501
Copyright-free design books, as well as a large selection of arts and crafts books. Takes four to six weeks to receive catalog.

Equipment and Supplies
Stewart-Superior
1800 Larchmont Ave.
Chicago, IL 60613
Send SASE for the location of an office nearest you.

Periodical
Rubberstampmadness
P.O. Box 610, Monroe Ave.
Corvallis, OR 97339
$24 per year, 6 issues.

Additional Business Ideas
✤ Teach how to decorate cards, envelopes, and posters with stamps.
✤ Teach how to make stamps.
✤ Sell handmade paper as a sideline to your stamps.

Books
Making & Decorating Your Own Paper by Kathy Blake and Bill Milne. 1994, Sterling Publishing Co., Inc., New York, NY.
Making Your Own Paper by Marianne Saddington. 1993, Storey Communications, Inc., Pownal, VT.

🌿 ● 🌿

MISCELLANEOUS CRAFT IDEAS

Decoupage:
Practical Decoupage by Denise Thomas and Mary Fox. 1996, Trafalgar Square, North Pomfret, UT.

Decoupage Sourcebook by Jocasta Innes and Stewart Walton. 1995, Trafalgar Square, North Pomfret, UT.

Music Boxes:
Making Marvelous Music Boxes by Sharon Ganske. 1996, Sterling Publishing Co., Inc., New York, NY.

Pottery:
The Encyclopedia of Pottery Techniques by Peter Casentino. 1990, Running Press Book Publishers, Philadelphia, PA.

Publish an Arts-and-Crafts Directory:
(See "Independent Publishing.")

Food-Related
Businesses

Americans love to eat! If you love food, love to cook, or have a special recipe, a food-related business may be something you want to do. Here are some helpful resources to get you started.

Food-Related Businesses: General Resources
Association

> National Association for the Specialty Food Trade, Inc.
> (NASFT)
> 8 W. 40th St., 4th Floor
> New York, NY 10018

Trade publication: *Showcase Magazine.* You must have had your food products selling in retail food stores for one year to qualify for membership. $200 per year.

Books

The Guide to Cooking Schools, Shaw Associates Educational Publishers, 625 Biltmore Way, Suite 1406, Coral Gables, FL 33134.

The Guide to Cooking Schools: Cooking Schools, Courses, Food Businesses, Snack Shops, Specialty Food, Restaurants, & Other

Ideas: A Business Workbook by Data Notes Staff. 1992, Prosperity Profits Unlimited Distribution Services, Denver, CO. *From Kitchen to Market: Selling Your Gourmet Food Specialty,* 2nd ed., by Stephen Hall, Upstart Publishing Co., Inc., Dover, NH.

Business Guides

How to Start and Manage a Specialty Food Store Business by Jerre G. Lewis and Leslie D. Renn. 1995, Lewis & Renn Associates, Inc., Interlochen, MI 49643.

Entrepreneur's Start-Up Guide, "Marketing a Family Recipe." (800) 421-2300; $69.50 + shipping.

Distributorship

The Pampered Chef, Ltd., 205 Fend Lane, Hillside, IL 60162. Home party sales of specialized cookware and kitchenwares.

Periodical

Income Opportunities
P.O. Box 55207
Boulder, CO 80323-5207
Offers a special food business issue every August. Look for copies at your local newsstand or see "Small Business Periodicals and Publications" in "General Resources."

Schools for Chefs

Educational Institute of American Culinary Federation
P.O. Box 3466
Saint Augustine, FL 32084
Send SASE for free brochures about certification for chefs and cooks.

Other Publications

The U.S. Department of Agriculture offers "Foreign Buyer Lists" for a variety of food products for $15 each. Call (202) 720-7130 or see your County Extension Agent.

≈ 46 ≈
SALT DOUGH ART AND CREATIONS

In this business, you put together a recipe of salt dough, roll it, form it, and bake it, but you *do not eat it!* You sell your creations as ornaments, for displays, as decorative accents, and to whatever markets want the "look" of food that is not for eating. You will have to experiment with the recipes, decorations, and dyes to get the product you want.

Start-Up Costs
$5,000 to $10,000 for kitchen equipment and rental of kitchen facilities.

Pricing Guidelines
* $4 to $5 for small items (cookies, muffins)
* $25 for pies
* $30 for turkeys, hams, etc.

Essential Equipment
* Access to large ovens.
* Bakery utensils: rolling pins, cutters, molds, commercial mixers, etc.
* Promotional materials: color brochures.
* Office: computer with fax/modem and mail-order software; telephone system, copier.

Marketing and Advertising Methods and Tips
* Direct mail of promotional materials to museums, antique stores, country furniture stores, theater groups, film studios, restaurants, food photographers.
* Antique shows.
* Advertisements in antique trade publications, craft magazines, consumer country decor magazines.
* Word-of-mouth referrals.

Recommended Training, Experience, or Skills
✤ Have personal baking experience or commercial bakery work experience.
✤ Experiment with doughs and dyes.

Income Potential
✤ Depends on your markets and demand.
✤ $10,000 per year part-time to $50,000 per year and up full-time and with good markets.

Best Customers
✤ Museums
✤ Historical homes and societies
✤ Antique and country furniture shops
✤ Country publications
✤ Interior decorators

Helpful Tips
✤ Experiment and develop your own recipes. Make them non-toxic and insect resistant.
✤ Experiment with other replicas of perishable foods: fruit, vegetables, fish, cheeses, etc.
✤ It will take time to develop your recipes, markets, etc. before you can realize a profit.

For More Information
Book
Fun Dough: Over One Hundred Salt Dough Projects for All the Family by Brenda Porteous. 1994, Seven Hills Distributors, Cincinnati, OH.

Additional Business Ideas
Gingerbread houses: sell at Christmas seasons to stores for displays; give private lessons, one-day workshops.

Gingerbread House by Christa Currie. Doubleday Co., Inc., New York, NY.

≈ 47 ≈
COUNTRY INN, RESTAURANT

This is a labor-intensive, time-consuming business with a high failure rate. It can also be a successful business if you do your research, study the industry, and get some experience, either managing a restaurant or working at a variety of restaurant jobs (being a chef or cook, waitress, menu planner). General advice is to get the needed training and experience, then start with a small luncheonette or by just serving breakfast.

Start-Up Costs
* From $50,000 to $200,000 and up; much more if you are buying and/or renovating a country or historic inn.

Pricing Guidelines
Depends on your location, the type of food on your menu, the type of restaurant you have, your customers, and which meal(s) you serve—breakfast, lunch, or dinner.

Essential Equipment
Cooking utensils, stoves, freezers.

Marketing and Advertising Methods and Tips
* Word of mouth from satisfied diners.
* Listings in restaurant guides, tourist brochures.
* Ads in the Yellow Pages and on radio and local cable TV.
* Display ads in local newspapers or other publications read by your customers.
* Offer specials and have meeting rooms for groups, associations, and businesses.

Recommended Training, Experience, or Skills
* Attend restaurant school.
* Have at least two years of on-the-job experience.
* Acquire management and business skills and/or training.

❖ Be able to work 80 + hours a week!
❖ Read restaurant trade publications, reference books.

Income Potential
❖ $20,000 per year for a small shop.
❖ $150,000 for a more established restaurant.

Best Customers
Satisfied customers will be repeat customers and spread the word!

Helpful Tips
❖ Research your market and your competition.
❖ Develop a detailed business plan and refer to it often.
❖ Get more financing than you need.
❖ Reconcile your books daily to keep up with profits and losses.
❖ Have adequate insurance and follow all food regulations; have required licenses.
❖ Consult a lawyer for contracts between partners and any investors.
❖ Have the best service at all times.

Franchises
There are many listed in franchise books and small-business magazines. (See "Franchise" chapter and/or "Small Business Periodicals and Publications," in "General Resources".)

For More Information
Association
National Restaurant Association
1200 17th St. NW
Washington, DC 20036
Write for membership information: send $10 (check or money order), to the attention of Library Services, for a starter kit.

Books

The Complete Guide to Food Service Success: What You Need to Know to Plan a Profitable Operation by Fred Schmid. 1992, RWI Publishing Group, Phoenix, AZ.

How to Open and Run a Successful Restaurant, 2nd ed., by Christopher Egerton-Thomas. 1994, John Wiley & Sons, Inc., New York, NY.

The Restaurant Planning Guide, 2nd ed., by Peter Rainsford and David H. Bangs, Jr. 1996, Upstart Publishing Company, Dover, NH.

The Upstart Guide to Owning and Managing a Restaurant by Roy S. Alonzo. 1995, Upstart Publishing Company, Dover, NH.

Business Guides

How to Start and Manage a Restaurant Business by Jerre G. Lewis and Leslie D. Renn. 1995, Lewis & Renn Associates, Interlochen, MI.

Entrepreneur's Start-Up Guide, "Restaurant Start-Up." (800) 421-2300; $69.50 + shipping.

Directories

Chain Store Guide Information Services
3922 Coconut Palm Dr.
Tampa, FL 33619-8321

Publishes directories/databases of food service and food retailing, distributors; profiles of supermarket, grocery and convenience store chains; wholesale grocers, food service operators, and other retailer profiles. Prices range from $195 to $325 for guides; $700 to $995 for CD-ROMs. Write for complete listings and ordering information.

Periodical

Nation's Restaurant News
425 Park Ave.
New York, NY 10022

Write for current subscription information.

Distance Education/Correspondence Course
Educational Institute of American Hotel & Motel Association
Stephen S. Nisbet Building
1407 South Harrison Rd.
P.O. Box 1240
East Lansing, MI 48826
Write for course listings.

Software
At-Your-Service Software, Inc.
450 Bronxville Rd.
Bronxville, NY 10708-1133
Write for listing or see "Software" in "General Resources."

Additional Business Ideas
❖ Breakfast-and-lunch-only café
❖ Muffin shop; sell soups for lunch
❖ See "Small Shops: Coffee and Tea Shop."

⌐ 48 ⌐

FOOD SPECIALTY

In this business, you have created a specialty food or foods to distribute to retail and small food shops and outlets, gift-basket businesses, booths at trade shows and craft fairs, catalogs, and via your own mail-order business. Selling to large stores or wholesalers requires a large investment of time and money, as well as expert consulting. Your food may get to that market level, but it is easier and financially safer to start small and expand as your markets demand.

Start-Up Costs
$5,000 to $35,000

Pricing Guidelines
❖ Conduct thorough market research to compare prices of similar products and to get an idea what percentage your

customers (food retailers) will add to your product to make a profit.

✤ Also determined by your costs to produce goods and run your business.

Essential Equipment

✤ Use of a commercial kitchen (you can rent a local institution's kitchen that is only used occasionally, or use a commercial kitchen during off-hours).

✤ Kitchen utensils.

✤ Ingredients; purchase, or raise your own if applicable.

✤ Computer with food software, including printing and designing software for your labels and brochures.

✤ Packaging materials.

✤ Promotional materials: brochures with product lists and display and ordering terms.

Marketing and Advertising Methods and Tips

✤ Start at local fairs and shows to get "taste tests" and opinions.

✤ Direct mail to local retailers; follow-up visits with samples.

✤ Exhibit at trade food shows

✤ Give samples to local restaurants to get feedback.

✤ Give away samples at community charity auctions.

✤ Take a space at a farmer's market. You never know who will shop there.

✤ Approach food catalogs with an application and sample.

✤ Send press releases out to food trade magazines, consumer food magazines; do test-market advertising in these. Track responses carefully.

Recommended Training, Experience, or Skills

✤ Background and/or education in marketing, sales, advertising, and business management.

✤ Determination to persist to find the answers and help you need.

Income Potential
Can range from $10,000 per year on a small scale or in the beginning, to $35,000 per year and even $100,000 to $200,000 per year and more if your sales go national.

Best Customers
❖ Small shops: gifts, food, country crafts.
❖ Gift basket businesses.
❖ Local restaurants.
❖ Small grocery stores.
❖ Neighborhood, privately-owned convenience stores.

Helpful Tips
❖ Do thorough market research as to what type of stores would be the best to sell your food product.
❖ Determine the best price for your product.
❖ Determine what type of foods your product should be placed near on shelves to increase sales.
❖ Carefully evaluate your packaging and design.
❖ Chose a display that will best complement your product.
❖ Check with your state's Department of Commerce or Agricultural to see if they have any assistance programs.
❖ Follow all food regulations.
❖ Determine how much of your product you can produce; you may need to have a manufacturer produce it for you.
❖ Test market your product with friends and family, then at local fairs and craft shows; have free samples.

For More Information
Association
See National Association for the Specialty Food Trade, Inc., in "Food-Related Businesses: General Resources," above.

Books
From Kitchen to Market by Stephen Hall. 1992, Upstart Publishing Company, Dover, NH.

Business Guide
Entrepreneur's Start-Up Guide, "Marketing a Family Recipe."
(800) 421-2300; $69.50 plus shipping.

Also see "Food-Related Businesses: General Resources" and
"Mail Order," in "General Resources."

Additional Business Ideas
❖ Jams and jellies
❖ Special condiments
❖ Special salsas and hot sauces
❖ Roasted nuts
❖ Boneless turkey rolls
❖ Gourmet popcorn

≤ 49 ⊵

COOKBOOK AUTHOR

If you have always wanted to write a cookbook, maybe now's
the time to start. Cookbooks are as popular as ever and are
not just written by world-famous chefs. If you like to write
and cook, you may have a best-selling combination.

There are two ways to have a cookbook published: have a
proposal accepted by a cookbook publisher or publish it
yourself. You should approach both ways like any new business: research the necessary steps toward being accepted by
a publisher and do your market research.

In approaching a publisher, you should know something
about what kind of cookbooks this publisher produces and
what the author-guidelines for submissions are.

With self-publishing, *you* will be paying for the printing,
advertising, and distribution, so you should read about self-
publishing and talk with successful self-publishers before
you pay for printing and end up with a garage or basement
full of books! It is possible to be a successful self-publisher,

and often a publisher will subsequently publish your book, especially if you have a good record of your own sales. In "For More Information," below, are three good books on self-publishing and marketing your books. They will give you insights on the publishing world that will help you make your decisions concerning a book idea. You will probably not earn thousands of dollars being published or self-published, but many people have, so you may choose to take the risk. Many new cookbooks are published annually, and one of those could be yours!

Start-Up Costs
* Self-publishing: $5,000 to $10,000 for a printing of 1,000 to 2,000 books; money for promotional materials, advertisements, mailings, and phone calls; $3,000 for a computer, software, and printer.
* For submitting to a publisher: money for equipment (computer, etc.), for postage, envelopes, telephone calls, and photocopies of your manuscript.

Pricing Guidelines
Self-publishing: On average, self-publishers say they price their books five to eight times their production costs.

Essential Equipment
* A computer with word processing software that is compatible with your publisher's software; a desktop publishing program for self-publishing.
* Fax/modem; laser printer or ink-jet printer.
* Business stationery—just your name, address, and phone number and good quality paper—and assorted mailing envelopes.

Marketing and Advertising Methods and Tips
* Self-publishing: know who your readers are likely to be and put ads and press releases in the publications they are most likely to read; teach courses and give workshops;

give cooking demonstrations at food trade shows or on local cable TV shows; attend book trade shows; write magazine articles on your food topic.

❖ Submitting to a publisher: give a short resumé of your credentials; tell why your book is different from others and who you think will read this book.

If submitting your book or proposal to a publisher include a cover letter, title page, synopsis, table of contents/recipe list, sample recipes, your background in cooking, and a SASE. Mention in your proposal, too, who you think would be the most likely people to buy your book and why. This helps the publisher determine if a market exists for this type of cookbook. If they like your book and offer you a contract, they will usually give you an advance (on future royalties).

Recommended Training, Experience, or Skills
❖ Write recipes for magazines.
❖ Teach cooking classes.
❖ Have training or experience in cooking; this establishes you as an expert in your field in the minds of the publisher and the reader.

Income Potential
From a few thousand dollars for an advance and royalties to more if your book is a best seller. Most publishers want to know if you have more than one book idea; they may want to do a series if your first book is successful.

Best Customers
Depends on the type of the food: is it low-calorie, desserts, budget meals? Then target the people who would be interested in your kind of recipes through ads in catalogs, magazines, etc.

Helpful Tips
❖ Look at other cookbooks like yours and be able to tell your publisher or reader how yours is different.

❖ Be able to say (in your advertisements or to a publisher) in just a few sentences why your cookbook is new and special, and why people would want to buy it.

For More Information
Books
The Complete Guide to Self-Publishing, 3rd ed., by Tom and Marilyn Ross. 1994, Writer's Digest Books, Cincinnati, OH.

Cookbook Author's Handbook edited and compiled by Linda Hayes. 1994, International Association of Culinary Professionals, Louisville, KY 40202. Covers all facets of the cookbook-writing process; $10 for nonmembers, $5 for members. Write to 304 W. Liberty St., Suite 201, Louisville, KY 40202.

For All the Write Reasons: Forty Successful Authors, Publishers, Agents and Writers Tell How to Get Your Book Published by Patricia Gallagher. 1992. Box 265, Worcester, PA 19490; $24.94 + $3 shipping; good tips and information on self-publishing and marketing.

1,001 Ways to Market Your Books, 4th ed., by John Kremer. 1993, Open Horizons, P.O. Box 205, Fairfield, IA 55256-0205; $19.95 + $3.50 shipping.

Self-Publishing Resources
Cookbook Publishers, Inc.
10800 Lakeview
Lenexa, Kansas 66219
This company has been in business since 1947, and puts together spiral-bound books for individuals and fund-raising organizations. You send them your manuscript, and you get to select your cover, type style, etc. They print and assemble your book. *Then it is up to you to sell them.* Send SASE for information.

Additional Business Ideas
❖ Mail-order food business.
❖ Publish a restaurant guide/directory.

❖ Specialized catering.

❖ Cooking school: add tours to restaurants and cooking seminars.

❖ Chocolate "factory".

❖ Food column: you can make $10 to $20 per week for a weekly column in a local paper; $15 to $100 per column for small- to large-circulation dailies.

❖ Cake baking and decoration:
Start-up costs: $4,000 to $5,000
Income potential: $15,000 to $40,000
First Steps In Cake Decorating: Over 100 Step-by-Step Cake Decorating Techniques and Recipes by Janice Murfitt. 1996, Sterling Publishing Co., Inc., New York, NY.

❖ Food cart:
From Dogs to Riches: A Step-by-Step Guide to Starting and Operating Your Own Mobile Cart Vending Business by Vera D. Clark-Ruglery. 1993, MCC Publishing, Los Angeles, CA.

❖ Specialized baking: a variety of breads, cakes, and desserts.
Professional Baking, 2nd ed., by Wayne Gisslen. 1995, John Wiley & Sons, Inc., New York, NY.

❖ Home canning instruction:
Better Homes and Gardens All-American Canning and Preserving Cookbook. Order through the Better Homes & Gardens Crafts Club, P.O. Box 8824, Camp Hill, PA, 17012-8824.

❖ Personal chef:
Professional Cooking, 3rd ed., by Wayne Gisslen. 1995, John Wiley Sons, Inc., New York, NY.

Green and Environmental Businesses

Many businesses are finding that being "environmentally conscious" is not only "earth-friendly," but economical as well. It helps decrease waste and saves money at the same time. Because of environmental regulations, many businesses and consumers need to find a way to recycle their wastes and waste products. This provides many entrepreneurial opportunities in the collection and recycling processes. Or you may choose other businesses that help our earth like those that involve plants or growing specialty foods.

Green Businesses: General Resources
Association
   American Horticultural Society
   7931 East Boulevard Dr.
   Alexandria, VA 22308-1300
Send SASE for membership information.

Books
Gardening by Mail: A Source Book by Barbara J. Barton. 1994, Houghton Mifflin, Boston, MA.

Just the Facts: Dozens of Garden Charts, Thousands of Gardening Answers by the editors of Garden Way Publishers. 1994.

Publishers of Gardening Books
(Write for a catalog of publisher's current books).

Better Homes & Gardens Books
110 Walnut St.
Des Moines, IA 50309-3400

Rodale Press, Inc., Dept. B
33 East Minor Street
Emmaus, PA 18098
Publisher of *Organic Gardening* magazine and numerous gardening books.

Storey's How-To Books for Country Living
Schoolhouse Rd.
Pownal, VT 05261

Mail-Order
Hannon House
5310 Mountain Rd.
Cheyenne, WY 82009
Carries an assortment of gardening books. Write for catalog.

Periodicals and Publications
Organic Gardening
Rodale Press, Inc.
P.O. Box 7320
Red Oak, IA 51591
$25 per year for nine issues. Call (800) 666-2206.

Home Gardener
Burpee Seed Co.
P.O. Box 5114
Warminster, PA 18974-0001
$9.95 per year, 4 issues.

Software

"The Gardener's Friend," Crystonix Software. Contains information on more than 1,800 flowers, trees, shrubs, etc. ($29.95 plus $3.50 shipping and handling). Call (408) 272-9343.

Government

U.S. Department of Agriculture Cooperative Extension Service: there is an office in every county in the U.S. They can help with gardening problems, crops, pests, etc. Call your county courthouse and ask for the number of the office nearest you.

Miscellaneous

National Wildlife Federation
310 Tyson Drive
Winchester, VA 22603

Write, or call (800) 432-6564, to order the low-cost packet on how to establish a backyard wildlife habitat.

⚞ 50 ⚟

GARDEN CENTER

It would be hard to compete with large garden centers, with the volume of plants, garden supplies, and assorted garden-related products they carry. It requires a substantial investment to say the least. Instead, many women who are knowledgeable about gardening start on a much smaller scale, working from their home gardens, and have thriving businesses. One woman specializes in herbs, another in many varieties of day lilies, and another, who also has a home day-care business, sells seedlings from a little greenhouse and small building located near her driveway.

If you have a special knack or knowledge of certain plants that large garden centers do not have, there may be a good market for your business. News about quality plants sold at good prices spreads rapidly among gardeners! If you have that green thumb, a small garden center may be the business for you.

Start-Up Costs
$10,000 (if operating from your property) to $40,000 at a local commercial location.

Pricing Guidelines
Compare prices in garden and seed catalogs and local nurseries.

Essential Equipment
* A small greenhouse, pots, gardening tools, a vehicle for picking up supplies.
* Office equipment: a computer with accounting, gardening, and mailing-list software; telephone system.
* Promotional materials: a list of plants available; business cards.

Marketing and Advertising Methods and Tips
* Word of mouth: establish a reputation for quality plants at reasonable prices.
* Direct mail to local gardening clubs; mailings to larger garden centers about specialized plants you may carry and they do not. Often, they will be happy to refer their customers to you.
* Promotional garden column in local newspapers.
* Articles and ads in local newspapers' spring home remodeling and garden sections.
* Free gardening seminars on special topics: gardening for people with disabilities, children's gardens, specific garden types (shade, perennial, dry, butterfly gardens, etc.).
* If you have the space, plant sample gardens for your customers to view.

Recommended Training, Experience, or Skills
* Acquire gardening education and work experience. Many greenhouses, nurseries, and garden centers need extra

help in their busy seasons. Enroll in horticultural courses at local schools, colleges, etc.
+ Have a love of plants and gardening.
+ Study gardening books; subscribe to gardening publications.
+ Grow the plants you sell so that you become an expert.

Income Potential
$12,000 per year part-time to $100,000 per year or more, depending on your location.

Best Customers
+ Homeowners
+ Gardening enthusiasts

Helpful Tips
+ Specialize in plants and products that other garden centers do not carry; it will give you the market niche you need for business.
+ Offer garden advice to your customers with informative booklets; send a seasonal newsletter to customers on your mailing list.
+ Offer dried flowers that you grow or buy from others to bring you off-season business if you live in an area with cold winters.
+ Look for ways to draw in your customers: locally made birdhouses and feeders, pond plants, creative garden containers.

For More Information
Books
The New Seed-Starter's Handbook by Nancy Bubel. 1994, Rodale Press, Emmaus, PA.
The Easy-Care Gardening Expert by Dr. D.G. Hessayan. 1996, Sterling Publishing Co., Inc., 387 Park Ave. South, New York, NY 10016.

Sterling Publishing Co., Inc., has an "Expert" gardening series including special books on bulbs, bedding plants, fruits, rock and water gardens, roses, etc. Write for a listing or check your local bookstore.

Business Guide
How to Start and Manage a Garden Center Business by Jerre G. Lewis and Leslie D. Renn. 1995, Lewis & Renn Associates, Inc., Interlochen, MI 49643.

Additional Business Ideas
Farm center: If you have a small farm not too far from suburban communities or large towns, you can offer various ventures on your farm:

❖ A petting area with farm animals.
❖ A pumpkin patch where families, school classes, and preschool groups can pick out their pumpkins.
❖ Apple-picking in an orchard in the fall; present an apple-press demonstration.
❖ Hay rides.
❖ Straw-bale mazes.
❖ A roadside stand selling your own fruit, vegetables, poultry.
❖ Greenhouse plants.
❖ Scarecrow contests.
❖ Homemade breads and pies.

◁ 51 ▷

GARDEN PROBLEM-SOLVER

Even people who love to garden have problems getting certain plants to grow and battling garden pests and critters; they need gardening advice of one sort or another. If you have the experience, training, education, or all three, you can start a garden problem-solving service. As a consultant, you can price according to your expertise, reputation, and the time it takes to research and remedy the garden problem.

You can offer free property evaluations and then give the customers a list of your services from which they can choose, for example: pruning, soil testing, plantings for difficult areas, and advice on how to treat plant diseases or discourage insect pests using safe, organic methods.

Start-Up Costs
$4,000 to $12,000 for a computer, references, and tools.

Pricing Guidelines
$25 to $30 per hour; you can charge $50 to $100 per hour if you have a degree or certification in horticulture, landscape design, or botany.

Essential Equipment
Reference books; computer, fax/modem, access to online gardening databases, garden problem-solving software; gardening tools; 4-wheel drive vehicle for reaching difficult spots.

Marketing and Advertising Methods and Tips
* Advertise: in gardening sections of local newspapers; flyers enclosed in classified-ad newspapers; cable TV classified ads.
* Publish a newsletter filled with problem-solving tips. Offer a free garden tips booklet (that you write) for the best reader tips.
* Have a call-in hour on a local radio show.
* Post flyers in hardware stores, garden centers, and farmer's markets.
* Give talks to local garden or women's clubs.
* Call homeowners in your area to let them know of your service and free evaluation.
* Take a booth at garden and/or home shows.
* Write a paid garden column for your local newspapers.
* Get magnetic signs for the sides of your vehicle.
* Post a lawn sign where you are working.
* Get referrals from satisfied customers.

Recommended Training, Experience, or Skills
* Have gardening experience and training in both traditional and organic methods of gardening.
* Have a degree in horticulture and/or attend classes at your local agricultural school or college, or see if they have correspondence courses.
* Work in a plant nursery, greenhouse, or garden center, or for a landscaping service. Many have tips they have garnered over the years.

Income Potential
$5,000 to $10,000 per year part-time; $20,000 to $50,000 per year full-time, depending on the demand for your service.

Best Customers
* Homeowners.
* Institutions such as nursing homes, where there are gardens and plants.
* Businesses that want good-looking grounds.

Helpful Tips
* Offer free evaluations.
* Know the common plant problems, how to identify them, and how to solve them.
* Make sure you have adequate business and liability insurance.
* Study organic and pesticide-free methods of pest and weed control.

For More Information
Books
Garden Magic: Hundreds of Motions, Potions, & Lotions for Your Lawn and Garden! by Jerry Baker, Box 1001, Wixom, MI 48393. 1995. $4.95 + $1 shipping and handling (check or money order).
Garden Problem Solver: 101 Solutions to Common Landscaping Problems. By Catriona Tudor Erler. 1995. Storey's How-To Books for Country Living, Pownal, VT.

Books from Rodale Press, Dept. B, 33 East Minor St., Emmaus, PA 18098:

Great Garden Shortcuts edited by Joan Benjamin.

The Organic Gardener's Handbook of Natural Insect and Disease Control edited by Barbara Ellis and Fern Marshall Bradley.

Rodale's All-New Encyclopedia of Organic Gardening edited by Fern Marshall Bradley and Barbara W. Ellis.

Rodale's Garden, Insect, Disease and Weed Identification Guide by Miranda Smith and Anna Smith.

Rodale's Landscape Problem Solver by Jeff and Liz Ball.

Start with the Soil: The Organic Gardener's Guide to Improving Soil for High Yields, More Beautiful Flowers, and a Healthy, Easy-Care Garden by Grace Gershunny.

Periodical
Organic Gardening
Rodale Press
P.O. Box 7320
Red Oak, IA 51591
$25 per year for nine issues. Call (800) 666-2206.

Additional Business Ideas
Plant doctor: you could offer a service saving "sick" plants, or caring for plants while people are on vacation.

The House Plant Expert by Dr. G. Hessayon. 1992, Sterling Publishing Company, Inc., New York, NY.

≤ 52 ≥
GREENHOUSE GROWER

With a greenhouse business, you can sell from your home or from a greenhouse with a store attached. You could sell wholesale and retail seedlings and plants—seedlings for outdoor spring planting or specialized plants such as orchids, begonias, etc. With the popularity of organic foods, you can grow chemical-free fruits and vegetables, herbs, and/or hydroponically grown vegetables like tomatoes.

This business takes experience and a willingness to work long hours. You will also need to find out the best markets for your business. Research what is popular or needed in plants and/or specialty foods in your area. If you love growing plants, being a greenhouse grower may let you enjoy your love while earning profits.

Start-Up Costs
$2,500 to $250,000; you can start small, with a small greenhouse attached to your house or garage, and then expand to a larger greenhouse with a small retail shop attached if you want.

Pricing Guidelines
Greenhouse growers usually come to a retail price at four times what it costs them to grow the plant. This depends on your location, the demand for your products, and the current market prices.

Essential Equipment
+ A greenhouse: free-standing or attached; can range in price from $300 on up to $25,000 for a larger steel structure.
+ A truck or vehicle for deliveries and pick-up of supplies.
+ Seeds, growing medium, pots, markers, fertilizer, reference books on plant care and prevention and treatment of insects and plant disease.
+ Office equipment: a computer with gardening and accounting software; a telephone system.

Marketing and Advertising Methods and Tips
+ Ads in local papers, local magazines, and gardening publications.
+ Direct calls to businesses that sell plants as part of their spring promotions: hardware stores, grocery stores, all-purpose department stores.
+ Fairs, craft shows, farmer's markets, large weekend flea markets.

* Word of mouth if you sell specialty plants such as unusual herbs, flowers, orchids, etc.
* A handpainted, attractive sign.
* A promotional newsletter to your steady customers.
* Flyers on apartment-house bulletin boards if you grow houseplants
* Lectures at garden clubs about propagation methods of their favorite plants.

Recommended Training, Experience, or Skills
* Horticultural experience or classes; courses on plant propagation and care and prevention of diseases.
* If possible, work in greenhouses that grow different crops to gain experience with a variety of plants, etc.
* Study the particular plants you want to grow.

Income Potential
$12,000 per year part-time; $30,000 to $60,000 per year full-time, and more depending on how the market is for your plants.

Best Customers
* Restaurants.
* Local grocery stores.
* Schools and institutions for spring fund-raising sales.
* Apartment dwellers for your houseplants.
* Plant-lovers of all kinds.
* Businesses that sell plants in the spring.

Helpful Tips
* Have enough money saved to support yourself for at least one year while you build up your business. It is easier to start part-time and test your markets with a variety of plants to see what grows best and what sells best.
* Try to find unusual plants, herbs for gardening enthusiasts, hobbyists, collectors.
* Take business courses on horticultural business.
* Try to have something for sale in all seasons at your greenhouse.

For More Information

Association
Hobby Greenhouse Association
8 Glen Terrace
Bedford, MA 01730-2048
A nonprofit organization that promotes greenhouse gardening as a hobby or avocation. Publishes *Hobby Greenhouse*, an excellent magazine on the operation of small greenhouses. $15 per year, 4 issues; sample copy $3. Write for membership information.

Books
The Complete Greenhouse Book by Ian G. Walls. 1996, Sterling Publishing Co., Inc., New York, NY.

The following can be ordered from Storey's How-To Books for Country Living, Schoolhouse Rd., Pownal, VT 05261 (write for catalog):
Greenhouse Gardener's Companion: Growing Food & Flowers in Your Greenhouse or Sunspace by Shane Smith. 1993.
Perennial Plants for Profit or Pleasure by Francis X. Jazwik, Ph.D.
Secrets of Plant Propagation: Starting Your Own Flowers, Vegetables, Fruits, Berries, Shrubs, Trees, and Houseplants by Lewis Hill. 1985.
Secrets to a Successful Greenhouse Business by T.M. Taylor.

Business Guide
National Business Library's Start-Up Guide, "Seedling Grower." (800) 947-7724, $39.95 + shipping.

Additional Business Ideas
✤ Growing orchids:
     American Orchid Society
     6000 South Olive Ave.
     West Palm Beach, FL 33405
Write for membership information.

Online: CompuServe: 71726.1741@compuserv.com
Orchidweb: *http://www.vg.com/Gardens/AOS*
Orchid Growing Basics by Gustav Schoser. 1993, Sterling
Publishing Co., Inc., New York, NY.
Orchid Growers Handbook by I.D. James. 1989, Sterling
Publishing Co., Inc., New York, NY.
Orchid Growers Manual, 7th ed., by B.S. and H. Williams.
1973, Lubrecht & Cramer, Ltd., Forestburgh, NY.

❖ Small-scale farming:
Backyard Market Gardening: The Entrepreneur's Guide to Selling What You Grow by Andy Lee. 1995, Good Earth
Publications, Columbus, NC.

The following can be ordered from Storey's How-To Books
for Country Living, Schoolhouse Rd., Pownal, Vermont
05261 (write for catalog):
Grow It!: The Beginner's Complete in-Harmony-with-Nature Small-Farm Guide: From Vegetable and Grain Growing to Livestock Care by Richard W. Langer. 1994, Farrar,
Straus, and Giroux, New York, NY.
How to Make $100,000 Farming 25 Acres by Booker T. Whatley and the editors of *The New Farm*. 1994.
Metro Farm: The Guide to Growing for Big Profit on a Small Parcel of Land by Michael Olson. 1995, T. S. Books,
Santa Cruz, CA.
Successful Small-Scale Farming by Karl Schwenke. 1996.

Periodical
Small Farm Today
3903 W. Ridge Trail Rd.
Clark, Missouri 65243-9525
"Its mission is to make small farms and acreages profitable." $21
per year, 6 issues; sample copy $4. Freelance queries welcome.

Business Guides
National Business Library's Start-Up Business Guides, "Backyard Farming," "Make Money Growing Herbs," "Make Money

Growing Mini Vegetables." (800) 947-7724, $39.95 each + shipping.

❖ Growing bonsai:
The Bonsai Workshop by Herb L. Gustafson. 1996, Sterling Publishing Co., Inc., New York, NY.

❖ Growing mushrooms:
Growing Gourmet and Medicinal Mushrooms, 2nd ed., by Paul Stamets. 1995, Ten Speed Press, Berkeley, CA.
Growing Shiitake Commercially: A Practical Manual for Production of Japanese Forest Mushroom Cultivation, 2nd ed., by Ed Harris. 1993, Second Foundation, Summerton, TN.
Shiitake Growers Handbook by Paul Przybylowicz and John Donoghue. 1990, Kendal Hunt Publishing Co., Dubuque, IA.
National Business Library's Start-Up Business Guides, "Magic Mushroom Growing." (800) 947-7724, $39.95 each + shipping.

❖ Make wreaths and centerpieces to sell during Christmas and Easter holidays:
The Wreath Book by Rob Pulleyn. 1996, Sterling Publishing Co., Inc., NY.

≈ 53 ≈

RAISING BENEFICIAL INSECTS

With the current concern for organic gardening—gardening without pesticides and commercial fertilizers—more gardeners, small farmers, and nature enthusiasts are looking for natural ways to protect against crop- and plant-damaging insects. There is a growing market for the raising of beneficial insects such as ladybugs, praying mantises, beneficial wasps, and green lace-wings for insect control. This is may be an unusual business for a woman, but if you have experience in gardening as a hobby, growing food crops or flowers, or creating a backyard wildlife habitat, you have probably already seen firsthand how beneficial insects can help keep harmful insects under control.

Start-Up Costs
$1,000 to $3,000

Pricing Guidelines
* Ladybugs: $6/1,500
* Spider-mite predators: $30/100
* Whitefly parasites: $16.50/500
* Praying mantis egg cases: $9.95/3

Essential Equipment
Containers for raising insects, food, packages for shipping.

Marketing and Advertising Methods and Tips
* Classified/display ads in gardening publications.
* Direct mail to gardening clubs.

Recommended Training, Experience, or Skills
* Take some entomology courses at local colleges.
* Read books on specific insects.
* Raise some insects on a small scale.

Income Potential
$20,000 to $30,000 full-time.

Best Customers
Garden catalogs, home gardeners, commercial greenhouses, organic growers.

Helpful Tips
* Interview entomologists and/or commercial insect-raisers to get tips and advice.
* Contact your County Extension Agent for information and referrals.
* Experiment on your own in raising the insects you want.

For More Information
Association
Entomological Society of America
9301 Annapolis Rd.
Lanham, MD 20706-3115
Not-for-profit educational organization serving entomologists and people in entomology fields. They do not have information about starting a business, but they can provide names of members who may be able to answer some questions about insects that interest you. Send SASE for information.

Book
Good Bugs for Your Garden by Allison M. Starcher. 1995, Algonquin Books of Chapel Hill, Chapel Hill, NC.

Additional Business Ideas
✤ Raise bees for honey and bee products:
  Backyard Beekeeping by C.N. Smithers. 1993, Seven Hills Book Distributors, Cincinnati, OH.
  Books from Storey's How-To Books for Country Living, Schoolhouse Rd., Pownal, VT 05261:
  Beekeeping: A Practical Guide by Richard E. Bonney. 1993, Storey Communications, Inc., Pownal, VT.
  Hive Management by Richard E. Bonney.
✤ Raise butterflies for show and hobbyists:
  The Case for Live Butterfly Habitats in the U.S. by W. Mark Cotham. 1992, Young Entomologists Society, Inc., Lansing, MI.
✤ Raise mealworms for bird lovers.
✤ Raise earthworms:
  For fishing, gardening, composting, etc. Start for less than $30.

  Facts About Nightcrawlers and Redworms, 7th ed., by George Sroda. 1995. $10.95 + $2 postage and handling from George Sroda, P.O. Box 97, Amherst Junction, WI 54407. Information on raising worms, including tips for worm breeders and worm merchandisers. George

Sroda is the "International Worm Czar"; he also wrote a fun book, *Herman the Worm* (same price and shipping as the other book; both for $19 including postage and handling).

How to Raise, Store, and Sell Nightcrawlers by Charlie Morgan. 1984, Shields Publications, Eagle River, WI.

❖ Raise snails for cooking in restaurants:

U.S. Snail
9755 Q St., Suite 226
Omaha, NE 68127
Send $5 for information.

⚐ 54 ⚑
UNIQUE PLANTERS

Gardeners who grow plants, indoors and out, are always looking for containers, decorative pots, window boxes, etc. in which to show off their plants. If your are talented with woodworking, ceramics, papier-mâché, decorative painting, pottery, etc. you can have a creative and profitable business making unique custom containers and planters for just about anything and everything that grows!

Start-Up Costs
❖ $100 for redoing already-made new and used containers.
❖ $2,000 to $3,000 for woodworking equipment and other assorted tools related to the materials with which you are working.

Pricing Guidelines
❖ Price your containers at two to three times your total costs (materials + labor + overhead).
❖ Compare prices for containers in local garden centers, florist shops, greenhouses, hardware stores, craft shops, etc.

Essential Equipment

* Tools: woodworking electrical equipment (see "Wood Crafts Wholesaler"), paints, brushes.
* Boxes for packaging and shipping.
* Materials for making your containers.
* Ceramic or pottery supplies and kiln.

Marketing and Advertising Methods and Tips

* Exhibit at craft fairs, flea markets, and garden shows.
* Take samples to garden centers, plant nurseries, greenhouses with retail stores, hardware stores.
* Put up lawn signs with samples in your front yard.
* Display at mall shows and art shows, depending on the type of planter you are making.
* Take out display ads with photos or illustrations of your products.
* Direct-mail flyers to garden clubs.
* Give talks about container gardening and demonstrations on transplanting.
* Sell to catalog houses: seed, home and garden (make sure you can produce a large quantity at wholesale prices and still make a profit).
* Start out with an album of photos of the containers you make with a price list that you can show to prospective customers. Then invest in a photo brochure with price list.
* Exhibit at garden trade wholesale shows if you can produce enough to fill large orders.

Recommended Training, Experience, or Skills

* Take woodworking, pottery, ceramic, and/or art classes, depending on your containers' materials.
* Read books, visit garden centers, etc. to see what kinds of containers or boxes are being sold in your community or in catalogs, and what their prices are.

Income Potential

$100 to $2,000 at a good weekend craft or garden show; $5,000 part-time; $25,000 full-time.

Best Customers

❖ Gardeners, garden centers, hardware stores, nurseries, florists catalogs.
❖ Antique stores, especially if you use rustic or antique-finished containers.
❖ Businesses, for their storefronts; offer different planters already planted with flowers and herbs.
❖ Country furniture shops.

Helpful Tips

❖ Develop your own trademark design and high-quality product that lasts under outdoor weather conditions.
❖ Read gardening magazines and home-and-garden magazines, to learn what is popular.
❖ Keep good business records to make sure you are charging enough to make a profit.

For More Information

Books

The Creative Container Gardener by Elaine Stevens and Dagmar Hungerford. 1995, Ten Speed Press, Berkeley, CA.

Garden Structures You Can Make by Paul Gerhards. 1996, Stackpole Books, Mechanicsburg, PA.

Making Decorative Lawn Ornaments & Patio Containers by Edie Stockstill. 1996, Sterling Publishing Co. Inc., New York, NY.

The Ornamental Gardener: Creative Ideas for Every Gardener by Miranda Innes. 1992, Stemmer House Publishers, Inc., Owings Mills, MD.

Traditional Garden Woodwork by Peter Holland. 1996, Sterling Publishing Co., Inc., New York, NY.

The following books can be ordered from Storey's How-To Books for Country Living, Schoolhouse Rd., Pownal, VT 05261 (write for a catalog):

101 Easy-to-Make Things for Your Garden, Home, or Farm by Ken Braren and Roger Griffith. 1977.

How to Build Outdoor Structures by Deborah Morgan and Nick Engler. 1988.
64 Yard & Garden Projects You Can Build Yourself by Monte Burch. 1994.

Additional Business Ideas

✤ Sell your containers via your own mail-order business (see "Mail Order" in "General Resources").

✤ Make and sell already planted containers as gifts.

⚞ 55 ⚟
RECYCLING BUSINESS

With the vast amount of garbage the U.S. creates every year, and fewer places to dump it, recycling businesses are not just a fad; they are a necessity if we are to keep from poisoning our world. Recycling businesses are using more and more products that were once thrown away: Plastic is converted into park benches; old rubber tires are made into shoes and racetrack turf; old newspapers are made into animal bedding; and so on.

Entrepreneurs are inventing new ways to corner the "green market" with consulting, environmental tours, educational games, books, and software. The business ideas will keep on arising as people and governments realize that it is both profitable and in all of our own interests to recycle. If you are interested in a recycling business, you will have to start researching what types of recycling businesses there are in your community, what your community needs most, and what new businesses could possibly work there. Also keep current on recycling and environmental trends by reading trade publications. It will take time, but it will be gratifying to you to not only make money, but also help our world be a little cleaner.

Start-Up Costs
As little as $500 for a used van to pick up recyclable items, to as much as $100,000 and more to purchase recycling equipment and start production.

Pricing Guidelines
+ Follow the business axiom: to make more profit, spend less and sell more. This means to spend what money you have thriftily and wisely, and re-invest it only in ways that will help your business grow. Decide what you would like your profit margin to be, and seek ways to increase it without sacrificing quality or customer service.
+ Test market your product or service to see what people would be willing to pay for such an item or service, and compare your prices with those of other similar businesses.
+ Make sure you check all governmental levels for regulations and licensing requirements.

Essential Equipment
+ Start with used equipment if possible, and invest in new equipment as you begin to make money.
+ Equipment needs depend on what kind of recycled materials and finished product you decide to work with.

Marketing and Advertising Methods and Tips
+ Send press releases to publications and television stations emphasizing the fact you are helping the environment with your business.
+ Write articles about recycling which may be related to your business; don't make them "infomercials" about your own company.
+ Publish a promotional newsletter.
+ Exhibit at trade shows.
+ Take out classified or display ads in local newspapers and trade publications.

❖ Place promotional articles in annual community business profiles in local papers.
❖ Promotional materials: brochures, business cards.

Recommended Training, Experience, or Skills
❖ If possible, work in the industry that produces the materials that you are planning to recycle. Do not copy your employer's methods, but originate ideas of your own. Tell your employer what you plan to do, and he or she may even give you some assistance.
❖ Read and research all you can in the industry that interests you. Talk with owners of recycling businesses for tips, etc.

Income Potential
$20,000 per year to as much as $1 million per year, depending on the demand for your business and what your product is.

Best Customers
❖ Consumers: Homeowners, nonprofit organizations, special events.
❖ Business customers: factories, manufacturers.

Helpful Tips
❖ Write a thorough business plan with at least a five-year projection.
❖ Keep current with recycling news.
❖ Be creative but practical in what you do with your recycled materials.
❖ Be prepared to persist in seeing an idea or service develop as it takes time to acquire a customer base.
❖ Be prepared to educate your customers about the qualities and purposes of this new product and how it can benefit them.
❖ Consumers: in your ads give information about the use of this product and how it will help them in its use and how it also helps the environment. Be honest and direct.

❖ Business customers: be ready to give samples, referrals, and demonstrations of your products. Offer free one-time service or evaluation to give you a chance to demonstrate your products' or service's quality.

For More Information
Association
National Recycling Coalition
1727 King St., #105
Alexandria, VA 22314-2720
Send SASE for more information.

Co-Op America Business Network
1612 K St. NW, Suite 600
Washington, DC 20077-2573
$60 membership fee. This is a nonprofit organization that supports businesses that are committed to the environment. If you pass their screening process, you will be listed in the *Co-op America National Green Pages,* a listing of more than 100,000 businesses. Membership also includes marketing, networking, and financial advice, and a subscription to the newsletter, "Co-op America's Connections."

Books
Ecopreneuring: The Complete Guide to Small Business Opportunities from the Environmental Revolution by Steven J. Bennett. 1991, John Wiley & Sons, Inc., New York, NY.
How to Start & Operate a Recycling Business by John P. Allison. 1991, RMC Publishing Group, Ltd., Fort Worth, TX.
Recycling Businesses: Suggestions for Types of Recycling Businesses by Research Division Staff. 1992, Center for Self-Sufficiency Publishing, Denver, CO.
Recycling Sourcebook by Gale Research Staff. 1992, Gale Research, Detroit, MI; a comprehensive source on recycling. Ask your reference librarian if they have a copy.

Online
  The Global Recycling Network
  271A Montauk Hwy
  Brookhaven, NY 11719
  World Wide Web: *http://grn.com/grn/#Whattis*

Periodical
  Resource Recycling Magazine
  P.O. Box 10540
  Portland, OR 97210
  $47 per year, monthly issues.

Additional Business Ideas
❖ Erasing graffiti
❖ "Green" store: Selling environmentally-safe and recycled products.
❖ Recycling consultant/broker:
  Entrepreneur's "Recycling Consultant/Broker." (800)421-2300, $69.50 + shipping.

  See also "Clothing Consignment Shop," "Clothing Recycling," in Additional Business Ideas.

꙳ ● ꙳

STILL MORE GREEN BUSINESS IDEAS

❖ Florist business:
  How to Start and Manage a Retail Florist Business by Jerre G. Lewis and Leslie D. Renn. 1995, Lewis & Renn Associates, 10315 Harmony Dr., Interlochen, MI 49643.
  The Upstart Guide to Owning and Managing a Florist Service by Dan Ramsey. 1995, Upstart Publishing Company, Dover, NH.

  Florist Magazine
  29200 Northwestern Hwy.
  P.O. Box 2227
  Southfield, MI 48037

$39 per year, 12 monthly issues, including annual Buyer's Directory.

✤ Grow gourds for crafters and painters:

The Complete Book of Gourd Craft by Ginger Summit and Jim Widess. 1996, Sterling Publishing Company, Inc., New York, NY.

✤ Create backyard ponds and water gardens:

The Complete Pond Builder: Creating a Beautiful Water Garden by Helen Nash. 1996, Sterling Publishing Company, Inc., New York, NY.

Hobbyist Guide to Successful Pond Keeping by Dr. David Pool, Tetra Press, Blacksburg, VA.

The Popular Guide to Garden Ponds by Dick Mills. 1992, Tetra Press, Blacksburg, VA.

Your Garden Pond by K.H. Wieser and Dr. Paul Loisell, Tetra Press, Blacksburg, VA.

Small Shops

Retail strategists say it appears shoppers are looking for something different in shopping. Consumers want to experience more than just going to a store. They want to enjoy their shopping, and want to encounter something different than the large, impersonal department store located at a huge shopping mall.

This gives the small retailer the opportunity to find her uniqueness and express her creativity in the decor and overall ambiance of her retail shop, and attracting her customers in ways the larger retail stores cannot. The store reflects her personality, and of course, special customer service will always help bring repeat customers. It is an exciting challenge for any woman contemplating opening a retail shop to make it quite unlike any other.

General Information
Books
How to Open Your Own Store by Michael Autoniak. 1994, Avon Books, New York, NY.

Make More Money Retailing by Barbara Lambesis and Susan Ratliff. 1994, order from Marketing Methods Press, (800) 745-5047.

Retail Store Planning & Design Manual, 2nd ed., by Michael J. Lopez. 1995, John Wiley & Sons, Inc., New York, NY
Run Your Own Store, 2nd ed., by Irving Burstiner, Ph.D. 1989, Prentice Hall Press, New York, NY.
Start and Run a Profitable Retail Shop, 1990 order through Front Room Publishers, P.O. Box 1541, Clifton, NJ, 07015-1541; write for Learning Extension Catalog.
Successful Retailing, 2nd ed., by Paula Wardell. 1990, Upstart Publishing Co., Dover, NH.

Business Guides
The following publishers produce many specific retail business guides; write or call for current catalogs:

Entrepreneur's Small Business Development Catalogs, (800) 421-2300.
Lewis & Renn Associates' Entrepreneur's Business Guides, 10315 Harmony Dr., Interlochen, MI 49643.
Nation Business Library's Small Business Catalog, (800) 947-7724.

Software
Silver Lining
1320 Standiford, Suite 170
Modesto, CA 95350
Business accounting software for retail operations, IBM compatibles; write for catalog.

The Software Directory for Retailers, 5th ed., by Coopers & Lybrand. 1995, John Wiley & Sons, Inc., New York, NY.

≥ 56 ≤

ANTIQUE SHOP

The rule of thumb is that an antique is any item that is at least 100 years old, but many items only half as old are collector's items. A good location is important for the success of this business so that you will get much traffic by car or by foot. Antiques are acquired through auctions, garage and yard sales, flea markets, and browsing through second-hand shops. If you love items with historical significance, and are knowledgeable about them, this may be an ideal shop for you.

Start-Up Costs
$15,000 to $25,000 to get a start-up inventory.

Pricing Guidelines
* Follow current antique price guides.
* Pricing also depends on what collectibles are the most popular at any given time, and what profit you hope to make on them.

Essential Equipment
* Office: computer for inventory and sales; fax/modem; sales receipts or cash register.
* Showcases and display cases.
* Promotional materials: brochures, business cards.

Marketing and Advertising Methods and Tips
* Advertise in local and antique trade publications.
* Get word-of-mouth referrals.
* Exhibit at antique shows and home shows.
* Teach a local course or seminar about how to price antiques or how to care for them.

Recommended Training, Experience, or Skills
* It really helps to have either worked in an antique business for a number of years, collected antiques yourself, or been in a family that has collected them.
* Study books and trade publications for business tips, or talk with one or more antique store owners.

Income Potential
$20,000 to $75,000 per year and up, depending on your inventory and customers' willingness to pay for antiques.

Best Customers
Individual collectors, other antique dealers, interior designers.

Helpful Tips
❖ Take your time in building an inventory so that you can learn the pricing and the little tricks of the trade.
❖ Look for other new items such as lace curtains or blacksmith hooks and iron work to attract more customers.

For More Information

Books
Buying & Selling Antiques & Collectibles for Fun & Profit by Joan and Dan Bingham. 1994, Charles E. Tuttle Co., Inc., Boston, MA.
Schroeder's Antiques Price Guide, 14th ed., by Collector Books Staff. 1995, Collector Books, Paducah, KY.
Upstart's Guide to Owning and Managing an Antiques Business by Lisa Rogak. 1994, Upstart Publishing, Dover, NH.

Publication
Antiques and Collectibles
P.O. Box 1565
El Cajon, CA 92022
$15 per year.

Software
Stellar Software, Inc.
6503 Slater Rd.
Chattanooga, TN 37412
Antique shop sales and inventory system.

Additional Business Ideas
❖ Antique house: If you own or have access to another house, or can section off a part of your house, decorate each room with appropriate antiques to sell.

✤ Antique sales and finding service: Collect and sell antiques to other dealers, collectors, shops, interior designers, businesses, and individuals.

✤ Antique show exhibitor.

✤ Restoring antique furniture:
    Discovering and Restoring Antique Furniture: A Practical Illustrated Guide for the Buyer and Restorer of Period Antique Furniture by Michael Bennett. 1996, Sterling Publishing Company, Inc., New York, NY.

✑ 57 ✎
CLOTHING CONSIGNMENT SHOP

Prices of clothing keep rising, yet we have a surplus of preworn clothing. If you have knowledge about good-quality clothing and materials, a clothing consignment shop may be an ideal venture for you. One young woman opened a consignment store in the ground floor of her house and offered mending and alterations as a side-service.

Start-Up Costs
Can range from $0 start-up to as high as $50,000 and more. It varies because of the location, whether you have to rent or buy a shop, the type of clothing and goods you carry, and whether you buy the clothing outright, take it on consignment, or both.

Pricing Guidelines
✤ Usually, the consignors are paid 50 percent of the sale price.
✤ Some shops charge from 100 percent to 600 percent mark-up.

Essential Equipment
✤ Tags, contracts, hangers, shoe and clothing racks, shelves, cash register.
✤ Office: computer with software for inventory.

Marketing and Advertising Methods and Tips
✤ Put up flyers on community bulletin boards.
✤ Take out ads in local newspapers.
✤ Hand out flyers in other consignment shops; often consignment shops will specialize, so they will keep a list of other shops to refer their customers to.
✤ Word-of-mouth referrals from satisfied customers.
✤ Mailings to regular customers to let them know of special sales, etc.

Recommended Training, Experience, or Skills
✤ It helps to have some clothing retail experience.
✤ Sewing and mending skills are helpful for making minor repairs, or to offer as an added service.
✤ You need attention to detail.

Income Potential
$15,000 to $38,000 per year and more, depending on your customers, the type of clothing you sell, and whether you have more than one store (successful owners of this type of store often open more than one shop).

Best Customers
Depends on the clothing you sell; most are people who want quality but are thrifty with their money.

Helpful Tips
✤ Find a theme for your shop and target your marketing and advertising to those customers.
✤ Take only good-quality items.
✤ Your store should have the "look" of a retail store in the way you set up and arrange your clothing and related items (cleaned and pressed, etc.).
✤ Keep a notebook of items people are looking for and notify them if you acquire them. They will appreciate the special attention.
✤ Keep your items moving; after some number of months, have a sale and bring in new items.

For More Information

Association

National Association of Resale and Thrift Shops
20331 Mack Avenue
Grosse Pointe Woods, MI 48236
Send SASE for membership information.

Books

Consignment Boutique Primer: Entrepreneurship for the Lady Who Loves Apparel and People by Mimi Wanek and Ken Meyer. 1992, Meyer-Man Books, Largo, FL.

The Consignment Workbook by Sue Harris. 1995, Scandia International, R.D. #1, Box 350, Petersburgh, NY 12138.
Send SASE for ordering information.

Business Guides

Entrepreneur's Start-Up Guide, "Consignment/Resale Clothing Store." (800) 421-2300, $69.50 + shipping.

National Business Library's Start-Up Guide, "Consignment Shop." (800) 947-7724, $39.95 + $5 shipping.

Software:

"Consignment Boutique Software"
Innovative Software Designers
1101 West Kennedy Blvd.
Tampa, FL 33606
Write for information.

Additional Business Ideas

❖ Fashioning old clothing into other products.
❖ Other consignment shops: Wedding, bridal, and formal gown shop and accessories; children's clothing, equipment, and toys; used sporting goods and equipment.
❖ Collector of antique clothing and accessories: Victorian, famous designers, costume jewelry.
   Clothing Recycling as a Home or Small Business by Data Notes Publishing Staff. 1992, Prosperity and Profits Unlimited, Denver, CO.

Daddy's Ties by Shirley Botsford. 1994, Chilton Book Co., Radnor, PA.

Second Stitches: Recycle as You Sew by Susan D. Parker. 1996, Chilton Book Co., Radnor, PA.

Starting and Operating a Vintage Clothing Shop by Rose Freeman Whitis. 1988, Pilot Books, 103 Cooper St., Babylon, NY 11702; $3.50. Send SASE for catalog.

◢ 58 ◣
USED BOOKSTORE

If you love books and reading, you will find that many others do, too. For every book in print, there are thousands that are out of print—some valuable, and others valuable only to those who want them. A used bookstore can specialize in a certain type of books, or it can carry a variety. You can start by researching the kinds of old and used books that are in demand; visit used bookstores and talk with the owners to get some advice and tips; attend old-book trade shows; then decide what types of books you will concentrate on.

This is a good way to meet people and travel as you search for books you want or as a professional book searcher.

Start-Up Costs
$3,000 to $20,000

Pricing Guidelines
+ Read the trade pricing books for prices.
+ Read trade publications.
+ Attend shows and visit shops to get an idea what is being charged for books.
+ Depends on the condition and value. First editions in mint condition get the highest price; if they are in good condition but not sought by collectors, then price at 20 percent to 25 percent of the original price.

Essential Equipment
+ A price guide and reference books.
+ A shop or other space for book inventory.
+ Tables and display cases for your store and for exhibiting at book trade shows.
+ A computer with accounting, bookkeeping, inventory, and mail-order software.
+ Promotional materials: business cards, flyers.

Marketing and Advertising Methods and Tips
+ Advertise in *Book Quote,* antique newspapers, the antique section of large Sunday editions of city newspapers, and the Yellow Pages.
+ Direct mail to customers and people whose names and addresses you acquire at book shows and fairs.
+ Write articles for trade magazines.

Recommended Training, Experience, or Skills
+ It helps to be an expert in at least one category of old books.
+ You need patience to learn and the persistence to find out the information you need.
+ Work in a used bookstore for some on-the-job training.

Income Potential
$28,000 per year and up

Best Customers
Other rare-book sellers who are searching for books for their customers, individual collectors, tourists.

Helpful Tips
+ Buy books on weekends and vacations as you get the money until you feel ready to open your shop.
+ Only buy books in the very best condition possible, preferably with dust jackets.
+ Use non-acid covers to protect your books.

❖ Avoid old encyclopedias, condensed books, book-club selections, and college textbooks unless you are doing a specific search for someone.

❖ Keep up with your business' bookkeeping tasks.

❖ Never sell a book without knowing its value.

For More Information
Books

Book Prices, Used and Rare, 1995 edited by Edward N. Zemple and Linda A. Verkler. The Spoon River Press (a division of Book Quote, Inc.), 2319-C West Rohmann Ave., Peoria, IL 61604-5072. $69 + $3 shipping. Write for catalog of other books on the collecting, pricing, and care of used and old books.

Buy Books Where, Sell Books Where, 1994-1995: A Directory of Out-of-Print Booksellers and their Author-Subject Specialties by Ruth Robinson. Ruth Robinson Books, Morgantown, WV.

Complete Guide to Starting a Used Bookstore, 2nd ed., by Dale L. Gilbert. 1991, Upstart Publishing Co., Inc., Dover, NH.

How to Open a Used Bookstore by Dale Gilbert. 1991, Upstart Publishing Company, Dover, NH.

Business Guide

Entrepreneur's "Used-Book Store." (800) 421-2300; $69.50 + shipping.

Periodical

Book Quote: The Book Trade Bi-Weekly for Buyers and Sellers of Out-of-Print, Used, and Rare Books. $32 per year, published every other Friday. Order from Spoon River Press (see above).

Additional Business Ideas

❖ Selling used and rare books by mail order:
Start-up costs: $3,000 to $5,000
Potential earnings: $25,000 to $30,000 per year and up; see "Mail Order," in "General Resources."

❖ New book retail store:
   How to Start & Manage a Bookstore Business by Jerre G. Lewis and Leslie D. Renn. 1995, Lewis & Renn Associates, 10325 Harmony Dr., Interlochen, MI 49643; $9.95 + $3 shipping.

⚞ 59 ⚟
COFFEE OR TEA SHOP

The Specialty Coffee Association of America (see "For More Information," below) predicts a coffee market of $4.5 billion by 1999. In the last few years, there has been an explosion of coffee-related businesses all across the country. Coffee ventures include simple coffee kiosks and carts, coffee bars, gift gourmet shops, specialty food stores and delis, cafés, and even bookstores with tables for coffee and tea.

Tea shops are also gaining in popularity. A number of women entrepreneurs sell specialized domestic and imported teas from tearooms that they have in their own homes or shops decorated with Victorian, English, and Scottish tables and antiques.

If you are a coffee or tea connoisseur, and you enjoy people, you may want to investigate what kind of venture you would like to start with these beverages.

Start-Up Costs
❖ Costs vary from $25,000 for coffee, tea, and a few tables to $80,000, and even up to $550,000 for a large coffee- or teahouse (or franchise) in a good location.
❖ A cart operation would cost $40,000 to $80,000.

Pricing Guidelines
Go by the industry guidelines given in the manuals and at the seminars.

Essential Equipment
❖ Assorted coffees, restaurant equipment, commercial coffeemakers, coffee grinders.
❖ Commercial licenses, permits.

Marketing and Advertising Methods and Tips
❖ You must put your customer service first.
❖ Develop a specialty that differentiates you from other coffee/tea shops: grind your own beans; offer to custom blend beans; serve special baked goods and foods with your beverages.

Recommended Training, Experience, or Skills
❖ Work in a coffee or tea shop.
❖ Research the industry thoroughly: read trade manuals and publications; visit different shops, carts, etc. and interview the owners and workers. Be a customer and take notes as to what you do or do not like.
❖ Research different franchises and distributorships.
❖ Attend industry trade shows and seminars.

Income Potential
$15,000 to $30,000 per year for a small shop or part-time tea- or coffeehouse. $70,000 to $90,000 per year for a larger shop.

Best Customers
❖ College students.
❖ Tourist areas with shops.
❖ Shopping districts in towns and cities; malls.
❖ Transportation stations.
❖ Wherever there is a considerable amount of foot traffic.

Helpful Tips
❖ Find your niche: what does your coffee or tea shop, cart, etc. offer that others do not?

❖ Start small and with used equipment until you build up your business.

❖ Pick a location that just "invites" coffee and tea drinkers to stop in.

❖ Follow good business rules: professionalism, keeping good books, good customer service, etc.

❖ Make your coffee or tea venture fun and delicious for your customers.

Franchises

There are a number of coffee franchises. Check magazines like *Entrepreneur* or *Small Business Opportunities,* which review franchises regularly. See Chapter 5 for how to select a franchise.

For More Information

Associations

Specialty Coffee Association of America
One World Trade Center, Suite 800
Long Beach, CA 90831-0800.

A nonprofit international trade association. Membership includes opportunities to participate in training seminars, conferences, exhibitions, and international site visits. Also includes subscription to newsletter, "In Good Taste," and starter subscriptions to other tea and coffee journals. Write for information.

The Specialty Tea Registry (STAR)
230 Park Ave., Suite 1460
New York, NY 10169

They will make a complete start-up package available for a nominal fee, which includes a six-month membership in the registry. Write for information.

Books

Espresso: Starting and Succeeding in Your Own Coffee Business by Joe Managhan and Julie S. Huffaker. 1995, John Wiley & Sons, Inc., New York, NY.

Start Your Own Coffee & Tea Store edited by JoAnn Padget. 1994, Pfeiffer Company, San Diego, CA.

Business Guides
Entrepreneur's Start-Up Guide, "Coffeehouse." (800) 421-2300; $69.50 + shipping.
National Business Library's Start-Up Guide, "Coffee & Tea Store." (800) 947-7724; $39.95 + shipping.

Additional Business Ideas
Develop a mail-order catalog for coffee and tea lovers.

Additional Shop Ideas
❖ Old-fashioned toy store
❖ Gift shop
❖ Hobby shop
❖ Candy store

Instructional Businesses

If you have a skill or knowledge in a certain subject that will help people earn more money, improve their relationships, empower and motivate them to change their lives, or learn a skill or craft, people will pay you to teach them. You can teach them privately, in a group, or in workshops or seminars in one- to seven-day sessions. You should have knowledge and firsthand experience in the topic you are teaching. You should like people, have patience, and be able to break the subject you are teaching into basic steps for learning.

One former teacher started tutoring out of her recreation room, and today has a full-time (licensed) tutoring business located in a three-story house with 20 teachers teaching part-time for her. Another woman teaches herb-growing in her garden. Whatever subject you would like to teach, here are some helpful tips:

❖ Be organized. For example, work from an outline and have handouts and related materials for each topic in separate folders.

❖ Be entertaining. Use examples (not too many personal ones), stories, and anecdotes to illustrate the points you are trying to emphasize.

❖ Introduce an overview of the course and then follow through with what you promised to teach your students.

❖ Keep in mind that people learn in three ways: by hearing, seeing, and doing. Use all three ways in your course: hearing from others, seeing visual aids, and doing the craft, project, or group activity.

❖ Give a five- to ten-minute break at least once an hour. It gives students a chance to get up and walk around and talk informally with you or other students.

❖ Provide an opportunity to let your students teach each other (and you). Adults have had varied experiences in their lives; you never know which one of your students can add to your course.

❖ Provide facts and statistics, and refer to them for credibility. It helps to keep you from talking in generalities.

❖ Make it fun! Students of all ages learn more if your course is interesting and active.

Instructional Businesses: General Resources

The Teaching Marketplace: Make Money with Freelance Teaching, Corporate Trainings and on the Lecture Circuit by Bart Brodsky and Janet Geis. 1991, Communication Resource Institution Press, Denver, CO.

Tutoring for Pay: Earn While You Help Others Learn by Betty O. Carpenter. 1990, Charles C. Thomas Publisher, Springfield, IL.

≈ 60 ≈
TEACHING ARTS AND CRAFTS

Teaching an art or craft can be both rewarding and frustrating. You are a skilled artist or craftsperson attempting to teach a beginner skills that you already take for granted.

Here are some possible options with arts and crafts instruction: teach beginners' and advanced classes on your topic at continuing education classes held at local schools, community colleges, art or craft centers, galleries, or folk centers. Put together a small instructional booklet to sell separately or with your course.

Start-Up Costs
* $100 to $500 for simple instruction materials, samples, and business cards.
* Optional: $3,000 for computer, printer, and desktop publishing software for booklets, etc.

Pricing Guidelines
* $35 to $50 an hour for private instruction.
* $18 to $25 an hour for group instruction.

Essential Equipment
* Materials for art or craft.
* Instructional sheets.
* Audio-visual aids: models, videos, charts.
* Promotional materials: business cards, brochures with price lists.

Marketing and Advertising Methods and Tips
* Apply directly to schools and craft centers for teaching positions.
* Hand out flyers at craft shows and fairs.
* Place classified ads for lessons in the newspaper and on cable TV.
* Get word-of-mouth referrals.
* Direct mail to those on your mailing list.

Recommended Training, Experience, or Skills
* Competence in your craft.
* An ability to communicate instructions well.

Income Potential
+ $200 to $500 per 6- to 8-week course meeting weekly at a school or college.
+ $1,000 for a one-day seminar, more if for multiple days.

Best Customers
+ Adults in continuing education programs or wanting private lessons.
+ Children in creative centers.

Helpful Tips
+ Bring more supplies than you expect to use.
+ If possible, know your students' skill levels beforehand for planning purposes.
+ Teaching a craft is a challenge because some students grasp the basic concepts more quickly than others. You have to be able to balance your time in helping everyone and still get your lessons completed in the time allotted.
+ Evaluate your classes' comments on your courses to see where you can improve.
+ Remember that you will not please everyone!

For More Information
The Art of Teaching Craft: A Complete Handbook by Joyce Spencer and Deborah Kneen. 1994, Sterling Publishing, Company, Inc., New York, NY.

Additional Business Ideas
Write and publish how-to booklets, manuals, and/or books on your craft (see "Businesses Involving Words").

⊿ 61 ⊾
INSTRUCTIONAL VIDEOS

The video industry has enabled people to bring the classroom right into their own homes. If you have taught courses, and have gotten good feedback, you might want to consider having a video made of your course to sell to your students or other consumers.

Start-Up Costs
$3,000 to $4,000 to make your own video or contract a videographer to do it for you.

Pricing Guidelines
* Compare the prices of other videos on your topic. Also view them to see how yours compares in quality, length, etc.
* How-to videos cost from $9.95 to $49.95 and up, depending on the length and type of instruction involved.

Essential Equipment
* Rent or buy a camcorder and VCR for playback and recording, simple editing equipment, and a digital switcher.
* Promotional materials: flyers and brochures about your video(s).

Marketing and Advertising Methods and Tips
* Advertise in trade publications; mail flyers and brochures to trade associations and to special interest groups that would be interested in your video.
* List your videos in video directories and guides.
* Direct mail to video distribution services.

Recommended Training, Experience, or Skills
* You need to be competent in filming and editing or hire a videotaping service.
* Be capable of writing the script and directing the filming.

Income Potential
Depends on the popularity of your video and how many people want to learn your craft; if your video is successful, you can earn $10,000 to $50,000 from it.

Best Customers
❖ Libraries.
❖ Individuals wanting to learn about your subject matter.

Helpful Tips
❖ Use graphics and titles to introduce and end segments.
❖ Make sure the video/audio quality is the best because it is a direct reflection on you.
❖ The content should be clear, sequential, and interesting. Much forethought and planning are required. One key to teaching is: "Say what you are going to say; then show it; then repeat what you have said."

For More Information
Books
Make Money with Your Camcorder: A Complete, Fully Illustrated Guide by Kevin Campbell. 1995, Amherst Media, Incorporated, Amherst, NY.
Videomaker's Comprehensive Guide to Making Videos by Butterworth-Heinemann. 1996, Video Magazine Editors, New York, NY.

Video
"Make Your Own 'How-To' Videos"
Wonderful World of Hats
897 Wade Rd.
Siletz, OR 97380
This video shows in easily understood step-by-step demonstrations how to use your video camera to make a "how-to" video in your own workspace. Also covers how to write a script, packaging, advertising tips, and more.

Additional Business Ideas
Sell/rent how-to videos:

Video Learning Library
15838 N. 62nd St., Suite 101
Scottsdale, AZ 85254

Write for information on a distributorship for renting and/or selling how-to videos. Also available: *The Complete Guide to Special Interest Videos.* $49.95 + $4 shipping for CD-ROM; $19.95 + $4 shipping for paperback.

≈ 62 ≈
COMPUTER INSTRUCTOR/TRAINER

In this business, you can teach individuals how to use different software programs in their homes, at their places of employment, or at your own computer learning center. You can specialize in your field or learn a number of software programs and applications. Start small and expand as you feel your business warrants it. This is a good business for someone who loves both computers and teaching.

Start-Up Costs
* $4,500 for a home office and equipment.
* $15,000 to $35,000 to set up a training center.

Pricing Guidelines
* For individual instruction: $30 to $75 per hour.
* For courses at your center: $165 to $175 for 9 hours (6 hours of instruction, 3 hours of practice); additional practice time: $10 per hour; can repeat a course at 50 percent off the regular price.
* Training employees at a business: $50 per student.

Essential Equipment
* Personal office equipment: computer with fax/modem; copier.
* Promotional materials: brochures with course prices and software programs you teach; business cards.
* Training materials: develop your own manuals or adapt those of the software you use to make them more user-friendly.

Marketing and Advertising Methods and Tips
* Advertise: Yellow Pages, Business Yellow Pages, local business newspapers and newsletters, classified ad newspapers.
* Direct mail to companies whose employees use computers and the business software you teach. Some software companies will refer their customers to you.
* Write a promotional information column in local papers.
* Write a promotional article in the annual business section of your newspaper.
* Get a booth or table in local business or trade shows.
* Make networking contacts through local Chambers of Commerce.
* Teach an evening continuing education course at local schools or colleges.
* Leave your business cards and flyers at computer stores.

Recommended Training, Experience, or Skills
* Computer knowledge, education, and training in the software programs that individuals and businesses need to learn.
* Patience and an ability to teach in progressive and logical steps that your students can comprehend.
* Knowledge of how the software can be specifically applied to an individual's or business' needs.

Income Potential
* $20,000 to $50,000 per year as a personal trainer/tutor.
* $35,000 to $65,000 per year as a corporate trainer.

Best Customers
* Individuals wanting a complete computer set-up and training in the use of their software.
* Individuals wanting to learn different software programs; they bring their software to your learning center and/or they pick courses from those you offer.
* Home-based business owners wanting to learn the software for their new business.

❖ Businesses wanting training and/or updating the latest business software.

❖ Business departments in high schools or vocational-technical schools.

Helpful Tips

❖ Decide whether you are going to be a generalist or specialist.

❖ Focus on businesses in which you have some background and expertise.

❖ Before you open a learning center, do market research as to what software and training individuals and businesses want or need. What is your competition?

❖ Join trade associations and computer training/consultant associations to stay current with the latest computer news.

Franchises, Distributorships, and Licenses

The Fourth R
1715 Market St., #103
Kirkland, WA 98033
Computer training for children and adults. Write for information.

For More Information

Association

Independent Computer Consultants Association
933 Gardenview Office Parkway
St. Louis, MO 63141
Write for membership information.

Books

The Computer Consultant's Guide: Real Life Strategies for Building a Successful Consulting Career by Janet Ruhl. 1993, John Wiley & Sons, Inc., New York, NY.

The Computer Training Handbook, 2nd ed., by Elliot Maise. 1995, order from Lakewood Publications, 50 South Ninth St., Minneapolis, MN 55402; also write for current catalog of general training books, newsletters, magazines, videos, and conferences.

Teaching Computer Applications by Carol A. Lundgren, Terry D. Lundgren, and George A. Mundrake. 1996, Delta Pi Epsilon, Inc., Little Rock, AR.

Business Guide

Entrepreneur's Start-Up Guide, "Computer Learning Center." (800) 421-2300; $69.50 plus shipping.

Online

Computer Training Forum on CompuServe; call (800) 848-8199 or (614) 457-0802 for more information.

Additional Business Ideas

✤ Be a trainer for software companies: teach to individuals and businesses.

✤ See also: "Computer Businesses" chapter and "Database Consultant," in "Business Services" chapter.

⚄ 63 ⚄

BUSINESS TRAINER

A business or employee trainer is a specialist in some aspect of business and is hired by firms to hold workshops, seminars, and training sessions to update or retrain employees in new technology, literacy skills, human resource matters (sexual harassment, employee recognition), customer relations, or any other matters that can help businesses improve their efficiency and operations. You can create your own presentations and accompanying materials or purchase them from training sources.

Start-Up Costs

$4,000 to $10,000

Pricing Guidelines
* $500 to $2,000 per day.
* $50 per employee.
* Charge a fee for an entire workshop based on length and number of employees attending.

Essential Equipment
* Office: computer with hard drive, fax/modem, software for business management and desktop publishing; telephone system, copier.
* Promotional materials: brochures, business cards, promotional newsletters, your own training video.
* Reference materials.
* Audio-visual aids, multimedia equipment, and materials to make your training more interesting and effective.

Marketing and Advertising Methods and Tips
* Direct mail to businesses in your industry with follow-up calls and visits.
* Promotional newsletter describing the latest employee training in the industry.
* Ads in your industry's trade publications.
* Exhibits at industry trade shows.
* A World Wide Web home page.
* Referrals from clients.

Recommended Training, Experience, or Skills
* Training, education, and work experience in your field.
* Human resources background or courses.
* Good organizational skills; ability to explain your material in logical steps.
* Attendance at employee training sessions to observe how different training sessions are conducted.
* Courses from other trainers in how to be an effective trainer.

Income Potential
$30,000 to $100,000 per year depending on your experience and the number of clients you add and return to each year.

Best Customers
+ Businesses that do not have employee trainers on their payrolls or who are downsizing and need to retrain their present employees or offer new training to employees they have let go.
+ Businesses that need to comply with laws concerning operations, etc.

Helpful Tips
+ You must be a good teacher and communicator.
+ You must know the industry or industries in which you are working.
+ Training sessions should be lively, fun, and organized such that each step builds on the previous one you presented.
+ Know the group you are training: their background, the purpose of their training, their relative age group.
+ Have related materials (for sale or included in the price) to help those who need to review your training principles: manuals, videos, books.

For More Information
Books
Corporate Training for Effective Performance edited by Martin Mulder, Wim J. Nijhof, and Robert O. Brinkerhoff. 1995, Kluwer Academic Publishers, Norwell, MA.
Make Training Work: How to Achieve Bottom-Line Results and Lasting Success by Berton H. Gunter. 1996, Lakewood Publications, Minneapolis, MN.

Lakewood Publications
50 South Ninth St.
Minneapolis, MN 55402
Write for current catalog of training books, newsletters, magazine, videos, and conferences.

Additional Business Ideas
+ Have a business trainers' referral service.
+ See also "Seminar Leader," in "Business Services."

ᴗ • ᴗ

OTHER INSTRUCTION BUSINESS OPPORTUNITIES

❖ One-on-one tutoring: SAT preparation; home schooling; languages for people who plan to travel; performance (acting, singing); grammar and English review for newly promoted executives.

❖ Personal Improvement: organization; public speaking; retention improvement.

❖ Free-time activities: lifetime sports instruction (tennis, golf, fitness); astronomy; cooking; painting.

❖ Professional skills: typing, word processing, business start-up information, SAT and graduate school counseling.

Medical Services

≈ 64 ≈

MEDICAL BUSINESSES

Health care will continue to be a growing and active industry, especially as our life expectancy lengthens due to medical advances and new technology. Thus, as our mature population increases, they will need an increase in medical services. The American Federation of Home Health Agencies in Washington says that "approximately 15% of the country's gross national product is spent on health care."

If your background or interests include training and expertise in one or more health fields, a medical-related business may be ideal for you. Here are some business ideas you may want to consider.

Agent for Home-Based Medical Caregivers
One of the fastest growth industries in medical care is home-based health care. With hospitals struggling to survive financially, home health care provides almost every kind of procedure except for major surgery. As an agent for home health-care agencies, you can refer people to the agency that

269

fits their needs. You would be paid a finder's fee by the family and by the agency.

Association
National Association for Home Care
228 Seventh St. SE
Washington, DC 20003
E-mail: nahc@nahc.org
Represents agencies that provide home care, but does not recommend specific agencies. Send SASE and request a publications list that includes consumer publications as well as those that focus on how to start a home care agency; or call (202) 547-7424.

Start Your Own Health Care Agency
Business Guides
Entrepreneur's Start-Up Business Guide, "Home Health-Care Agency." (800) 421-2300; $69.50 plus shipping.
How to Start and Manage a Home Attendant Business by Jerre G. Lewis and Leslie D. Renn. 1995, Lewis & Renn Associates, 10315 Harmony Dr., Interlochen, MI 49643; $9.95 plus $3 for shipping.

Franchises
Home Instead Senior Care
1104 S. 76th Ave., #A
Omaha, NE 68124

WovenHearts
7617 Mineral Point Rd.
Madison, WI 53717

Personal Medical Data Research
If you have access to the Internet and your expertise and interest is in medical research, you can do research for individuals on the latest information, treatment, and centers worldwide for their medical conditions. You can search medical databases and prepare individual medical reports for them.

Book
The Information Broker's Handbook, 2nd ed., by Sue Rugge and Alfred Gloss-Brenner. 1995, McGraw-Hill, New York, NY. See also "Clipping Service," and "Fact Finder."

Nurse Entrepreneur

Nurses who are frustrated with slow bureaucracies and increasingly limited salaries are creating and inventing new health products, publishing, and starting their own medical businesses. You may want to research such ventures.

Association
National Nurses in Business Association (NNBA)
56 McArthur Ave.
Staten Island, NY 10312
1-800-331-6534
"Promotes the growth of health-related businesses owned and operated by nurses." Publishes *How I Became a Nurse Entrepreneur* ($24.95, including shipping and handling) and a directory of nurse entrepreneur businesses (a good net working source; $45). Membership costs $95 per year. Write or call for more information.

Postpartum Care Services

These health and personal enterprises provide personal, basic, and educational support to babies, their mothers, and their families in the days following birth. They give moral support, childbirth and nursing support, help with household chores, and overall support for approximately three months after the birth of the child. It is a much-needed service with many people living away from family support, and health insurance companies urging the early release of mothers and newborns. Even though state and federal legislators are beginning to prevent health insurance companies from requiring the early hospital release of babies and mothers, many women still need that emotional support and care to help them make the transition to a normal schedule again.

Additional Business Ideas

❖ Ambulatory care center: private walk-in centers for medical attention.

❖ Home drug delivery business.

❖ Medical halfway homes/centers: patients recuperate from surgery, a non–life-threatening illness, or an injury in a motel-like setting, but not in a hospital. A nurse checks the patients regularly, but there is less cost since the patients are no longer in the hospital.

❖ Mobile medical laboratory.

❖ Medical records consultant:

Medical Records: Management in a Changing Environment by Susan M. Murphy-Muth. 1987, Aspen Publications, Inc., Gaithersburg, MD.

Personal Services

PERSONAL SERVICE PROVIDER

It is part of the nineties—so much to do and so little time to do it all. Young singles trying to establish themselves in a profession, two-career families—everyone trying to do it all. That is where a personal service provider business can help. The people who have money and little time are willing to trade money for your time. Personal service providers help organize people's lives and homes by doing the tasks and running the errands that people do not have the time to do. If you are well organized, and like doing a multitude of different jobs, you might try venturing into this type of service.

Start-Up Costs
$200 to $3,500, depending on whether or not you purchase a computer.

Pricing Guidelines
$20 to $40 per hour.

Marketing and Advertising Methods and Tips
* Send out press releases.
* Post flyers in grocery stores and on restaurants' community bulletin boards.
* Take out ads on cable TV and radio, and in local papers.
* Donate some of your business hours to a charity auction.
* Get word-of-mouth referrals from satisfied customers.

Essential Equipment
Telephone answering system, contracts for services, daily planner, transportation.

Recommended Training, Experience, or Skills
* Know how to run a household and manage its expenses.
* Enjoy meeting people.
* Be well organized and know how to organize, plan, and direct a household.
* Be trustworthy.

Income Potential
$50,000 to $100,000 per year, depending on the number of clients.

Best Customers
* Dual-income couples with or without children.
* Single professionals.

Helpful Tips
* Check with your insurance agent about being bonded.
* Realize that it is demanding work, but it is gratifying to help your customers gain some valuable time.
* Give good service: be prompt and honest.

Additional Business Ideas
* Waiting service: wait in customers' homes or offices for deliveries, repair persons, or utility inspectors (charge $10 per hour).

+ Personal shopping service:
  Entrepreneur's Start-Up Guide, "Personal Shopping Service." (800) 421-2300; $69.50 plus shipping.

◢ 66 ◣
APARTMENT FINDING/ROOMMATE SERVICE

With the rising cost of housing and apartments, it is increasingly difficult for a single, young person to pay for an apartment herself. With a roommate/apartment service, you can help people find affordable housing and a compatible roommate.

Start-Up Costs
$8,000 to $12,000

Pricing Guidelines
$60 to $195 flat fee, or on a weekly or monthly basis (try to make your fees affordable for all income levels).

Marketing and Advertising Methods and Tips
+ Advertising: Yellow Pages, classified ads in local papers.
+ Direct mail, flyers to local churches, colleges, companies, hospitals, and other institutions.
+ Contact real estate agents who handle apartment rentals.
+ Promotional materials: brochures, business cards.
+ Referrals from satisfied clients.

Essential Equipment
Computer for mailings, record-keeping, and bookkeeping; telephone system, fax machine, and copier; promotional materials.

Recommended Training, Experience, or Skills
+ Have people skills and sales skills.
+ Interview roommate service businesses in other towns to see how they conduct business.

❖ Be able to communicate well on the phone.
❖ Understand the needs of your target market.

Income Potential
$30,000 to $100,000 per year (the high end applies to a large city).

Best Customers
❖ Single men and women.
❖ Young professionals.
❖ Recent graduates.
❖ Divorced men and women.
❖ Widowed men and women.
❖ People newly located to your town or city.

Helpful Tips
❖ Research your area to see if there is enough of a market in your area for a service business like this to be profitable.
❖ Start small, and expand to an office or larger facilities as your business builds.
❖ Have a thorough screening process with questionnaires and interviews. Have potential roommates personally meet one another at your office.
❖ Check with a lawyer about the wording of your questionnaires, and your liability.

Additional Business Ideas
Apartment preparation service:
Entrepreneur's Start-Up Guide, "Apartment Preparation Service." (800) 421-2300; $69.50 plus shipping.

≈ 67 ≈
BOARDING HOME

There are a number of individuals who cannot afford housing because they cannot hold a full-time job due to mental or physical disabilities and do not have family available to help them. These people may be receiving support from the state or federal government, but not enough to allow them independent housing. You may be able to open one or more boarding homes to provide these individuals with safe and affordable housing and some supervision and guidance. You will have to check with the social services departments in your county and state as to applicable regulations and licenses you will need to open such a facility. You could also have a boarding home for young singles, single mature persons, and/or college students.

Start-Up Costs
❖ $150,000 to $200,000 for purchase of a building and remodeling it to fulfill any regulations.

Pricing Guidelines
Charges can be weekly, monthly, or for longer periods, and might include meals.

Marketing and Advertising Methods and Tips
❖ Referrals through human services agencies.
❖ For young and mature singles, classified ads in newspapers.
❖ Flyers on community bulletin boards in stores and senior centers.
❖ For college students: contact a college's off-campus housing office; flyers on student bulletin boards.

Essential Equipment
❖ Adequate housing with rooms that may or may not have private bathrooms.
❖ Operational kitchen in which residents can either cook their own meals or have them prepared as part of their fees.
❖ Furniture for bedrooms, recreation rooms, and kitchen.
❖ Office equipment: a computer for bookkeeping, record keeping, and mailings.

Recommended Training, Experience, or Skills
✤ Read the state's guidelines and manuals.
✤ Talk to social services, human services, and housing agencies as to the needs and legalities involved in having a licensed boarding home.
✤ Visit as many boarding homes as possible and interview the owners and residents for tips and recommendations.
✤ It helps to have background, training, or education in sociology, psychology, or special education, and experience working with the type of people who will be residing in your home.

Income Potential
$40,000 to $100,000 per year and up

Best Customers
✤ Persons unable to afford housing due to financial, physical, or mental limitations.
✤ Older single people who are independent and capable of taking care of themselves, but do not want to live alone and do not want to live in a retirement community or a nursing home.
✤ College students who need housing.

Helpful Tips
✤ Follow all regulations.
✤ If you cannot reside in the boarding home, hire a supervisor or manager to either live there or work there daily.
✤ Check with your lawyer for liability coverage and contracts.
✤ Consult with your insurance agent about the coverage you will need.
✤ Have rules and regulations and contracts to define your residents' rights and obligations, and your rights as a provider.

For More Information
Check with your state for regulations regarding boarding homes and licenses required.

Additional Business Ideas
Rent furnished rooms in your house if you have extra space available (a separate entrance will help facilitate your privacy).

⚞ 68 ⚟
MATURE ADULT SERVICES:
MOVING/UNPACKING SERVICE

According to statistics from the U.S. Census Bureau, seniors are the fastest-growing segment of the nation's population. By the year 2020, there will be around 53 million senior citizens in this country. Thus, the need for services for this mature adult population will also increase, creating a number of entrepreneurial opportunities. You could start one or more of these service businesses, or one business to handle several of them. Seniors basically want to be independent, to be in control of their lives, to enjoy leisure activities, to feel needed and worthwhile to their community, and to live safely and securely.

A moving and unpacking service is ideal for seniors without family nearby. This business helps clients pack, find an auctioneer if they want to have a sale of household goods, unpack, prepare their new room or residence, and perform any other errands they may need.

Start-Up Costs
$3,000 to $5,000

Pricing Guidelines
+ $40 to $60 per hour.
+ Or a flat fee of $2,000 to $3,000.

Essential Equipment
+ Office equipment: computer with accounting and bookkeeping software; laser printer; telephone system; fax, copier.
+ Promotional materials: brochures, business cards, flyers.

Marketing and Advertising Methods and Tips
❖ Notify nursing homes, social services for the elderly, hospitals, gerontologists, senior citizen centers, local real estate agencies, and local churches.
❖ Take out Yellow Pages and classified ads.
❖ Get word-of-mouth referrals.
❖ Target advertising to the adult children of seniors, who often make such arrangements for their parents.

Recommended Training, Experience, or Skills
❖ Volunteer to help move friends or family to see what is involved.
❖ Be well organized, have good attention to detail, and be able to coordinate a number of services simultaneously.
❖ Have experience working with seniors and enjoy helping them.

Income Potential
$40,000 to $65,000 a year, depending on the number of seniors living in your area.

Best Customers
❖ Persons moving from a large house into a retirement community or a smaller residence.
❖ Persons with families who live too far away to help or who are unable to help.

Helpful Tips
❖ Try to keep your rates reasonable, as many seniors are on a fixed income.
❖ Be patient and sensitive, as moving and selling personal items can be a traumatic and emotionally trying experience.
❖ Give caring, personal attention to your customers, striving to make the transition and moving experience as smooth as possible.
❖ Do not rush your clients; urge them to get adequate rest and nourishment. Many become overwhelmed by the entire experience.

For More Information
Business Guide
Entrepreneur's Start-Up Guide, "Unpacking Service." (800) 421-2300; $69.50 plus shipping.

Additional Business Ideas
❖ Chauffeur service.
❖ Dating or companion service.
❖ Employment service: add volunteer opportunities as a side-service at no charge.
❖ Retirement counselor: financial counseling, leisure recommendations.
❖ Senior day-care center:
Entrepreneur's Start-Up Guide, "Senior Day-Care Center." (800) 421-2300; $69.50 plus shipping.
Also see "Medical Businesses."

⚜ 69 ⚜
TRANSPORTATION COORDINATOR

With rising traffic congestion in and around our cities, and the rising price of commuting, many people and companies wish they could carpool with others. A transportation coordinator would match up riders and destinations for a fee. You could offer your services to commuters, companies, and college students.

Start-Up Costs
$15,000 to $25,000

Pricing Guidelines
❖ Charge a basic fee of $25 to $30, and $15 for a re-assignment.
❖ Or sign a contract with different companies to coordinate their carpooling and/or van pools.

Essential Equipment
* A computer with travel software to help plan routes, etc.; telephone system, fax-modem, mailing list software.
* Local maps.
* Promotional materials: business cards, brochures, flyers.

Marketing and Advertising Methods and Tips
* Advertise in business and auto sections of local and regional newspapers; take out cable TV and radio ads.
* Send direct mail and flyers to companies that have a number of commuters coming from one area; follow up with calls and visits.
* Post flyers on community bulletin boards and at bus and train stations.
* Get referrals from employers and commuters.

Recommended Training, Experience, or Skills
* Be a good organizer and coordinator.
* Enjoy helping people.
* Interview those who do have a car- or van-pooling service in another region to see how they run it.

Income Potential
$30,000 to $65,000 per year.

Best Customers
* Large companies with many employees commuting from the same direction.
* People traveling across the state or country.
* College students commuting daily to community colleges or on weekends.

Helpful Tips
* Do a market survey or other research to see what people or companies would be willing to pay for your service.
* Ask customers to fill out a questionnaire of travel times and days, home address and destination, as well as asking

if they prefer to smoke, go to work early, work late, etc. to better facilitate your matches.

For More Information

Business Guide
Entrepreneur's Start-Up Guide, "Transportation Service." (800) 421-2300; $69.50 plus shipping.

Additional Business Ideas

❖ Franchise:
   Mobility Center, Inc.
   6693 Dixie Hwy.
   Bridgeport, MI 48722
   Sells battery-powered motorized vehicles for people with walking limitations and disabilities, and other related merchandise. Write to Richard Zimmer for information.
❖ Children's taxi.
❖ Limousine services:
   Entrepreneur's Start-Up Business Guide, "Limousine Service." (800) 421-2300; $69.50 plus shipping.
❖ Pet taxi.
❖ Commuter services: stand by a bus or train station and take customers' clothes to the cleaners, pick up prescriptions, etc., and have them ready when they return home that evening. Charge a service fee.

⚜ 70 ⚜

CLOCK REPAIR

This is a business that lovers of clocks can operate from a small shop or a building attached to their home. Most of the clocks you would repair would be older models and/or antiques (usually driven by weights or the windup kind) or those with sentimental value. Because there are not many people who do this service, there is usually a good demand for this business.

Start-Up Costs
$1,500 to $3,000

Pricing Guidelines
❖ Hourly fees $35 to $50 plus parts.
❖ $600 to $700 for house visits to adjust and set a grandfather clock.
♣ Go by industry guidelines.

Essential Equipment
Jeweler's lathe and accessories, tweezers, jeweler's magnifier, assorted pliers, screwdrivers, wires, and clock parts.

Marketing and Advertising Methods and Tips
❖ Classified ads in local papers and antique trade newspapers; Yellow Pages ad.
❖ Flyers on community bulletin boards and distributed to antique shops.
❖ Word-of-mouth referrals.

Recommended Training, Experience, or Skills
❖ Work as an apprentice.
❖ Study manuals.
❖ Practice on clocks bought at sales, flea markets, or auctions.
❖ Enjoy close work, attention to detail, and mechanical work.

Income Potential
$30,000 to $65,000, depending on the local population.

Best Customers
Individual collectors, antique dealers, individuals with family heirlooms.

Helpful Tips

❖ Start with secondhand pieces for practice.
❖ Treat the pieces as if they were your own valuable possessions.
❖ Give prompt, reliable service.

For More Information

Books

Clock Repair: Part-Time Hours, Full-Time Pay by John R. Piercon. 1992, Clockworks Press, Shingle Springs, CA.
Clock Repairer by Jock Rudman. 1994, National Learning Corporation, Syosset, NY.
Clock Repairer's Handbook by Laurie Penman. 1993, Sterling Publishing Co., Inc., New York, NY.
Striking and Chiming Clocks: Their Working and Repair by Eric Smith. 1996, Sterling Publishing Co., Inc., New York, NY.

Institute

American Watchmaker's Institute
701 Enterprise Dr.
Harrison, OH 45030
Send a SASE for more information.

Additional Business Ideas

❖ Making wooden clocks: see "Wood Crafts Wholesaler," "Wood Carver."
❖ Making clocks out of unusual objects or wood burn (pyrography), or polishing unusual pieces of wood and putting in clock parts.
❖ Buying old clocks at flea markets and fixing them for resale.

⊰ 71 ⊱

PERSONAL HELP COUNSELOR

A personal help counselor is a professional who provides psychological assistance to people to help them deal with personal problems. Marriage, divorce, substance abuse, and relationships with children are just a few of the psychological problems clients must face. A personal counselor helps her clients using individual and group therapy. Most counselors must have a master's degree in psychology or counseling, and more education may be required for specialization.

Start-Up Costs
$1,000 to $5,000 for office set-up, advertising.

Pricing Guidelines
Counseling is priced by the hour; the average is $80 per hour.

Marketing and Advertising Methods and Tips
✣ Advertising: Yellow Pages, ads in local papers.
✣ Referrals from other professionals.
✣ Seminars on selected topics held at health clinics and other institutions.
✣ Talks to organizations and community groups.
✣ Articles in professional journals or magazines.
✣ Word-of-mouth referrals.

Essential Equipment
Office equipment: computer, copier, fax machine, telephone system.

Recommended Training, Experience, or Skills
✣ Master's degree in counseling.
✣ Experience working in clinics, institutions, and/or a multi-member practice.
✣ Ongoing study and courses.
✣ A license if required by your state.
✣ Empathy for your patient's feelings.

Income Potential
$40,000 to $75,000 per year

Best Customers
People who need professional help to deal with problems such as substance abuse or depression, and then need advice as to the steps they can take to resolve their dilemma or problem.

Helpful Tips
It will take some time to build a reputation as a counselor, so it may be best to start part-time until your practice builds enough to be open every day.

For More Information
Association
American Counseling Association (ACA)
5999 Stevenson Ave.
Alexandria, VA 22304-3300
For general information on counseling as a career, contact the ACA Library.

Book
How to Start & Manage a Counseling Business: A Guide for Churches, Ministers, and Professionals by Kathie T. Erwin. 1993, Word Publishing, Grand Rapids, MI.

Additional Business Ideas
✤ Investment counseling and financial planning.
✤ Marketing consulting.
✤ Career and vocational counseling.
✤ Credit counseling/consulting:
   Everything You Need to Know about Credit by Deborah McNaughton, 1993. Order from Deborah McNaughton, 1100 Irvine Blvd., #541, Tustin, CA 92680. Also inquire about credit and financial strategies seminars and "Yes You Can" distributorship.

Business Guide
Entrepreneur's Start-Up Guide, "Credit Consultant." (800) 421-2300; $69.50 plus shipping.

⚜ 72 ⚘

GENEALOGIST

As a professional genealogist, you help people search for their "roots," or family histories. You interview the families and help find their ancestors and native countries (if they are not Native Americans). It is fascinating work. A person in this business has to know the sources to tap in to and be persistent and tenacious.

Start-Up Costs
$3,000 to $4,000 for office equipment and reference books.

Pricing Guidelines
* $20 to $50 per hour or a flat fee per project.
* Go by professional recommended pricing.

Marketing and Advertising Methods and Tips
* Advertise in classified sections of newspapers.
* Place flyers on bulletin boards.
* Send out press releases when you open for business.
* Give talks to groups about researching their family's past.
* Write a promotional column in a local paper with tips for people who want to research their family background.

Essential Equipment
* Computer with fax/modem, printer.
* Promotional materials: business cards, flyers.

Recommended Training, Experience, or Skills
* Take courses offered by genealogical and historical societies, community colleges, or continuing education evening programs.
* See *The Independent Study Catalog* (Peterson's Guides) for genealogy correspondence courses.

Income Potential
$10,000 to $30,000 per year, depending on whether you work part- or full-time.

Best Customers
People interested in finding out more about their family history.

Helpful Tips
* Be persistent.
* Use your sources (the Internet, libraries, genealogy records kept by the Mormon church) to help you in your research.

For More Information
Books
Becoming a Professional Genealogist by Nancy Carlberg. 1991, Carlberg Press, Anaheim, CA.
The Genealogist's Companion & Sourcebook by Emily Anne Croom. 1994, Betterway Books, Cincinnati, OH.
The Genealogist's Handbook: Modern Methods for Researching Family History by Raymond S. Wright, III. 1995, American Library Association, Chicago, IL.

Reference Books
Genealogical Sourcebook Series: *African American, Asian American, Hispanic American, Native American Genealogist Sourcebooks.* 1995, Gale Research, Detroit, MI. Look for them in a public library's reference section.

Online
If you have access to the Internet, you can subscribe to "Roots-1" by sending e-mail to listserv@mail.eworld.com. In the body of the letter, write "Subscribe Roots 1." Follow that with your name, and you will be placed on the genealogy mailing list. You will receive large amounts of daily information in your e-mail box.

Also check out Everton Publishers Inc.'s *Online Search,* an online genealogical subscription service. Information can be found at *http://www.everton.com.*

Additional Business Ideas

✤ Writing family histories: compile in booklets for the families.

   Writing Family Histories and Memoirs by Kirk Polking. 1995, Betterway Books, Cincinnati, OH.

✤ Video biographies of older persons.

✤ Research the history of people's homes—when they were built, who built them, etc.

⚞ 73 ⚟

INSURANCE AGENT

With the high cost of insurance, individuals and businesses are always looking for good coverage and reasonable rates. If you like selling and want to help people get the best policies for them, you might consider starting your own independent or franchise insurance agency. Many women like the flexible hours and the satisfaction of guiding people to make the best insurance decisions for themselves, their families, and/or their businesses.

Start-Up Costs

$2,000 to $5,000 for an office set-up (some insurance companies will help with office and equipment costs).

Pricing Guidelines

Follow industry guidelines for the percentage you earn from each policy you sell.

Marketing and Advertising Methods and Tips

✤ This depends on whether you specialize, or if you are an independent agent who provides several kinds of insurance.

✤ Direct mail, Yellow Pages listing, referrals.

Essential Equipment
* A computer with insurance, accounting, and bookkeeping software.
* A fax machine, copier, and office furniture.
* Trade manuals: reference books, directories.

Recommended Training, Experience, or Skills
* Take insurance courses and training.
* Get a state license.
* Work in an agency before you start your own.

Income Potential
$25,000 to $100,000 (when you have built up a clientele).

Best Customers
Individuals, homeowners, business owners, and home-based business owners—a fast-growing market.

Helpful Tips
* This business can require long hours, and it may take a while before you build up a client list that can support you.
* Be persistent in finding the best coverage for each client. Keep in touch with them about upgrading their coverage as their lives and their insurance needs change.
* Keep personal contact with your clients; too many insurance agents overlook the personal attention that can be crucial to customer satisfaction, preventing problems, and getting referrals to potential clients.
* Focus on women's insurance needs and help educate them so they can make wise choices in purchasing insurance.

For More Information
Association
Independent Insurance Agents of America
127 South Peyton
Alexandria, VA 22314
Send SASE for membership information.

Books

Agency Operations & Sales Management, 2 vols., 2nd ed., by Carol A. Hammes, Peter R. Kensicki, Daniel Hussey, Jr., and Christopher J. Amrhein. 1992, Insurance Institute of America, Inc., Malvern, PA.

Insurance Smart: How to Buy the Right Insurance at the Right Price by Jeff O'Donnell. 1991, John Wiley & Sons, Inc., New York, NY. For anyone about to buy insurance or for individuals beginning a career as an insurance agent.

The Merritt Company
1661 Ninth St.
P.O. Box 955
Santa Monica, CA 90406-0955
(800) 638-7597

Order the following books and courses, and ask for their current catalog:

Insurance Principles: A Basic Course, $23.95. 1995.
Life Insurance Policy Comparisons & Underwriting, $19.95. 1994.

Software:

"Insurance Perfect"
Micro Perfect Corporation
225 W. 34th St.
New York, NY 10122
Comprehensive management program; write for information.

Additional Business Ideas

Insurance restoration service: this service makes arrangements to help clients repair property damage from natural or man-made disasters.

Entrepreneur's Start-Up Guide, "Insurance Restoration Service." (800) 421-2300; $69.50 plus shipping.

≈ 74 ≈

LEGAL SERVICES

There are a number of legal services one can offer from home, freelancing, or in one's own office: law practice, paralegal, independent legal secretary, research, pension valuations, etc. Your education and training in the law will determine the nature of your customers: individuals needing legal advice, businesses, and/or law firms. The focus here is on the practice of law itself, which is ideal for a small and/or home-based business for women.

Start-Up Costs

Relatively low for basic office set-up and equipment: approximately $1,000 to $6,000, depending on whether you already have a computer and work from your home office or have a separate office away from your home.

Pricing Guidelines

Depends on the going rate in your area, your clients, and professional guidelines (see Jay Foonberg's books in "For More Information"). One woman attorney works from two offices, one home-based; she has "call-in" hours when her clients may call to talk with her about any concerns at no cost to them. If they call at other times, however, they are billed her usual rate.

Essential Equipment

* Office equipment: computer with legal/paralegal software; copier, fax machine, telephone system.
* Reference books.

Marketing and Advertising Methods and Tips

* "The best marketing source is referral. A satisfied client is worth his/her weight in gold."
  —K.L. Barndt, family law attorney

❖ Yellow Pages listing (you do not need a full-page ad; two lines will do).

❖ Contacts in the community from volunteer work, school, or church.

Recommended Training, Experience, or Skills

❖ Lawyer: law degree and passing of the bar exam in your state.

❖ Belong to a state or county bar association.

❖ Paralegal: two to four years of college; paralegal training, distance education courses.

❖ Experience: "Good to work several years for an experienced attorney or legal services group to familiarize oneself with the system. Local legal service providers are overworked and underfunded and often welcome volunteer service. Volunteer for some pro bono work. It's good experience for you and good for society too!"
—K.L. Barndt

Income Potential

❖ Lawyer: $50,000 to $100,000 per year and up, depending on your clients, training, education, and experience.

❖ Paralegal: $25,000 to $40,000.

Best Customers

❖ Lawyer: those individuals and businesses who need your specialized legal services.

❖ Paralegal: law firms, individuals, and businesses who need your specialized services.

Helpful Tips

Lawyer

❖ "It's essential to figure out what your clients need and want and to try to provide it in an innovative way."
—Barndt

❖ "Although not necessary from the start, you will soon need support staff. It is possible to start with a part-time office clerk to free you from some of the mundane details, which gives you uninterrupted meetings, research, etc."—Barndt

✤ "Don't be afraid to answer the telephone yourself; clients are surprised and delighted when you do."—Barndt

Paralegal
You work under the direct supervision of attorneys and help to make legal assistance more affordable by doing anything an attorney does except signing documents, giving clients legal advice, and appearing in court in contested cases.

For More Information
Books
How to Start and Build a Law Practice, 3rd ed., by Jay G. Foonberg. 1992, ABA Professional Education Periodicals and Publications, Chicago, IL.

The Independent Paralegal's Handbook, 3rd ed., by attorney Ralph Warner. 1994, Nolo Press, Berkeley, CA.

Marketing Legal Services: Developing & Growing Client Relationships for the 1990's by Richard K. Rodgers. 1993, Kelley Rodgers Group, Atlanta, GA.

Starting and Managing Your Own Business: A Freelancing Guide for Paralegals by Dorothy Secol. 1994, John Wiley & Sons, Inc., New York, NY.

Distance Education/Correspondence Courses
Write for brochures:

International Correspondence Schools
925 Oak St.
Scranton, PA 18515

Graduate School
U.S. Department of Agriculture (USDA)
Ag Box 9911
Room 1112, S. Agriculture Bldg.
14th St. & Independence Ave. SW
Washington, DC 20250-9911

296 101 BEST SMALL BUSINESSES FOR WOMEN

Distance Education and Training Council
1601 18th St. NW
Washington, DC 20009-2529

Software
Micro Perfect Corporation
225 W. 34th St.
New York, NY 10122
Write for information about legal profession software.

Forms
E-Z Legal Forms
384 Military Trail
Dearfield Beach, FL 33442
Software, legal forms and agreements, books, certificates. Write for catalog.

Additional Business Ideas
See "Court Services," in the "Business Services" chapter.

⚉ 75 ⚉
PERSONAL MATCHMAKER

Many singles hate going to bars to meet people. You have no idea of their background, and it can be unsafe at times. If you enjoy meeting people and helping them meet people, then an introduction service may be a venture you want to look in to.

Unfortunately, according to the International Society of Introduction Services (ISIS), "20% of the introduction services get 80% of the media coverage, most of it negative." An ISIS spokesperson says that these unscrupulous and mismanaged introduction services have hurt the entire industry.

Thus, if you decide to start an introduction service, you should follow the ISIS "Code of Ethics," and also your state's consumer protection laws.

Start-Up Costs
* $12,000 to $25,000
* Budget enough for adequate advertising.

Pricing Guidelines
Introduction services charge a monthly or yearly fee: $50 per month, $600 per year. This varies from location to location and depends on what services you offer—videotaping, meetings at restaurants, etc.

Essential Equipment
* A computer with billing and mailing software; telephone system; fax machine, copier.
* Access to a videotaping service or equipment.
* Contracts and agreements (check with a lawyer and insurance agent).

Marketing and Advertising Methods and Tips
* The ISIS says that the number one advertising tip is "Location! Location! Location!" It also advises that you review a media source's readership and call current advertisers who use a medium that appeals to a similar demographic group as your target group to find out if they have had positive responses. If so, you probably will, too.
* Press releases and promotional stories in your local media.
* Yellow Pages listing; classified and display ads in local newspapers and magazines.
* Community bulletin boards.
* Direct mailings.
* Advertisements in periodicals and publications that reach your target market.

Recommended Training, Experience, or Skills
* Work for an introduction service.

* Study and talk with as many introduction services as you can, especially those that have been in business for a number of years.
* Be honest, and build up your reputation for having made successful matches.

Income Potential
* It may take two years to begin to earn enough of a profit for you to take an income.
* Annual earnings can range from $15,000 to $75,000 and up.

Best Customers
Young singles, young professionals, mature individuals, persons with disabilities, etc.; decide which audience you want to target.

Helpful Tips
* "Fair business practices, a genuine concern for the well-being of your clients, and your professional reputation are factors critical to your success." (from the ISIS Interface newsletter, Fall 1995)
* Abide by the ISIS "Code of Ethics," and make sure your dating service is seen in a positive light in your community.
* Do your market research to see if there are enough singles in your area to support your service.
* Owners of introduction services say that this is a very enjoyable business to run, but that many go out of business in six months because they do not manage it like a business or understand the commitment and difficulty involved in making an introduction service successful.

For More Information
Association
International Society of Introduction Services
P.O. Box 4876
West Hills, CA 91308

Does not have start-up information; send SASE for membership information. Has a "Code of Ethics" and suggested questions consumers should ask when shopping for an introduction service.

Books
Dating (How to Pick & Choose Your Date) by John R. Craig. 1992, Rite Books Publishing, Warren, OH.
The Dating Service Maze: The Experts Guide to Dating Services by Lynda M. Johncock. 1994, Queen of Hearts Publishing, Phoenix, AZ.
Mate Selection: How to Make Things Start and Go Right by Roosevelt Gentry and William T. Henderson. 1987, Colonial Press, Birmingham, AL.

Business Guide
Entrepreneur's Start-Up Business Guide, "Dating Service." (800) 421-2300; $69.50 plus shipping.

Additional Business Ideas
See "Apartment Finding/Roommate Service."

☙ 76 ☙
REAL ESTATE

Buying and selling homes, buildings, businesses, land, etc. is an industry that involves more than 1 million real estate agents, according to the National Association of Realtors. You can study and get your state license and work for an established agency, working independently (under a broker's supervision) and setting your own hours, or eventually open your own one-person business or build a larger agency, hiring your own agents.

You can also start other businesses related to real estate, but it is wise to study and work in real estate to gain working knowledge before you specialize or expand into other areas.

Start-Up Costs
About $1,500 to get a real estate license; $40,000 to open your own firm.

Pricing Guidelines
Find out the going commission for selling a property in your area.

Marketing and Advertising Methods and Tips
❖ Classified and display ads in local newspapers and in free real estate booklets put in grocery stores, etc.
❖ Annual promotions: sponsor local youth teams, plant give-aways.
❖ Teach home-buying tips in community continuing education courses.
❖ Send out flyers, make direct calls to local homeowners.
❖ Get referrals from satisfied customers, friends, and family.
❖ Write a promotional column in a local newspaper.
❖ Offer related services, such as appraisals for lending institutions.

Essential Equipment
❖ Office: computer, related software; fax machine, telephone system, copier.
❖ Promotional materials: brochures, business cards, signs.

Recommended Training, Experience, or Skills
❖ Take real estate college courses, training, and education.
❖ Pass your state's test to get your license.
❖ Apprentice with an established broker for two years or more.
❖ Apply to the state licensing board to find out if will be approved if you want to become a broker with your own agency.

Income Potential
❖ $29,000 to $40,000 per year for an agent.
❖ $55,000 per year and up for a broker.

Best Customers
❖ Families that want houses.
❖ Business owners who want commercial buildings.
❖ Builders who want land.

Helpful Tips
❖ Know your industry: how to help your buyer get loans, which mortgage is best for your buyer.
❖ Understand your buyers and sellers and what they are looking for.
❖ Be good at salesmanship.
❖ Have an attractive office and car (especially if you are driving your clients).
❖ Keep looking for new buyers through mailings, offers for free home evaluations, etc.
❖ This is often a seasonal business, and one that fluctuates with interest rates.

Franchises
There are many real estate franchises; refer to a franchise book or publication, such as *Entrepeneur Magazine*'s annual franchise issue published in January, to review those that exist.

For More Information
Buying and Selling Real Estate by Everette L. Gracey. American Literary Press, Inc., Baltimore, MD.
The Complete Guide to Buying & Selling Real Estate by Lowell R. Hodgkins. 1989, Betterway Books, Cincinnati, OH.
Modern Real Estate, 5th ed., by Charles H. Wurtzebach and Mike E. Miles. 1995, John Wiley & Sons, Inc., New York, NY. For real estate professionals and those preparing for a State Real Estate License.
Real Estate Agent's Business Planning Guide by Carla Cross. 1994, Dearborn Financial Publishing, Inc., Chicago, IL.

Business Guide
Entrepreneur's Start-Up Guide, "Flat-Fee Real Estate Agency." (800) 421-2300; $69.50 plus shipping.

Software
"Real Estate Office Management"
YARDI Systems
819 Reddick St.
Santa Barbara, CA 93103
Write for information and prices.

Additional Business Ideas
✦ Home inspection service:
  The Home Buyer's Inspection Guide by James Madorma.
  1990, Betterway Books, Cincinnati, OH.
  Inspecting a Home or Income Property, rev. ed., by Jim Yuen,
  R.S. 1996, Ten Speed Press, Berkeley, CA.
  Profits in Buying & Renovating a House or Income Property, 2nd
  ed., by Jim Yuen, 1986, Ten Speed Press, Berkeley, CA.
✦ Property tax consultant: these consultants put together
  property tax appeals for property owners and sometimes
  businesses. Earnings come from a percentage of the
  refund.
  Property Tax Consultant's Guide by Lynn Tyckzak and Chris
  Malburg. 1992, Prentice-Hall, New York, NY.
  Entrepreneur's Start-Up Guide, "Property Tax Consultant."
  (800) 421- 2300; $69.50 plus shipping.
✦ Real estate appraisal:
  National College of Appraisal and Property
    Management (NCAPM)
  3597 Parkway Lane, Suite 100
  Norcross, GA 30092
  Courses in real estate appraisal and property manage-
  ment. Write for information.

≈ 77 ≈
PERSONAL SECURITY CONSULTANT

Even though experts sometimes say that crimes are not on
the rise, many people, especially women, still perceive that
there is more crime and fear for the safety of their families

and themselves. As a personal security consultant, you could offer a range of services: personal safety devices, a home security analysis, self-defense lessons, etc.

Start-Up Costs
$15,000 to $20,000

Pricing Guidelines
+ $50 to $75 per hour for consulting: evaluating your customer's house, recommending home and personal devices.
+ $40 to $400 for self-defense courses, depending on the length and type of course.

Essential Equipment
+ Office equipment: computer with mailing list, accounting software; fax machine.
+ Personal safety devices.
+ Equipment, mats, and rented room to hold self-defense classes.

Marketing and Advertising Methods and Tips
+ Classified ads in newspapers, Yellow Pages listing, ads on local radio and cable television channels.
+ Talks to women's groups.
+ Demonstrations at shopping malls.
+ Flyers on community bulletin boards.
+ Word-of-mouth referrals.
+ Direct mail to businesses.
+ Flyers on college bulletin boards.

Recommended Training, Experience, or Skills
+ Take courses in self-defense.
+ Education and training in police work, criminal justice, etc. may be helpful.
+ Work in a security services company for experience.
+ Read up on the latest trends in the industry.
+ Teach self-defense for local YMCA's at first to get experience in teaching.

Income Potential
$20,000 to $80,000 per year and up; will grow as your reputation and the number of clients increase.

Best Customers
Single women, families, and businesses that want to have their employees aware of self-protection.

Helpful Tips
* Do your market research to see what kinds of security people have and would like.
* Talk to police officers and criminal attorneys to find out what kind of crimes are happening in your area.
* Be an expert in your business; know what devices are available, how they work, and who should and should not use them.
* Have the training and skill to teach your self-defense courses.
* Keep current as to the latest trends and products in the security industry.

For More Information
Books
Comprehensive Self-Defense by Jose G. Paman and Rod Goodwin. 1993, Eighty-Three Brixton-Hill Associates, North Highlands, CA.

Personal Safety: A Training Resource Manual by Chris Cardy. 1992, Ashgate Publishing Company, Brookfield, UT.

Self-Defense by Jonathan Kellerman. 1995, Bantam Books, Inc., New York, NY.

Self-Defense and Assault Protection for Girls and Women by Bruce Tegner and Alice McGrath. 1977, Thor Publishing Company, Ventura, CA.

Self-Defense for Women by Eva Shaw. 1996, Ingram, Emory Dalton Books, Del Mar, CA.

Additional Business Ideas
* Training dogs in customers' homes for protection and obedience.

❖ Inventions for the security field: alarms, dummies for cars, anti-theft devices, etc.

❖ Locksmith:
ICS Learning Systems
925 Oak St.
Scranton, PA 18515

McGraw-Hill Continuing Education Center
4401 Connecticut Ave. SW
Washington, DC 20008

NRI Schools
4401 Connecticut Ave. NW
Washington, DC 20008

❖ Mail-order catalog of home and personal safety devices (see "Mail Order," in "General Resources").

≈ 78 ≈
BUSINESS AND JOB COUNSELING FOR PERSONS WITH DISABILITIES

With the passage of the Americans with Disabilities Act (ADA) in 1990, new opportunities opened up. If you are knowledgeable about the ADA and can interpret it to both employers and people with disabilities, you may be able to provide helpful consulting and counseling.

In consulting for businesses about the ADA, you can help companies find practical and inexpensive ways to make their workplaces accessible to people with disabilities. You can evaluate their job sites and then make recommendations for compliance.

For individuals with disabilities, you can help counsel them about getting jobs and/or starting their own businesses.

Start-Up Costs
$2,000 to $15,000 for a home office or small office set-up with support staff.

Pricing Guidelines
❖ $50 to $100 per hour to companies for an audit of their facilities followed by recommendations.
❖ A flat, one-time fee for helping persons with disabilities find jobs.

Essential Equipment
❖ Standard office equipment: computer with modem and online services; telephone system.
❖ Presentation equipment, promotional materials, brochures.

Marketing and Advertising Methods and Tips
❖ For companies, do a direct mailing and follow up with a phone call and visit.
❖ Give talks to the Chamber of Commerce about hiring people with disabilities and compliance with ADA standards.
❖ Place classified ads on cable television and in larger local newspapers.
❖ Network and volunteer at nonprofit organizations that serve the disabled.
❖ Call builders to see if they need advice on complying with ADA regulations.

Recommended Training, Experience, or Skills
Have a background in human services, job counseling, psychology, special education, and/or business management.

Income Potential
$20,000 to $35,000 per year and up

Best Customers
❖ Businesses that need to comply with the ADA recommendations.
❖ Individuals with disabilities.

Helpful Tips
As you help businesses comply with ADA regulations, keep a database of the companies and the qualifications of employ-

ees they are looking for. Then see if you can match up their jobs with your clients with disabilities. You can help the employer accommodate the job to fit a potential client with disabilities who has the needed qualifications.

For More Information
Association
Disabled Businesspersons Association (DBA)
9625 Black Mountain Road, Suite 207
San Diego, CA 92126-4564
E-mail: DBAnet@ix.netcom.com

America's largest nonprofit organization for entrepreneurs and professionals with disabilities. Membership ($15 per year) is not a prerequisite for services. Write, or call (619) 586-1199, for more information.

The National Organization on Disability was founded in 1982 to promote full participation of America's 49 million men, women, and children with disabilities in all aspects of community life. The organization has established a Community Partnership Program (CPP) with more than 4,500 towns, townships, cities, and counties to concentrate on eliminating barriers that keep people with disabilities from participating fully in the life of their community. Awards, periodicals, and publications. Send SASE for more information about the community partnership program to help people in your community with disabilities: 910 16th St., Washington, DC 20006.

Books
Complying with the ADA: A Small Business Guide to Hiring and Employing the Disabled by Jeffrey G. Allen. 1993, John Wiley & Sons, Inc., New York, NY.

Get the Marketing Edge: A Job Developer's Toolkit for People with Disabilities. 1993, Training Resource Network, St. Augustine, FL.

The Job Developer's Guide to the American Disabilities Act: Using the ADA to Promote Job Opportunities for People with Disabilities edited by Susan M. Bruyere and Thomas P. Golden. 1996, Training Resource Network, St. Augustine, FL.

Job-Hunting Tips for the So-Called Handicapped or People with Disabilities, (booklet) by Richard Nelson Bolles. 1995, Ten Speed Press, Berkeley, CA.

Successful Job Search Strategies for the Disabled: Understanding the ADA by Jeffrey G. Allen. 1994, John Wiley & Sons, Inc., New York, NY.

Additional Business Ideas

❖ Invent or create new devices to help people with disabilities (see "Inventor").

❖ Teach people with disabilities how to drive.

⚜ ● ⚜

MISCELLANEOUS PERSONAL SERVICES

❖ Computer cleaning business.

❖ Facialist: give facials in people's homes or create your own line of facial products. Check for licensing requirements.

❖ Home inventory cataloging; organizing keepsakes.

❖ House calls for house plants.

❖ Personal chef: cook the ordered meal in your home or your customer's home.

Sewing Services

The American Home Sewing and Craft Association estimates than more than 21 million people sew from their homes. For some it is a skilled hobby that enables them to make clothes and gifts, decorate their homes, create functional items, etc. For others, their sewing skills have enabled them to earn money with their creative ideas such as children's clothing, items made from recycled clothing, soft jewelry, toys, vests, banners, and many more.

Check with your state's Department of Revenue or a lawyer about using home sewers to produce a line of goods for your business, to see if they should be classified as independent contractors or employees receiving minimum wage or better.

If you would like to profit from your sewing skills, here are some resources to help you get started.

Sewing: General Resources
Associations
American Home Sewing and Craft Association
1375 Broadway
New York, NY 10018
(212) 302-2150
Offers a sewing guild, educational materials, quarterly publication, show directories, and conventions. Send SASE for membership information.

The National Quilting Association
P.O. Box 393
Ellicott City, MD 21041-0393
Send a large SASE (with two stamps) for membership information.

Professional Association of Custom Clothiers (PACC)
P.O. Box 8071
Medford, OR 97504
A nonprofit organization for designers, custom dressmakers, tailors, teachers, writers, pattern makers, retailers, sewing contractors, and interior sewing specialists. There are 22 chapters in the U.S. and Canada. Send SASE for membership information.

Books

The Business of Sewing by Barbara Wright Sykes. 1992, Collins Publications, 3233 Grand Ave., Chino Hills, CA 91709-1318.

The Expert's Book of Sewing Tips & Techniques: From the Sewing Starts of America. 1995, from the editors of Rodale Press, Erasmus, NJ. Order through Better Homes & Gardens Crafts Club, P.O. Box 8824, Camp Hill, PA 17012-8824.

Price It Right by Claire Shaeffer. 1993, self-published. Look in your bookstore or send SASE for ordering information to Ms. Shaeffer, Box 157, Palm Springs, CA 92263.

Setting Up Your Sewing Space by Myrna Geisbrecht. 1996, Sterling Publishing Company, New York, NY.

Sewing As a Home Business by Mary Roehr. 1987. For ordering information send SASE to Mary Roehr, 500 Saddlebrook Circle, Sedona, AZ 86336.

Sewing As a Home or Small Business: Possibilities by Staff of Center for Self-Sufficiency Publishing. 1992, Center for Self-Sufficiency Publishing, Denver, CO.

Sewing for Profits, new ed., by Judy & Allan Smith. 1995, Success Publications, 3419 Dunham, Box 263, Warsaw, NY 14569; $12.

Chilton Book Company
1 Chilton Way
Radnor, PA 19809-0230
Publishes many sewing books; write for book list.

Business Guide
How to Start and Manage a Sewing Service Business by Jerre G.
Lewis & Leslie D. Renn. 1995, Lewis & Renn Associates,
Inc., 10315 Harmony Dr., Interlochen, MI 49643; $9.95 +
$3 for postage and handling.

Newsletters
"Cause I Said Sew!"
Maryanne Burgess, editor
Carikean Publishing
P.O. Box 11771
Chicago, IL 60611-0771
$12 a year.

"The Sewing Primer"
P.O. Box 376
Fanwood, NJ 07023-0376
$20 per year, 6 issues.

Supplies
Clotilde
2 Sew Smart Way
P.O. Box 8031
Stevens Point, WI 54481
(800) 772-2891
Call or write for catalog.

Nancy's Notions
333 Beichl Ave.
P.O. Box 683
Beaver Dam, WI 53916-0683
(800) 833-0690
Call or write for catalog.

The Crafts Supply Sourcebook, 3rd ed., by Margaret Boyd. 1994, Betterway Books, Cincinnati, OH.

Designer Source Listing, 1995-96 ed., edited by Maryanne Burgess. Carikean Publishing, P.O. Box 11771, Chicago, IL 60640. Has 21 categories from "Beads" through "Workshops." $19.95.

501 Sewing Hints from the Viewers of "Sewing with Nancy" edited by Nancy Zieman. 1995. Order from Oxmoor House, P.O. Box 2463, Birmingham, AL 35201.

⚞ 79 ⚟

ANIMAL SPECIALTIES

If you are an animal lover and a good seamstress, you may be able to pamper people's pets and earn money at the same time. Your specialty may depend on the animals with which you have had experience. One woman designed a special headband with a screen to protect horses' eyes from flies. You can come up with both practical designs and funny ones. Either way, Americans love their pets, and hopefully they'll love what you make for them!

Start-Up Costs
$1,200 to $2,500 to set up your sewing room and purchase an industrial sewing machine.

Pricing Guidelines
+ Material/supply costs + your labor + overhead + the percentage of profit you can realistically make = your price.
+ Clothing: dog and cat sweaters and jackets run from $5 for small items to $20 and up.
+ Check in pet stores and catalogs to get an idea of going prices.

Essential Equipment
+ Industrial sewing machine and notions.
+ Computer with mailing list software; telephone system.
+ Price tags, business cards, brochures.

Marketing and Advertising Methods and Tips
+ Post flyers in veterinarians' offices and on community bulletin boards and in animal feed stores.
+ Exhibit at animal shows, pet trade shows.
+ Have samples made up for pets of family and friends, to test them and get feedback on the product.
+ Place display ads in animal trade publications.

Recommended Training, Experience, or Skills
Working in a pet store or a veterinarian's office can give you both ideas and experience with the animals for which you want to make your creations.

Income Potential
At a good trade or animal show, you can make $500 to $1,000 in a weekend.

Best Customers
+ Pet owners, horse owners, pet shops.
+ Catalogs carrying animal and pet products.
+ Feed stores, hardware stores.

Helpful Tips
+ It helps to specialize in your breed of cat, dog, horse, etc.
+ Try your designs and finished product on your own pets.

For More Information
Books
Coddle Your Cat: Practical Projects to Prove You Care by Jane Burton. 1996, Anness Publishing, Ltd., New York, NY.
Pamper Your Pooch: Practical Projects to Prove You Care by Jane Burton. 1996, Anness Publishing, Ltd., New York, NY.
Selling to Catalog Houses. 1994. Order from Success Publications, 3419 Dunham Rd., Box 263, Warsaw, NY 14569. Send SASE for current publications listing.

Trade Show
International Pet Expo
Western World Supply Association
406 S. 1st Ave.
Arcadia, CA 91006-3829
Send SASE for information.

Additional Business Ideas
❖ Catnip bags and toys for cats.
❖ Sew "life-size" animals for lovers of specific animal breeds.

⊱ 80 ⊰
ARTFUL SEWING

A sewing machine has long been used as a tool for creative expression, and with the popularity of hobbies and crafts, books and other resources have become available to help sewers explore their unique ideas. Soft sculpture, textile art, quilts, and even teddy bears are just a few of the ways in which sewers are creating and selling their machine artwork.

Start-Up Costs
$1,200 to $2,500 to set up your sewing room and purchase an industrial sewing machine.

Pricing Guidelines
❖ Material/supply costs + your labor + overhead + the percentage of profit you can realistically make = your price.
❖ Quilts: Prices of finished quilts will vary, depending on your markets, your reputation, and the area in which you are selling. Expect $200 for small pieces, and $500 to $1,000 and up for larger pieces.
❖ Teddy bears: $10 to $12 per inch for a plain mohair bear. Other prices will vary depending on your market

and whether you are mass-producing or selling to collectors.

Essential Equipment
* Industrial sewing machine and notions.
* Computer with mailing list software; telephone system.
* Price tags, business cards, brochures.

Marketing and Advertising Methods and Tips
* Exhibit at trade shows, craft shows, and artist's shows.
* Sell through crafts shops, galleries, antique shops, and catalog houses.
* Teach courses at fabric shops and trade show workshops.
* Place display ads in trade and home decor publications.
* Offer to exhibit at free, local displays—libraries, banks, institutions.
* Donate an item for a nonprofit organization's fund-raising raffle or drawing.
* Give personal lessons.
* Do direct mailings to customers who have bought your items before.

Recommended Training, Experience, or Skills
* Take sewing courses at fabric shops, textile and design schools, trade shows, or through continuing education.
* Take private lessons.
* Study books and trade publications, and strive to improve your skill.

Income Potential
* Teaching courses: $20 to $40/hr.
* $10,000 to $20,000/yr, depending on your reputation.

Best Customers
* Collectors, those who have bought from you before.
* Shops, galleries.
* Interior designers.

Helpful Tips

❖ As with any art, you have to perfect your skill, develop your own style, and search for the best markets for your work.

❖ Keep abreast of the latest news in your particular art and/or craft by attending trade shows, reading trade publications, and comparing your work with others in your field.

For More Information

Books

Sewing Art Instruction by Inetta Samuel. 1995, Carlton Press Corporation.

Sewing Fun Stuff: Soft Sculpture Shortcuts by Lynne Farris. 1996, Sterling Publishing Co., New York, NY.

Texture with Textiles, Texture with Textiles and More and *Companion Project Book*, three books by Linda McGehee (1991, 1993, 1995). Order from Ghee's, 2620 Centenary Blvd., 3-250, Shreveport, LA 71104. Ideas and techniques for the sewing machine artist; write for prices and ordering information.

Textile Artistry edited by Valeria Campbell-Harding. 1996, Chilton Book Company, Radnor, PA.

Book Club

Better Homes & Gardens Crafts Club
P.O. Box 8824
Camp Hill, PA 17012-8824

Book club with many sewing, quilting, and craft books; write for catalog.

Publishers of Sewing Books

Chester Book Co.
4 Maple St.
Chester, CT 06412

Write for catalog; many art, sewing, and craft books.

Chilton Book Company
1 Chilton Way
Radnor, PA 19089-0230

Sterling Publishing Co., Inc.
387 Park Ave. South
New York, NY 10016-8810

Teddy Bear Books
Learn Bearmaking by Judi Maddigan. 1996. Order from Chilton Book Company.
Teddy Bear Magic: Making Adorable Teddy Bears from Aunt Louise's Bearlace Cottage by Anita L. Crane. 1995, Sterling Publishing Co., Inc., New York, NY.
The Teddy Bear Sourcebook edited by Argie Manolis. 1995, North Light Books, Cincinnati, OH.

Quilting Books
From Sterling Publishing Co., Inc., New York:
Learning to Quilt the Traditional Way by AnnLee Landman. 1996.
Speed Quilting by Cheryl Fall. 1996.
Treasury of Appliqué Quilt Patterns by Maggie Malone. 1996.

Soft Sculpture Books
Fabric Sculpture: The Step-by-Step Guide & Showcase by Nick Grego and Kathleen Ziegler. 1995, North Light Books, Cincinnati, OH.
Sewing Fun Stuff: Soft Sculpture Shortcuts (Great Sewing Projects Series) by Lynne Farris. 1996, Sterling/Sewing Information Resources, New York, NY.
Soft Sculpture & Beyond: An International Perspective by Jutta Feddersen. 1993, Gordon & Breach Science Publishers, Inc., Newark, NJ.

Additional Business Ideas
✤ Appliqué: design and sew custom appliqué pictures, pillows of people's houses, pets, etc. from photographs.
✤ Sewing stuffed toys (anything that is stuffed with a material may have to pass state inspection).

≥ 81 ≤

CANVAS REPAIR/CUSTOM WORK

Sewing custom-fitted covers or repairing canvas covers for boats, outdoor furniture, etc.

Start-Up Costs
$5,000 to $8,000

Pricing Guidelines
$80 to $380 and up per project

Essential Equipment
❖ Bookkeeping and accounting systems; billing forms; telephone system.
❖ Industrial sewing machines: straight sewer, serger, button machine; sewing supplies, cutting and assembling table.

Marketing and Advertising Methods and Tips
❖ Get word-of-mouth referrals
❖ Post flyers at camping and boating supply stores, marinas, and recreational vehicle establishments.
❖ Sell to boating supply catalogs.
❖ Exhibit at outdoor recreation and boating shows.

Recommended Training, Experience, or Skills
❖ If possible, work for a canvas business, then specialize in doing custom work, especially if you see a niche that is not being filled (be honest with your employer and she may be your first customer or refer customers to you when you start out on your own).
❖ Become skilled in sewing with canvas: take sewing courses at fabric stores.
❖ Start sewing cushions and covers for yourself, friends, etc.

Income Potential
$20,000 to $80,000 depending on the demand and whether you work alone or hire part-time employees.

Best Customers
❖ Camping and boating supply stores, marinas, recreational vehicle establishments, outdoor tour companies.
❖ Boating and recreational supply catalogs.
❖ Individuals (campers, boaters, hikers) who buy your custom canvas work.

Helpful Tips
❖ Research the market and what canvas products are being produced. Compare prices, products, etc. with your own work. Look for a niche market that no one has covered yet and try to fill it.
❖ Be able to visualize what your customer wants and give the best quality product you can produce.
❖ Be willing to work long hours during your busy season.

For More Information
Books
Canvas Work by Jeremy Howard-Williams. 1993, Sheridan House, Inc., Dobbs Ferry, NY.

Additional Business Ideas
Repair of vinyl-covered items in vehicles, homes, and offices.

The Vinylman Company
13453 Pumice St.
Norwalk, CT 90650
Vinyl repair supplies.

Foley-Belsaw Company
6301 Equitable Rd.
Kansas City, MO 64120-9957
Write for vinyl repair course information.

Dr. Vinyl & Assocs. Ltd.
13665 E. 42nd Terr.
Independence, MO 64055
Write for franchise information.

≤ 82 ≥

CHILDREN'S CLOTHING

When a former fashion model could not find the quality and style of clothing she wanted for her children, she designed her own. Soon, family and friends began asking for her to create classic clothing for their children. Her styles became so popular that she turned an upstairs floor into a workroom and began a business in which she sells her children's clothing at exclusive boutiques and by mail-order. Each of the outfits is packaged like a gift, in tissue paper and a decorated box.

If you have a background in clothing design and sewing, you might want to investigate this venture. It is highly competitive, but if you can originate a special design or style, you may have a successful business for your custom-made children's clothing.

Start-Up Costs

$4,000 to $10,000, including advertising, and protecting designs (Contact the Professional Association of Custom Clothiers (PACC) at P.O. Box 8074, Medford, OR 97504).

Pricing Guidelines

❖ Follow the guidelines of professional associations.
❖ Survey custom children's clothing in shops, stores, and specialty catalogs.

Essential Equipment

❖ Sewing room set-up: Industrial sewing machine, overlock machine to finish seams, serger; cutting table, sewing notions, storage space for patterns, sources for fabric, mannequin, design and reference sewing books, design table.
❖ Office: computer with mailing list, design, and mail-order software; fax machine, telephone system.

Marketing and Advertising Methods and Tips

❖ Make direct calls to shops followed up by appointments to show your samples.

❖ Have children of friends and family wear your clothing for advertising.

❖ Advertise: local papers, parents' newspapers, local cable TV shopping channels; display ads in women's specialty magazines.

❖ Network with women's clubs that hold charity fashion shows, and have your clothes modeled.

❖ Take a booth at local craft shows and fairs.

❖ Get word-of-mouth referrals

Recommended Training, Experience, or Skills

❖ Clothing design and fashion merchandising education, training, and/or experience. Take courses at local colleges, fabric stores, design schools.

❖ Experience in the children's fashion industry; knowing what is current in the industry.

❖ Design talent, sewing ability, knowledge of fabrics.

Income Potential

$25,000 to $100,000, depending on who your customers are, the complexity of design, and how much time is put into each garment.

Best Customers

Grandparents, customers of boutiques.

Helpful Tips

❖ Thoroughly research the children's clothing market by studying trade publications and attending fashion and trade shows.

❖ Develop your own style and line; it could be a totally new concept or based on classic fashions. Look for a market niche.

✤ Make sure your production can keep up with the demand if you decide to sell nationally and/or by mail order.

✤ Make your clothes easy to care for and easy to wear.

For More Information
Association
Professional Association of Custom Clothiers (PACC)
P.O. Box 8071
Medford, OR 97504

A nonprofit organization for designers, custom dressmakers, tailors, teachers, writers, pattern makers, retailers, sewing contractors, and interior sewing specialists. There are 22 chapters in the U.S. and Canada. Send SASE for membership information.

Books
Embellishments: Adding Glamour to Garments by Linda Fry Kenzle. 1993. Chilton Book Company, Radnor, PA.

Sewing for Children by Cy DeCosse, Inc., Staff (Singer Sewing Reference Library). 1988, Cy DeCosse, Inc., Minnetonka, MN.

Distance Education/Correspondence Schools
Write for course information.

ICS Learning Systems
925 Oak St.
Scranton, PA 18540-9888
"Dressmaking and Design."

Lifetime Career Schools
101 Harrison St.
Archbald, PA 18403
"Sewing/Dressmaking."

For your own mail-order business, see also "Mail Order," in "General Resources."

Additional Business Ideas

✤ Children's clothing store (purchasing clothing):
Entrepreneur's Start-Up Business Guide, "Children's
Clothing Store." $69.50 plus shipping.

✤ Unique baby clothes, gifts, christening gowns, etc.:
Sewing for a New Baby by Jane Fisk and Lois Kinsman.
1996, Sterling Publishing, Co., Inc., New York, NY.

◢ 83 ◣
CUSTOM TIES

In this business, you design and sew ties, bow ties, and match-
ing accessories, such as cummerbunds, to sell at men's and
contemporary clothing shops, at fairs, shows, and possibly
through mail-order and custom orders. Once exclusively
men's wear, some women's contemporary fashions also
include coordinating ties. The secret here is to fashion your
own style and line.

Start-Up Costs
$1,000 to $4,000 for sewing machine and related equipment,
and advertising.

Pricing Guidelines
$10 to $25 per tie depending on the material, complexity of
design, your customers, and the market.

Essential Equipment
✤ Sewing room set-up: Industrial sewing machine, overlock
machine to finish seams, serger; cutting table, sewing
notions, storage space for patterns, fabric, patterns, forms,
reference sewing books, design table.

✤ Office: computer with mailing list, design, and mail-order
software; fax machine, telephone system.

Marketing and Advertising Methods and Tips
* Make direct calls to shops followed by appointments with your samples.
* Have friends and family wear your clothing for advertising.
* Advertise: local cable TV shopping channels; display ads in men's and women's magazines
* Take a booth at local craft shows, fairs, bridal fairs.
* Get word-of-mouth referrals for custom-designed ties.
* Have a kiosk or cart in a shopping mall, especially before Christmas and Father's Day.
* Sell to catalogs.

Recommended Training, Experience, or Skills
* Training in fashion design and retail sales is helpful.
* Skill in tailored sewing.
* Knowledge of your market and the current tie fashions.

Income Potential
$10,000 to $25,000/yr

Best Customers
* Shops: formal wear, men's, children's, and women's fashions; shops in tourist and recreational areas for whimsical and fun ties.
* Women buying for men's gifts or themselves.
* Young people if the ties are of a unique design, color, shape, etc. that appeals to them.
* Catalog shoppers.

Helpful Tips
* Most important: develop your own design and line of ties, and test-market different types and styles, for different ages, and for men and women, until you find your market niche.
* Make sure your production can keep up with the demand if you advertise in magazines or catalogs.
* Have fun—make ties you like!

For More Information
Books

Ties, Ties, Ties: A Guide to Designing Wearable Art for Men by Janet Elwin. 1996, Collector Books, Puducah, NY.

See also "Mail Order," in "General Resources," for information about starting a mail-order business.

Additional Business Ideas
Unique gifts and items from old ties:

Daddy's Ties by Shirley Botsford. 1995, Chilton Book Company, Radnor, PA.

⚞ 84 ⚟
HATS

According to the Millinery Information Bureau, the $700 million hat industry is growing by 15 percent annually. If you have basic dressmaking and sewing knowledge and a sewing machine, you can design and custom-make your own hats. You will need to work and/or study this growing fashion industry to be competitive. You may want to sell coordinating accessories of scarves and evening bags.

Start-Up Costs
$6,000 to $12,000; more if you open your own shop.

Pricing Guidelines
Your time (at $25 to $40 per hour) + 25 percent to 30 percent added to the total of the cost of the materials, supplies, and business expenses (overhead, shipping, packaging, etc.)

Essential Equipment
- Industrial sewing machine, notions, fabrics, veils, hat wire and forms, patterns.
- Office equipment: computer with software for bookkeeping, business plan, mailing list, mail order; online access to keep you abreast of industry trends.

Marketing and Advertising Methods and Tips
+ Have your hats modeled in local fashion shows.
+ Word-of-mouth referrals from satisfied customers.
+ Wear your own creations.
+ Display ads in local papers and national magazines.
+ Show samples at fashion boutiques.
+ Exhibit at fairs and shows.

Recommended Training, Experience, or Skills
+ Acquire basic dressmaking and sewing skills.
+ Take courses locally or order correspondence courses, including courses on entrepreneurship and business management
+ Have manual dexterity and a flair for design.
+ If possible, work in the millinery industry, retail shops, hat factories.

Income Potential
$20 to $500 and up per hat, depending on your skill, reputation, customers, etc.

Best Customers
+ Specialty clothing boutiques.
+ Fashion-conscious women, readers of women's fashion magazines.
+ Mail-order catalogs.

Helpful Tips
+ If your market is exclusive shops, monitor the industry and latest fashion trends.
+ Start small and locally and experiment with different hat styles and age groups to see what sells best for you. Then, try national ads for your best sellers.
+ Familiarize yourself with the millinery industry through work experience, training, etc.

❖ Develop your own style and design that is your "signature."
❖ Know basic business management skills and keep good records.

For More Information

Books
The Hat Book by Juliet Bawden. Order through the Better Homes & Gardens Crafts Club, P.O. Box 8824, Camp Hill, PA 17012-8824.
Hats Made Easy by Lyn Waring. 1996, Sterling Publishing, Co., Inc., New York, NY.

Course/Video
Wonderful World of Hats
897 Wade Rd.
Siletz, OR 97380
Hat-making course/home study with videos; 15 lessons. $3 for catalog; $10 for catalog and an introductory video.

Also publishes *Hat Lovers Dictionary* and offers a designer shoe-covering course. Send large SASE for information.

See also "Mail Order," in "General Resources."

Additional Business Ideas
❖ Custom-made cowboy hats
❖ Paper hats:
  "Hats Incredible"
  P.O. Box 425
  Paoli, PA 19301-0425

These patented, novelty hats are made of recycled honeycomb paper that stretches to fit the wearer. Sell finished ($6 to $8 each), or let customers paint their own at fairs, outdoor functions, etc. Introductory kit includes five hat "blanks," a florescent paint set, foam paint brushes, glue sticks, ties, and assembly instructions (you provide the glue gun). $19.95 plus $5 for shipping and handling.

◢ ● ◣

MISCELLANEOUS SEWING BUSINESS IDEAS

❖ Clothing recycling:
Clothing Recycling as a Home or Small Business: Possibilities by Data Notes Publishing Staff. 1992, Prosperity & Profits Unlimited, Distribution Services, Denver, CO.

❖ Sewing banners:
The Banner Book by Ruth Ann Lowery. 1995, Chilton Book Company, Radnor, PA.

❖ Sewing pincushions:
Making Fabulous Pincushions: 93 Designs for Spectacular & Unusual Projects. 1996, Sterling Publishing Company, Inc., New York, NY.

❖ Sewing draperies:
"International Newsletter for Professional Drapery
    Workrooms"
Sew WHAT
P.O. Box 867
101 Strickland Terrace
Swannanoa, NC 28778
Write for subscription information.

❖ Start a sewing school:
Starting a Sewing School. 1995. Order from Success Publications, 3419 Dunham, Box 263, Warsaw, NY 14569; $10.

❖ Sewing casual slippers.

❖ Sewing tote bags:
Hold It! How to Sew Bags, Totes, Duffels, Pouches, and More by Nancy Resfurcia. 1995, Chilton Book Company, Radnor, PA.

❖ Sewing vests:
The Vest Book by Jacqueline Farrell. 1995, Chilton Book Company, Radnor, PA.

❖ Artists' clothing.

❖ Chef's uniforms.

❖ Barbecue and gardener's aprons.
❖ Dance costumes.
❖ Bathing suits and beachwear.
❖ Halloween costumes.
❖ Bridal gowns and accessories.
❖ Jewelry pouches for traveling.

Travel-Related Businesses

BED-AND-BREAKFAST INN

In the last 30 years, the bed-and-breakfast (B&B) industry has grown from 5,000 to 6,000 B&Bs in 1980 to almost 20,000 in 1991 (from a published study by the U.S. Travel Data Center). The American Bed & Breakfast Association says that, with the increase in B&B establishments, large hotel and motel chains, and resort lodgings offering complimentary breakfast, "this is no longer a hobby or second investment opportunity ... this is a hardball, entrepreneurial business."

This business requires not only a sizable investment of money, but also a 100 percent commitment of hard work and attention to the needs of your guests. If this is something you have always dreamed about, take your time to learn and study the industry and then decide if this lifestyle and business is for you.

Start-Up Costs
* $300,000 to $450,000
* Financing suggestions: SBA business loan; "angel" investors; venture capital firms.

Pricing Guidelines
$80 to $100 a room, depending on what part of the country you're in and the demand for your rooms.

Marketing and Advertising Methods and Tips
* Promotional materials: brochures, business cards, stationery.
* Advertisements in guidebooks and B&B national directories.
* Membership in a local B&B association for networking and referrals.
* National advertising in travel publications.

Essential Equipment
* An establishment of 1 to 25 rooms, furnished with all the amenities of guest rooms.
* Kitchen and dining facilities.
* Office: computer with management, mailing list, accounting, and bookkeeping software.

Recommended Training, Experience, or Skills
* Courses in hospitality and hotel management, B&B apprenticeship programs and seminars.
* Work in a B&B, visit as many as you can, talk to owners, and read books and industry publications.

Income Potential
* $10,000 to $80,000 depending on the number of rooms and occupancy rates.
* The American B&B Association recommends having at least a 10-room inn to support a couple with equity of 25 percent of the project cost and operating capital to cover negative cash flow during start-up.

Best Customers
Tourists, businesspeople, retired couples, satisfied previous customers.

Helpful Tips
❖ Comply with state licensing regulations.
❖ Be prepared for long hours and hard physical work.
❖ Be special or unique in some way to make guests want to stay at your inn over the competition.
❖ Do thorough research and/or hire an industry consultant to help you evaluate the market where you will be opening your B&B.

For More Information
Association:
American Bed & Breakfast Association
P.O. Box 1387
Midlothian, VA 23113-1387
Offers two starter kits, Basic ($45) and Deluxe ($160), which include how-to books, industry newsletter, sourcebook, directory, and more. Also offers an apprenticeship program. Send SASE for more information.

Books
How to Start & Operate Your Own Bed-&-Breakfast: Down-to-Earth Advice from an Award-Winning Bed & Breakfast Owner by Martha W. Murphy. 1994, Henry Holt & Co., Inc., New York, NY.
Open Your Own Bed and Breakfast, 3rd ed., by Barbara Notarius and Gail Storza Brewer. 1996, John Wiley & Sons, Inc., New York, NY.
The Upstart Guide to Owning and Managing a Bed & Breakfast by Lisa Rogak. 1994, Upstart Publishing, Dover, NH.

Business Guide
Entrepreneur's Start-Up Guide, "Bed & Breakfast Inn." (800) 421-2300; $69.50 plus shipping.

Distance Education/Correspondence Courses
Educational Institute of the American Hotel & Motel
Association
Stephen S. Nisbet Bldg.
1407 Harrison Rd.
P.O. Box 1240
East Lansing, MI 48826
Write for information.

Additional Business Ideas
Offer a full-service restaurant with your inn (see "Country Inn,
Restaurant").

◢ 86 ◣
BOATING SERVICES

A boating service business could offer small boats that you
design and build yourself, cleaning and detailing, tours and
transportation, and/or navigation, and/or sailing instruction. Of course you have to have knowledge, skill, and training about boating, but if this is second nature to you
because of your background and education, it may be a
good venture for you.

Start-Up Costs
+ Boat tours: $50,000.
+ Navigation and boating instruction: $5,000 (more if you
  buy a boat for this purpose).
+ Cleaning and detailing: $1,000 to $5,000.
+ Small boat (craft) building: $3,500 to set up workshop.

Pricing Guidelines
+ Boat tours: Seasonal rates; charge the going tourist rates
  in the busy season and off-season rates according to the
  distance traveled and demand for your boat.
+ Navigation and boating instruction: $40 to $75 per hour.

❖ Cleaning and detailing: $40 to $50 per hour.
❖ Boat building: $300 for a small boat; $1,000 to $1,500 for a large boat.

Marketing and Advertising Methods and Tips
❖ Boat tours: brochures at travel bureaus; ads in boating magazines and local newspapers
❖ Navigation and boating instruction: flyers at marinas and marine retail centers.
❖ Cleaning and detailing: word-of-mouth referrals.
❖ Boat building: ads in recreational publications.

Essential Equipment
❖ Boat tours: boat, promotional materials, record-keeping system, telephone system.
❖ Navigation and boating instruction: manuals.
❖ Cleaning and detailing: cleaning equipment.
❖ Boat building: woodworking tools, wood, waterproof glues, paints.

Recommended Training, Experience, or Skills
❖ Boat tours: work on or for a boat tour company.
❖ Navigation and boating instruction: U.S. Coast Guard boating courses; other boating training, private lessons.
❖ Cleaning and detailing: work for a detailing company; have your own boat for practice.
❖ Boat building: apprentice or work with a boat builder; take boat-building courses.

Income Potential
❖ Boat tours: $30,000 to $80,000 per year, depending on how busy your seasons are.
❖ Navigation and boating instruction: $400 to teach a course; $6,000 to $30,000 per year.
❖ Cleaning and detailing: $30,000 to $60,000 per year.
❖ Boat building: $2,000 to $3,000 for small boats.

Best Customers

* Boat tours: tourists, residents who have to get to other islands or shores.
* Navigation and boating instruction: new boat owners.
* Cleaning and detailing: commercial fishers, recreational boaters.
* Boat building: hobby boaters, young boaters.

Helpful Tips

* Boat tours: have several different tours planned from which your customers can pick.
* Navigation and boating instruction: knowledge and practical experience are your strengths. Make sure safety and emergency procedures are taught, and have your students practice them often.
* Cleaning and detailing: pay attention to detail. If you cannot do it, hire people with the experience to do the very best job for your customers.
* Boat building: develop your boat specialty.

For More Information

Book

Boatkeeper: The Boatowner's Manual to Maintenance, Repair, and Construction edited by Bernard Gladstone and Tom Bottomley. 1984, William Morrow & Co., Inc., New York, NY.

Distance Education/Correspondence Course:

Westlawn Institute of Marine Technology
733 Summer St.
Stamford, CT 06901
Courses in boat and yacht design and related marine technology subjects. Write for information.

Video

"The Sail Boat" is a video about building a small (one-person) sailboat. Order from The New Yankee Workshop, P.O. Box

9345, South Burlington, VT 05407; write or send SASE for brochure.

Additional Business Ideas
Marine retail business:
How to Start and Manage a Marine Retailing Business by Jerre G. Lewis and Leslie D. Renn. 1995, Lewis & Renn Assocs., 10315 Harmony Dr., Interlochen, Michigan 49643; $9.95 + $3 for shipping and handling.

⚞ 87 ⚟

TOUR OPERATOR

If you are a tour operator, you will organize, plan, and guide your customers on specialized tours while charging a price that will cover the expenses and make a profit for you. You can have tours based on your personal interests, which means there are unlimited tour possibilities in this multi-million dollar industry.

Start-Up Costs
❖ Low start-up: $5,000
❖ Average start-up: $35,000 to $45,000

Pricing Guidelines
Follow industry guidelines as how much to add to your costs to make a profit: about 40 percent to 50 percent above your costs.

Essential Equipment
❖ Depends on what kind of tour you offer—adventure, scientific, art, etc. You can purchase your own equipment or contract with local suppliers.
❖ If you do contract for supplies and equipment, make sure their quality is excellent, because their products and services will reflect positively or negatively on your tours.

Marketing and Advertising Methods and Tips

✤ Notify travel agencies.
✤ Get listings in travel guides and tour books.
✤ Place ads in trade magazines and hobby and special interest magazines.
✤ Exhibit at travel trade shows.
✤ Get word-of-mouth referrals from satisfied travelers.
✤ Place online advertisements.

Recommended Training, Experience, or Skills

✤ It is highly recommended that you have training, education, and experience in the travel industry—taking tours and being a tour director or group leader.
✤ Know your specialty.
✤ Be a good business manager; be organized, patient, able to withstand stress and pressure.
✤ Have a good balance of sales and administrative skills.

Income Potential

✤ It is recommended that you have a large reserve of capital because it may take years before your business is profitable.
✤ Income can range from $20,000 to hundreds of thousands and more, depending on the popularity of the tours, how often they are run, and whether you work alone or hire others to run the tours.

Best Customers

✤ Repeat customers from previous tours.
✤ Those whose interests relate to the tour's theme or purpose (birders, rafters, historians, etc.).

Helpful Tips

✤ Develop specialized tours that are based on your experiences, training, and knowledge so that you can target your advertising to those specific customers and meet those customers' special needs.

❖ Be creative with financing, advertising, and finding a tour niche not yet discovered.
❖ Stay within your budget and fill your tours
❖ Concentrate on giving your customers the best possible time on the tours.

For More Information
Associations
National Tour Association
546 E. Main St.
Lexington, KY 40508
For those already involved in the tour industry. Send SASE for membership information.

The Adventure Travel Society, Inc.
6551 S. Revere Parkway, #160
Engelwood, CO 80111
For travel agents and professionals in the travel business. Write for membership information.

Books
Marketing Tourism Destinations: A Strategic Planning Approach by Ernie Heath. 1992, John Wiley & Sons., Inc., New York, NY.

Astronomy Book Club, A Newbridge Book Club
3000 Cindel Dr.
Delran, NJ 08075-1185
Books on science and nature, and an annual catalog of travel books. Write for membership information.

Distance Education/Correspondence Courses
Echols International Tourism Institute
676 N. St. Clair St., Suite 1950
Chicago, IL 60611
Write for information on travel training.

Distance Education & Training Council
1601 18th St. NW
Washington, DC 20009-2529
Send SASE for a free list of other distance-education schools.

Additional Business Ideas

❖ Travel agency:
Entrepreneur's Start-Up Business Guide, "Travel Agency."
(800) 421-2300; $69.50 plus shipping.
How to Start and Manage a Travel Agency Business by Jerre
G. Lewis & Leslie D. Renn. 1995, Lewis & Renn Assocs.,
10315 Harmony Dr., Interlochen, MI 49643; $9.95 +
$3 postage and handling.
National Business Library's Start-Up Guide, "Travel Agency."
(800) 947-7724; $39.95 plus $5 shipping.

❖ Publish travel newsletters or a tourist video directory for
travel agencies (see "Independent Publisher," in "Businesses
Involving Words").

❖ Travel videos for tourists:
*Make Money with Your Camcorder: A Complete, Fully Illus-
trated Guide* by Kevin Campbell. 1995, Amherst Media,
Inc., Amherst, NJ.
Videomaker's Comprehensive Guide to Making Videos by Butter-
worth-Heinemann. 1996, Videomaker Magazine Editors,
Chico, CA.

Videomaker
P.O. Box 469026
Escondido, CA 92046-9938
$14.97 per year, 12 issues.

❖ Travel writing:
Travel Writing: A Guide to Research, Writing, and Selling by L.
Peat O'Neal. 1996, Writer's Digest Books, Cincinnati, OH.

❖ Make and sell fishing lures (women enjoy fly fishing, too):
*Luremaking: The Art and Science of Spinnerbaits, Buzzbaits,
Jigs & Other Leadheads* by A.D. Livingston. 1993, Inter-
national Marine Publishing Company, Camden, ME.

Mastering the Art of Fly-Tying by Richard W. Talleur. 1994, Stackpole Books, Mechanicsburg, PA. (Stackpole also publishes many related books; write for current list to Stackpole Books, 5067 Ritter Rd., Mechanicsburg, PA 17055-6921.)

Tying and Fishing the NYMPH by Taff Price. 1996, Sterling Publishing Co., Inc., New York, NY.

Fly Fisherman
Cowles Magazines
6405 Flank Dr.
Harrisburg, PA 26947
$20 per year, 6 issues.

✤ Teach fly-fishing.
✤ Lead fly-fishing tours.

Businesses
Involving Words

If you love to read, love books and the English language (and foreign languages), and are good with writing and communications, a business involving words may be an interesting and rewarding venture for you to investigate. You will need a good grammar background and possibly additional college courses or training, depending on the business you want to start.

Businesses Involving Words: General Resources
Books: The Business of Writing
Editorial Freelancing: A Practical Guide by Trumbull Rogers. 1995, Aletheia Publications, Bayside, NY.

Guide to Literary Agents, Writer's Digest Books, 1507 Dana Ave., Cincinnati, OH 45207.

How to Start and Run a Writing and Editing Business by Herman Holtz. 1992, John Wiley & Sons, New York, NY.

National Writers Union Guide to Freelance Rates & Standard Practice, National Writers Union. 1995, Writer's Digest Books, Cincinnati, OH.

Writing for Money by Loriann Hoff Oberlin. 1995, Writer's Digest, Cincinnati, OH.

Writing: Getting Into Print—A Business Guide for Writers by J. Frohbieter-Mueller. 1994, Glenbridge Publishing Ltd., 6010 W. Jewell Ave., Lakewood, CO 80232.

Market Books
(Check your local library to see if they have the latest copies.)

Insider's Guide to Book Editors, Publishers, and Literary Agents, 1997-1998 edition, by Jeff Herman. 1996, Prima Publishing, Rocklin, CA.

Literary Market Place. R.R. Bowker, 121 Chanlon Rd., New Providence, NJ 07974.

Writer's Market Books. Writer' Digest Books, 1507 Dana Ave., Cincinnati, OH 45207:
Children's Writer's & Illustrator's Market
Mystery Writer's Sourcebook
Novel & Short Story Writer's Market
Poet's Market
Romance Writer's Sourcebook
Science Fiction Writer's Market Place
Writer's Market

Books: Business Writing
The Business Writer's Companion by Charles T. Brusow, Gerald J. Alred, and Walter E. Oliu. 1996, St. Martin's Press, Inc., New York, NY.

Business Writing Quick & Easy by Laura Brill. 1989, Amacon, New York, NY.

Powerful Business Writing: Say What You Mean, Get What You Want by Tom McKeown. 1992, Writer's Digest Books, Cincinnati, OH.

Distance Education/Correspondence Courses
Write for catalogs:

USDA Graduate School (U.S. Department of Agriculture)
Ag Box 9911, Rm 112
S. Agriculture Bldg.
14th St. & Independence Ave. SW
Washington, DC 20250-9911
Editing, proofreading, and indexing courses.

McGraw-Hill Continuing Education Center
4401 Connecticut Ave. NW
Washington, DC 20008

NRI Schools
4401 Connecticut Ave. NW
Washington, DC 20008

Online Sources
✤ America Online: (800) 827-6364; "The Writers Club."
✤ CompuServe: (800) 336-6823; various writers' forums.
✤ Prodigy: (800) 822-6922; "Books & Writing."
✤ Genie: (800) 638-963; writer's "Roundtables."
✤ Delphi: (800) 695-4005; updating its offerings.
✤ Microsoft Network: (800) 386-5550; "Journalism Forum" and others.
✤ Explore the Internet and Web for others.

Periodicals
Byline
P.O. Box 130596
Edmond, OK 73013
A monthly for writers and poets.

Children's Writer
95 Long Ridge Rd.
West Redding, CT 06896
Very good market newsletter.

The Writer
120 Boylston St.
Boston, MA 02116

Writer's Digest
1507 Dana Ave.
Cincinnati, OH 45207

Writer's Journal
27 Empire Dr.
St. Paul, MN 55103

Reference
  Gale Directory of Publications and Broadcast Media
  Gale Research
  835 Penobscot Bldg.
  Detroit, MI 48226-4094
Includes lists of magazines, newspapers, and radio and television stations located throughout the country.

Association
  Society of Children's Book Writers and Illustrators
  22736 Vanowen St., Suite 106
  West Hills, CA 91307
$50 per year. Trade association with excellent market newsletter.

≥§ 88 ≥≤

LITERARY AGENT

If you love books and reading, and can identify writing talent, you may want to consider becoming a literary agent. It goes without saying that you should have worked for a literary agency or a publisher as a reader, editor, writer, etc. You have to have both current knowledge of the market and ongoing networking contacts with editors and publishers. You must also study the market to know what publishers want.

To a writer/client, an agent is a critic, an advocate, a caretaker, a negotiator, and a business partner. Your job as an agent is to get the most money or the best deal for your client's work. You will help a client hold onto his or her rights so that he or she can get the most profits from any one piece of work.

Start-Up Costs
$5,000 to $15,000 for equipment and office set-up.

Pricing Guidelines
❖ Commissions range from 10 percent to 20 percent for domestic sales, and sometimes a little higher for foreign or dramatic sales.
❖ Additional charges: some agents charge reading fees, marketing fees, fees for expenses such as foreign postage, fax charges, long-distance phone calls, photocopying, express mail, etc. This depends on your philosophy and how you conduct your business.

Essential Equipment
❖ Computer with business and mailing software; telephone system; fax/modem, fax machine; laser printer.
❖ Contracts, files, and an office for receiving clients.

Marketing and Advertising Methods and Tips
❖ Place ads in writer's trade publications.
❖ Meet clients at writer's conferences.
❖ Get referrals from clients, agents, and publishers.
❖ Make online queries.
❖ Send notices to writer's trade associations and clubs.

Recommended Training, Experience, or Skills
❖ Education in writing, journalism, and law.
❖ Work experience in the publishing world and/or knowledge about it.
❖ Professionalism and ability to communicate well with your clients, editors, and publishers.
❖ Patience with clients and persistence with publishers.

Income Potential
$20,000 first year; $45,000 and up after established.

Best Customers
+ Publishers that are looking for your clients' type of manuscripts.
+ First-time writers looking for representation to help them get started in writing.

Helpful Tips
+ Be straightforward with your client; have contracts that clearly define what your client can expect of you and vice versa.
+ Join a professional agents' association.
+ Develop a specialty by representing certain kinds of books.
+ Study and keep abreast of the market as to the latest trends in reading and what publishers want.

For More Information
Books
How to Be a Literary Agent: An Introductory Guide to Literary Representation by Richard Mariotti and Bruce Fife. 1995, Picadilly Books, Colorado Springs, CO.
Literary Market Place. 1996, R.R. Bowker, 121 Chanlon Rd., New Providence, NJ 07974.

Periodical
Publisher's Weekly
Cahners Magazines
249 W. 17th St.
New York, NY 10011
$107 per year.

Additional Business Ideas
Book proposal consultation and writing:
Consultation: $25 to $75 per hour.
Book proposal writing: $165 to $3,000, depending how much research you have to do.

⚐ 89 ⚐
BOOKBINDING

Repairing and restoring books and bindings.

Start-Up Costs
$2,000 for basic equipment.

Pricing Guidelines
$50 and up to $500 for valuable books.

Essential Equipment
Frames, presses, papers; you have to be creative and resourceful sometimes in getting new materials to match old, damaged pages.

Marketing and Advertising Methods and Tips
* Word-of-mouth referrals.
* Letters to libraries, book collectors, shops, and museums.
* Yellow Pages advertisements.

Recommended Training, Experience, or Skills
* Take courses on bookbinding from the Guild of Book-workers. There are chapters all over the country. Send SASE to the Guild of Book Workers, Membership, 521 Fifth Ave. New York, NY 10175.
* Read books on bookbinding and then practice on old books that have no value.

Income Potential
$50 to $500 per book, $10,000 to $26,000 per year. This is more a labor of love for all the hours you can put in to one book.

Best Customers
Individual collectors, local and state libraries, museums, stores that sell old books.

Helpful Tips

❖ There are two basic categories of binding: art binding (more a creative art) and conservator binding (dealing with restoration of books, maps, plates, etc.).

❖ Take courses and workshops, and develop your own style.

❖ Practice and perfect your skill until you feel you can begin to charge for your services.

For More Information

Books

Bookbinding: A Manual of Techniques by Pamela Richmond. 1995, Trafalgar Square, North Pomfret, VT.

Bookbinding Notes: How to Repair and Rebind Paperback Books, Pamphlets, and Magazines by Robert F. Cross. 1988, Booker's, Wooster, OH.

The Business of Bookbinding by Alexander Philip. 1989, Garland Publishing, Inc., New York, NY.

Books from Dover Publications:

Basic Bookbinding by A.W. Lewis. 1957. $3.95.

The Craft of Bookbinding by Manly Banister. 1994. $7.95.

Creative Bookbinding by Pauline Johnson. 1990. $12.95.

Dover Publications, Inc.
31 East 2nd St.
Mineola, NY 11501

Add $3 (book rate) for any order (U.S. only); $4.50 UPS any order (U.S. only), Write for catalog (allow 3 to 4 weeks).

Books from The Spoon River Press:

Bookbinding and the Care of Books, 4th ed., by Douglas Cockerell. 1920.

Japanese Bookbinding: Instructions from a Master Craftsman by Kojiro Ikegami. 1986.

The Spoon River Press
2319-C West Rohmann
Peoria, IL 61604

Write for catalog.

Additional Business Ideas
Paper conservation: restoring and preserving old documents.

≥ 90 ≤
INDEPENDENT PUBLISHING

Independent publishing encompasses everything from self-publishing and desktop publishing to publishing newsletters, magazines, small books, simple how-to booklets, manuals, reports, and directories. The main considerations are: know the audience for whom you are writing and what they want to know, and get them to know that you have this information and how they can purchase it.

Many writers prefer this method instead of contacting a major publisher because they feel that they have full control of what they write and sell. By thoroughly researching and reading about this independent industry, you can be successful in your own publishing ventures. The following information represents an average of all the above-mentioned independent publishing ventures.

Start-Up Costs
✤ $3,000 to $25,000

Pricing Guidelines
✤ The going rates of publications similar to yours.
✤ Desktop publishing: $25 to $90 per hour, depending on whether there is color work, etc.

Essential Equipment
✤ A computer with word processing, desktop publishing, and mailing software; fax/modem; printer (high dpi), scanner, copier, etc.; telephone system.
✤ Promotional materials.

Marketing and Advertising Methods and Tips
❖ Advertisements: in trade publications and category-specific magazines (don't pay for advertising until you have exhausted "freebies").
❖ Press releases.
❖ Booths at bookseller conventions.
❖ Attending writer's conferences.

Recommended Training, Experience, or Skills
❖ Work experience, education, and training in writing, journalism, publishing, marketing, etc.
❖ Expertise in your topic from experience and/or training.
❖ Experience in book sales and publishing is helpful.
❖ Courses and seminars in the publishing methods you plan to use.

Income Potential
Varies with the demand for your books. As much as $50,000 to $100,000 per book.

Best Customers
There is a demand for "niche" books, such as children's, singles, or hobbyists, and for nonfiction.

Helpful Tips
❖ Don't work with other self-publishers.
❖ Make your book look as professional as possible.
❖ Write for a specific market.
❖ Don't attempt to publish until you know the business well. Study, attend workshops, books, etc.

For More Information
Associations
American Booksellers Association (ABA)
828 S. Broadway
Tarrytown, NY 10592
Write for convention information.

Magazine Publishers of America
919 Third Ave., 22nd Floor
New York, NY 10022
Send SASE for membership information and requirements.

The National Association of Desktop Publishers
462 Old Boston St.
Topsfield, MA 01983
Membership: $95 per year; $48 per year for subscription to monthly magazine. Does not have start-up information.

National Association of Independent Publishers
P.O. Box 430
Highland City, FL 33846-0430
E-mail: NAIP@aol.com
Geared to the beginning publisher. Membership: $75 per year, $40 subscription to newsletter only; a sample can be obtained upon request; send SASE.

Newsletter Publishers Association
1401 Wilson Blvd., Suite 207
Arlington, VA 22209
$395 membership includes discounts on insurance, supplies, newsletter, and the books *How to Launch a Newsletter* and *Success in Newsletter Publishing*, plus a current directory of members and industry suppliers.

Books

Bookselling: How to Know Your Target Audience, Plan Special Sales Strategies and Develop Flexible Marketing Methods. David C. Cook Foundation, 1993, Elgin, IL.

The Copyright Handbook by Attorney Stephen Fishman. 1996, Nolo Press, Berkeley, CA.

For All the Write Reasons by Patricia C. Gallagher. 1992, Young Sparrow Press, Worcester, PA. Order from Patricia Gallagher, Box 555 PG, Worcester, PA 19490; $24.96 + $3 for shipping and handling (PA add 6% tax). Account of various authors' publishing experience, plus good self-publishing information.

How to Write a Manual by Elizabeth Slatkin. 1991, Ten Speed Press, Berkeley, CA.

The Magazine: Everything You Need to Know to Make it in the Magazine Business by Leonard Mogel. Globe Pequot Press, Old Saybrook, CT.

Newsletter Sourcebook by March Beach. 1993, Writer's Digest Books, Cincinnati, OH.

Self-Publishing, 3rd ed. by Tom and Marilyn Ross. 1994, Writer's Digest Books, Cincinnati, OH.

The Upstart Guide to Owning & Managing a Desktop Publishing Business by Dan Ramsey. 1994, Upstart Publishing, Dover, NH.

101 Ways to Market Your Books by John Kremer. 1993, Open Horizons, P.O. Box 205, Fairfield, IA 52556-0205.

Communicators Bookstore
Hudson Associates
44 W. Market St.
P.O. Box 311
Rhinebeck, NY 12572
Many books on newsletters; write for catalog.

Reference Books
(Check library reference sections.)

Books & Magazines: A Guide to Publishing & Bookselling Courses in the U.S. 1991, Peterson's/Pacesetter Books, Peterson's Guides, P.O. Box 2123, Princeton, NJ 08543-2123.

Literary Market Place. R.R. Bowker, 121 Chanlon Rd., New Providence, NJ 07974.

Newsletters in Print, Gale Research, Detroit, MI.

National Directory of Magazines, Gale Research, Detroit, MI.

Business Guides
Entrepreneur's Start-Up Publishing Guides, "Desktop Publishing," "Newsletter Publishing." (800) 421-2300; $69.50 each plus $6.75 shipping.

National Business Library's Start-Up Guides, "Desk Top Publishing," "Newsletter Publishing." (800) 947-7724; $39.95 each plus $5 shipping.

Distance Education/Correspondence Courses
Distance Education and Training Council
1601 18th St. NW
Washington, DC 20009-2529
Send SASE for a listing of home-study schools.

Periodicals and Publications
Desktop Publishers Journal
462 Boston St.
Topsfield, MA 01983-9914

Publisher's Weekly
249 W. 17th St.
New York, NY 10011
The primary book-trade magazine that regularly tracks book expos, shows, conferences, fairs, and other industry news.

Small Press
Kymbolde Way
Wakefield, RI 02879-1915
A magazine for independent publishers. Published quarterly; send SASE for subscription information.

Report
How to Make Money with Information Marketing. Better Life Publishing, 3002 Penna Ave., Charleston, WV 25302. $3; request by title.

Resource Guide
Resource Guide for Publishers. $5 for printed version; $7 on $3\frac{1}{2}$-inch disk in Word format; send SASE for more information to The Small Business Advisor, Box 579, Great Falls, VA 22066.

Desktop Publishing Software
* Adobe Systems: (415) 961-4400.
* Corel: (800) 772-6735.
* Microsoft: (206) 882-8080.
* Serif: (603) 889-8650.

Additional Business Ideas
* Personalized children's books:
  "Personalized Children's Books on Your Home Computer"
  Hefty Publishing Co.
  1232 Paula Circle
  Gulf Breeze, FL 32561
  Write for costs and information.
* Selling specialty and/or how-to books by mail (see "Mail Order" resources, in "General Resources").
* Directory publisher: Arts & Crafts, Women's Businesses, etc.

ᴇ 91 ᴇ
GRANT PROPOSAL WRITING

Every year, private foundations, government agencies, and business interests give away millions of dollars in the form of grants. The federal government and U.S. businesses spend billions of dollars to purchase services and products through competitive bids. Many organizations—a number of them community action and service groups—do not have the time, know-how, or staff to apply for these grants. Many groups are not even aware of the grant opportunities that are available.

As a grant writer, you would make sure your client is hired (if it is a job for bidding) or receives the funding needed for a specific project. Your role is to convince an agency that your client can solve its problems (in the case of being hired) or can help improve society (as with a grant to open a homeless shelter, etc.).

If you have been involved in writing grants and have strong writing, communication, and verbal skills, you may find this an interesting and a rewarding venture.

Start-Up Costs
$1,000 to $4,000

Pricing Guidelines
It is recommended that you offer your services on a flat-fee basis, based on the hours you estimate the proposal will take you to complete. For example, if you estimate that a proposal will take 40 hours and your rate is $60 an hour, you would charge a flat fee of $2,400.

Essential Equipment
Current computer equipment with accounting, word processing, and spreadsheet software; fax/modem, copier, separate fax, telephone system.

Marketing and Advertising Methods and Tips
❖ Get referrals to other foundations and/or businesses based on the volunteer grant work you have already performed.
❖ Search for grants that may apply to a certain group or business, notify the group of the grant's existence, and offer to write a proposal.

Recommended Training, Experience, or Skills
❖ Volunteer with a nonprofit agency helping to apply for grants, or work with an agency that provides grant-writing services.
❖ Read copies of successful grant applications.
❖ Be able to understand a group's or business' purpose in applying for a grant, and be able to communicate that purpose effectively in the proposal you write.

Income Potential
$25,000 to $40,000 per year; can realize a profit within two years.

Best Customers

❖ Nonprofit groups and organizations (look in the telephone book and read local papers for listings of nonprofit groups).
❖ Public and private schools.
❖ Centers for persons with mental disabilities.
❖ Shelters for the homeless or abused.
❖ Business advising groups for minorities.
❖ Senior citizen centers.
❖ Small businesses seeking government contracts.

Helpful Tips

❖ Concentrate in an area with which you are familiar and which you support.
❖ Make the proposal stand out from others.
❖ Understand the area in which you are writing.
❖ Adhere to deadlines.
❖ Make sure you go over the final draft with the organization with which you are working.
❖ Understand the terminology and the questions asked so that you can be specific in your answers.

For More Information

Books

The Consultant's Guide to Proposal Writing: How to Satisfy Your Client and Double Your Income, 2nd ed., by Herman Holtz. 1990, John Wiley & Sons, Inc., New York, NY.

Government Contracts, Proposalmanship, and Winning Strategies by Herman Holtz. 1988, Plenum Publishing, New York, NY.

What It Takes to Write a Winning Grant Proposal by Lynnette R. Porter and William O. Coggin. 1993, American Vision Publishing, Inc., Findlay, OH.

CD-ROM

Grants on Disc, Detroit, MI; electronic access to more than 300,000 cash grants available four times a year (for a total of $120,000 per year). Find out if it is available at a large public or college library near you, or call (800) 877-GALE.

Other reference sources
Available at some large public and college libraries:
+ *Federal Domestic Assistance*
+ *Foundation Directory*
+ *Federal Registry*

Additional Business Ideas
Write complaint letters for consumers:
Consumer's Information Center
Pueblo, CO 81009
Write for a free copy of the *Consumer's Resource Handbook,* which includes addresses and 800 numbers of major companies and Better Business Bureaus, and tips on how to write a consumer complaint letter.

ᓆ 92 ᕁ
LANGUAGE TRANSLATION SERVICE

A translation service provides people who are fluent in foreign languages for the purpose of translation and communication in correspondence, publications, business conferences and meetings, sales literature, technical manuals and interpretation, legal documents and court appearances, and so on. You can work on your own, especially if you are fluent in more than one language, or you can hire others, covering a wider range of languages and clients.

Start-Up Costs
+ $12,000 to $25,000 for a high-end start-up.
+ $5,000 to $11,000 low-end start-up.

Pricing Guidelines
Payment is by the word.

Essential Equipment

* Computer with business-related software; fax/modem; copier, telephone system; dictaphone.
* Business cards.

Marketing and Advertising Methods and Tips

* Research what businesses in your area do business with foreign companies, and contact them about your services.
* Place ads and articles in business publications.
* Get word-of-mouth referrals.
* Have a listing in a translation directory.

Recommended Training, Experience, or Skills

* Gain knowledge, education, and training in one or more foreign languages.
* Work for a translation services agency or as a volunteer for nonprofit agencies.
* Preferably, have some background in the businesses and agencies that contract for your service so that you can translate into the correct terminology.
* If possible, take specialization courses in medical, legal, and technical areas in your language specialty, to be able to concentrate in specific areas of business.

Income Potential

$50,000 to $90,000 per year.

Best Customers

Local governments, businesses, institutions, law firms, hotels, large retail stores.

Helpful Tips

* It is beneficial also to have an area of specialization, such as law or business.
* It is helpful to have additional office skills such as typing, proofreading, typesetting, and transcribing.
* You will need a high level of proficiency in a foreign language.

Franchises, Distributorships, and Licenses
Berlitz International, Inc.
Worldwide Headquarters
400 Alexander Park
Princeton, NJ 08540-6306
Language instruction, publications, and translations. Write for information.

For More Information
Books
Basic Concepts & Models for Interpreter & Translation Training, 2nd ed., by Daniel Giel. 1995, John Benjamins North America, Inc., Philadelphia, PA.
Guide for Translators, 2nd ed., by Morry Sofer. 1995. Schrieber Publishing, Rockville, MD.
A Practical Guide for Translators, 2nd ed., by Geoffrey Samuelson-Brown. 1995, Taylor and Francis, Inc., Bristol, PA.

Business Guide
Entrepreneur's Start-Up Business Guide, "Language Translation Service." (800) 421-2300; $69.50 plus shipping.

Directory
The Translation Services Directory,
American Translators Association
1800 Diagonal Rd., Suite 220
Alexandria, VA 22314
There are certain requirements for being listed as a translator such as passing accreditation exams or demonstrating your expertise through your work experience. Send a large SASE for information.

Additional Business Ideas
❖ Court interpreter/translator
❖ Sign language interpreter

◄ 93 ►

PUBLIC RELATIONS WRITING

The Bureau of Labor statistics projects a 40 percent increase in the number of public relations specialists beyond the year 2000. Public relations writing is a combination of journalism and advertising. A public relations specialist's job is to promote the merits and qualities of the individuals, businesses, and/or agencies it represents. A public relations writer helps to organize and write the copy for promotional literature—brochures, newsletters, feature articles, personal profiles, press releases, annual reports—that make the public aware of her client's services.

If you have an advertising and/or business background and you are skilled in writing and communications, you may want to investigate being a public relations writer.

Start-Up Costs
$4,000 to $12,000

Pricing Guidelines
✤ Public relations for businesses: $200 to $600 per day plus expenses; $1,800 per day for large corporations.
✤ Public relations for nonprofit or small groups: $100 to $500 monthly retainer.
✤ Public relations for libraries and schools: $15 to $25 per hour.

Essential Equipment
✤ Office equipment: computer with hard drive, fax/modem, and business-related and desktop publishing software; telephone system with attachments (headsets, fax machine, recorder); copier.
✤ Office set-up; reference books and industry books

Marketing and Advertising Methods and Tips
✤ Direct mail your brochure and literature to companies and institutions; make follow-up calls and visits.

* Volunteer work for politicians and fund-raising events.
* Networking in your trade and business associations.
* Referrals to other firms from your satisfied customers.

Recommended Training, Experience, or Skills
* Advertising writing, newspaper work, and business writing experience.
* Education in journalism, advertising, and English.
* Sales experience.
* Knowledge in the industry for which you are writing.
* Personal characteristics: drive, enthusiasm, energy, persistence, self-assurance, creative flair.
* Good people skills; a memory for names and networking contacts.

Income Potential
* $600 to $1,000 a day or per project.
* $30,000 to $70,000 per year or more.

Best Customers
* Businesses in your field of specialization that do not have a public relations department.
* Nonprofit groups.
* Private and public schools.
* Countywide library systems.
* Museums.
* Hospitals.
* State and local politicians.

Helpful Tips
* Work in one or more public relations firms or volunteer to help with promotions for community events, to give you experience and help you decide which kind of public relations you like best.
* Be professional at all times, and be constantly looking for work or projects.

For More Information
Books
The Public Relations Writer's Handbook by Merry Aronson and Dan Spetner. 1993, Lexington Books (Macmillan), New York, NY.

Six Steps to Free Publicity: And Other Ways to Win Free Media Attention for You or Your Business by Marcia Yudkin. 1995, Plume/Penguin, New York, NY.

Business Guide
Entrepreneur's Business Start-Up Guide, "Public Relations Agency." (800) 421-2300; $69.50 plus shipping.

Online
CompuServe: (800) 336-6823; various writers' forums, including "PR and Marketing Forum" for those interested in corporate writing.

Association
Public Relations Society of America
33 Irving Place, Third Floor
New York, NY 10003-2376
Send SASE for membership information.

Additional Business Ideas
✦ Political writing: speeches, press releases, brochures, candidates' profiles.
✦ Fund-raising specialist:
   The Complete Book of Fund-Raising by Don Fey. 1995, Morris-Lee Publishing Group, New York, NY.

⚜ 94 ⚜
TYPESETTING

A typesetter uses computers, scanners, design software, etc. to prepare professional-looking printed materials for clients without the need of paste-up and typesetting that printers once needed. It eliminates costly design, typesetting, and mechanical charges. It involves high-resolution scanning of logos, photographs, and anything else that is needed. The scans are then placed on disk, SyQuest cartridge, or CD-ROM and given to the client, who can take them directly to a printer.

Other services that can be offered in a typesetting business are design, printing, photography, signs, silk screening, and more. This business is ideal to run from a home or small office, and offers a considerable savings for businesses with printing and design needs.

Start-Up Costs
* $8,000 to $20,000
* One typesetter recommends that you buy only the equipment you need to get started, and add pieces only when the work is there to warrant the purchase.
* Another option is to start this business part-time while holding another job until the new business grows enough to stand on its own.

Pricing Guidelines
* Do your research and call local companies in the same line of business to ask for pricing; compare with yours and make sure you are competitive.
* $7.50 for a simple scan, more for more complex designs.
* $30 for a color screen for silk screening.
* $25 to $90 per hour for other services (depending on the going rates), or by the job.

Essential Equipment
* A computer with large hard drive and a full-page monitor.
* A high-resolution printer, color scanner, and high-resolution color laser printer.
* Fax machine; telephone system.
* Promotional materials: business cards, brochures, and samples of designs.

Marketing and Advertising Methods and Tips
❖ Advertise: Yellow Pages ad; display ads in local papers several times a year, especially any business feature issues; write your own promotional article.
❖ Begin by building a good reputation to gain word-of-mouth referrals.
❖ Investigate developing a Web page on the Internet.
❖ Donate your services to local functions: community days, senior center events, etc.; it is a great way to get your name out.
❖ Offer incentives to get repeat customers (e.g., 10 percent off the client's next bill for any referrals).

Recommended Training, Experience, or Skills
❖ Training and education in computers, graphic design, desktop publishing and printing, typesetting, layout, and printing operations. Enroll in college, vocational-technical schools, or art schools.
❖ Work experience with a printer or other related business.

Income Potential
$25,000 to $45,000 per year

Best Customers
❖ Advertising agencies.
❖ New businesses for start-up promotions.
❖ Schools for public relations materials, yearbooks, calendars.
❖ Established businesses for design of direct-mail promotions.

Helpful Tips
❖ Target your market, then send personalized mailings that are signed by you. Hand-address the envelopes; they have a five times greater chance of being opened!
❖ Plan software/hardware purchases carefully and investigate when upgrades will be available so that you do not buy a "leftover." Find the software and hardware that you

like, then contact the company directly to ask them about new products, upgrades, recommendations.

❖ Keep up on current developments.

❖ Have a backup plan—especially if you are the sole proprietor—and network with similar businesses in the event that you are unable to meet a deadline or become overwhelmed with work and need their help. Customers in the printing industry do not like excuses for why a deadline was not met.

❖ If you do a project for an annual event (e.g. a school yearbook), make a note of the date so that you can ask them in advance for repeat business.

For More Information
Books
Type and Typography: The Designer's Type Book by Ben Rosen. 1989, Van Nostrand Reinhold, New York, NY.
From North Light Books, Cincinnati, OH:
Great Type & Lettering Designs by David Brier. 1992.
Typographics 1 by Roger Walton. 1995.

Additional Business Ideas
See also "Graphic Design."

≥ 95 ≤
COPYWRITING

Copywriting is writing meant to sell a product, service, or idea. It explains to potential customers how an item or service will be of benefit to their lives if they purchase it. Everyone defines life according to his or her needs. If you, as a copywriter, can make the customer realize how the product or service will help make them smarter, make their lives easier, save them money, etc., so that they buy it over another brand or service, then you will be a successful copywriter. A copywriter also has the obligation to do this at the best price for her client.

Copywriters generally specialize in a particular industry and will write copy for ads, brochures, product literature, scripts, booklets, and a variety of other promotional materials. Freelancing can be lucrative, but it will take some time to build up your client base for a business. It is a competitive industry, but if you like creative and challenging writing, being a freelance copywriter may be a venture for you.

Start-Up Costs
$3,000 to $10,000

Pricing Guidelines
* For brochures: $30 to $700 per published page, or a flat fee per project.
* For advertising: $25 to $80 per hour, depending on your experience and the demand for your services.

Essential Equipment
* Computer system with fax/modem, hard drive, and word processing and desktop publishing software; copier, telephone system, separate fax machine and telephone line; trade and industry directories, reference books.
* Promotional materials: samples of your work, business cards, brochures.

Marketing and Advertising Methods and Tips
* Direct mail to the advertising departments of the industry you wish to target, followed up by telephone calls and visits.
* Samples of your work.
* Referrals from satisfied clients.
* Articles in trade publications.
* Networking at trade shows and business conferences.

Recommended Training, Experience, or Skills
* Acquire training and education in journalism or advertising.
* Take courses at local colleges in copywriting, business management, and desktop publishing.

❖ Work in an advertising department for a company, writing copy.

❖ Volunteer to write promotional materials for fund-raising events for nonprofit groups.

Income Potential
$20,000 to $25,000 as you start out; double or triple that amount eventually, depending on how long it takes you to build a reputation and a steady client base.

Best Customers
❖ Businesses selling products or services to consumers or other businesses.

❖ Professionals who want to expand their practices.

❖ Retail stores.

❖ Institutions.

❖ Home-based businesses and small businesses that need publicity to expand.

❖ Organizations that want copy explaining who they are, what they do, and their future goals.

Helpful Tips
❖ If the product or service is new, your copywriting must explain it so that the customer will understand how it will be beneficial to him or her.

❖ If the product is new, your copywriting should also explain how it is better than the "older" product.

❖ Your copywriting should appeal to the emotional motivations of the targeted customer.

❖ Specialize and write copy for an industry that appeals to you and in which you have some knowledge and experience.

For More Information
Books
The Copywriter's Handbook, updated ed., by Robert Bly. 1990, Henry Holt and Company, New York, NY.

Write Great Ads: A Step-by-Step Approach by Erica Levy Klein. 1990, John Wiley & Sons, Inc., New York, NY.

Additional Business Ideas
✤ Freelance copy editing, editing, and proofreading:

Association
Editorial Freelancer's Association
71 W. 23rd St., Suite 1504
New York, NY 10010
Send SASE for membership information and a publications list.

Books
How to Make $50,000 A Year or More as a Freelance Business Writer by Paul D. Davis. 1992, Prima Publishing, Rocklin, CA.

Handbook for Proofreading by Laura K. Anderson. 1994, N T C Publishing, Lincolnwood, IL.

Proofreading by Souder. 1995, Houghton-Mifflin Company, Boston, MA.

Periodical
✤ Professional reader:
  Reading for a Living: How to Be a Professional Story Analyst for Film & Television by T.L. Katahn. 1990, Blue Arrow Books, Pacific Palisades, CA.
✤ Technical writing:
  Writing High-Tech Copy That Sells by Janice King. 1996, John Wiley & Sons, Inc., New York, NY.

◣ 96 ◢

FACT FINDER

A fact finder is an information specialist or broker who can find facts, data, etc. online and via other sources, and compile it in such a way as to be useful for the customer's purposes. You are selling your knowledge and your time, but you need marketing and business management skills, or your business will not succeed.

Start-Up Costs
$5,000 to $13,000

Pricing Guidelines
❖ Rates range from $25 per hour to $100 per hour and more, giving your customers an estimate of the total cost. Your prices will vary per project depending on whether you are finding facts as they exist, or if you are analyzing the facts and compiling them into a report.
❖ Some charge extra for copies, etc.
❖ Compare prices with other information specialists and look at the recommendations listed in industry trade books.

Essential Equipment
❖ A computer with a hard drive, fax/modem (high speed), printer, and bookkeeping, billing, and word processing software; fax machine, telephone system.
❖ Promotional materials: business cards, brochures.
❖ Report folders.

Marketing and Advertising Methods and Tips
❖ Network with other information specialists in your industry.
❖ Get word-of-mouth referrals from satisfied clients.
❖ Place ads in trade publications of the industry in which you specialize.

* Give workshops and talks at business conferences in the information field.
* Join professional and trade associations to stay current with both your trade and specialty.

Recommended Training, Experience, or Skills
* Gain computer skills and familiarity with databases that can supply you with specialized information for your service.
* Know how to do research using other sources; take courses at local colleges if you feel you need more training.
* Do free searches and reports for business friends or family to get experience at finding the information.

Income Potential
* $20,000 to $80,000 per year, depending on the growth of your business. Much of your business will come from word-of-mouth referrals.
* Keep good business records to check regularly from where your business is coming, and which sources are not as profitable.

Best Customers
* Businesses and individuals who need your kind of specialized information.
* Institutions and foundations needing help in locating information sources.
* Companies that do not have in-house research departments.

Helpful Tips
* Anyone can take information off a computer. An information broker must know how to gather, analyze, and interpret the information gathered, and tailor it to the needs of her customer.
* Do some market research in your community to see if there is a market close to home and if you need to "educate" your community through talks and articles about

how an information specialist can be useful to their lives or their businesses.

❖ Send evaluation sheets to customers to see if your information was helpful to them and in what ways the information was used.

For More Information
Also see "For More Information," in "Clipping Service," and "Medical Businesses."

Associations
Association of Independent Information Professionals
245 Fifth Ave., Suite 2103
New York, NY 10016
For professional information specialists. Send SASE for membership information.

Alliance of Information and Referral Systems (AIRS)
P.O. Box 3546
Joliet, IL 60434
This "is a service that helps people in need find the (human) services that can best alleviate or eliminate that need." Members are agencies and human service professionals. Write for more information if this is your profession.

Books
Find It Fast by Robert I. Berkman. 1993, HarperCollins Publications, New York, NY.

Find It Online by Robert I. Berkman. 1994, TAB Books, Blue Ridge Summit, PA.

Freelance: Research for Pay by BevAnne Ross. 1992, BAR Publications, Novato, CA.

Information Broker's Handbook by Sue Rugge with Alfred Glossbrenner. 1995, The McGraw-Hill Companies, New York, NY.

Information for Sale by John H. Everett and Elizabeth P. Crow. 1994, The McGraw-Hill Companies, New York, NY.

Researching on the Internet: The Complete Guide to Finding, Evaluating, and Organizing Information Effectively by Robin Rowland and Dave Kinnaman. 1995, Prima Publishing, Rocklin, CA.

Business Guides
Entrepreneur's Small Business Start-Up Guide, "Information Broker." (800) 421-2300; $69.50 plus shipping.
National Business Library's Start-Up Guide, "Information Broker." (800) 947-7742; $39.95 plus shipping.

Online
> Dow Jones & Company, Inc.
> Business Information Services
> P.O. Box 300
> Princeton, NJ 08543-0300
> Write for information.

Additional Business Ideas
Professional finder: a professional finder matches qualified buyers with qualified sellers, or the reverse, for a fee.

> "Finder's Fees—The Easiest Money You'll Ever Make"
> Philander Co.
> P.O. Box 5385
> Cleveland, TN 37320
An information course available for $100 plus $5 shipping and handling.

Also see "Clipping Service," in "Business Services."

≈ 97 ≈

REAL ESTATE BROCHURE WRITER

This type of business assists real estate agencies and individual brokers in preparing their brochures and sales literature for the houses and properties they have for sale.

Start-Up Costs
3,000 to $10,000

Pricing Guidelines
$20 to $600 per published page, or $100 to $500 or more per project.

Essential Equipment
✤ Computer, copier (multi-functional), fax machine on separate line.
✤ Scanner, graphics tools.
✤ Desktop publishing software and multi-faceted graphics program.
✤ Clip-art packages.

Marketing and Advertising Methods and Tips
✤ When the opportunity arises, offer your services for free to make contacts (but only to a point!).
✤ Join local service clubs.
✤ Do a direct mailing followed by visits with samples.
✤ Get word-of-mouth referrals.

Recommended Training, Experience, or Skills
✤ Take basic writing, marketing, desktop publishing, and art courses.
✤ Freelance for publications in their real estate advertising departments.
✤ Subscribe to trade publications to stay current.

Income Potential
$15,000 part-time; $30,000 to $50,000 full-time.

Best Customers
Real estate agencies, small builders, insurance agents, local restaurants, retailers.

Helpful Tips

❖ Be creative; do not copy. Compare with other similar services, but be sure to find your own "space," style, niche.

❖ Watch the competition to see what is missing and fill the gap.

❖ Read and study real estate books, newspapers, and your own mail. PC magazines and technique publications are very helpful, as they regularly review the latest software and technology.

❖ Use your own imagination and draw from past educational and business experiences.

For More Information
See also "Graphic Designer" in "Creative Businesses."

ADDITIONAL BUSINESSES INVOLVING WORDS

❖ Book reviewer
❖ Columnist
❖ Custom poems for all occasions
❖ Indexing
❖ Scriptwriter
❖ Scriptwriter for audio-visual productions
❖ Lists of many ways to earn money, and suggested rates to charge, are listed in the introductory pages of every *Writer's Market* (see "Businesses Involving Words: General Resources," above).

Miscellaneous
Businesses

◢ 98 ◣
SOAP MAKING

People concerned with protecting the environment and with
chemicals in commercial products are always looking for alternative natural products. Soap making, once a common household chore, has experienced a resurgence in popularity recently
with handmade soaps. Soap makers enjoy experimenting with
different recipes using natural oils and fragrances and coming
up with a variety of soaps that can appeal to everyone.

You can start by making soap in your own kitchen or
workshop, and then decide if this is a business you would
like to start. You need to find out what other kinds of handmade soaps are being sold, and then develop your own line
and market.

Start-Up Costs
$300 to $700; more if you purchase a computer to do bookkeeping and mail-order.

Pricing Guidelines
$3 to $4 for a three-ounce bar of soap; $7 for animal-shaped soaps; $12 for a soap-making kit.

Essential Equipment
❖ Stainless steel kettles, scales, lye, oils, fragrances, wooden stirrers, thermometer, coloring agent, decorative labels and wrappers, rubber gloves, apron, tallow, plastic wrap, other miscellaneous supplies; order forms.
❖ Promotional materials: business cards, flyers, brochures.

Marketing and Advertising Methods and Tips
❖ Advertise in women's and country magazines, newspapers.
❖ Exhibit at craft shows, fairs, and trade shows.
❖ Give soap-making demonstrations at folk festivals.
❖ Get word-of-mouth referrals.
❖ Print brochures and flyers.
❖ Sell through catalogs.
❖ Give samples to gift shops.
❖ Teach a soap-making course through a continuing education program.
❖ Direct mail new products to previous customers (develop your mailing list at shows).

Recommended Training, Experience, or Skills
❖ Take continuing education courses.
❖ Contact your local USDA extension service to find out if they offer pamphlets or reference books.
❖ Take lessons.
❖ Find the right combinations and recipes by trial and error.
❖ Have a knowledge of herbs, oils, and fragrances.

Income Potential
❖ $12,000 to $60,000 per year.
❖ $1,000 a day at some craft shows and fairs.

Best Customers
+ Boutiques and gift shops.
+ Organic product or "natural" product stores.
+ Specialty catalogs.
+ Country inns and bed-and-breakfast inns.
+ Spas, health clubs, facialists, beauticians.
+ Antique shops.

Helpful Tips
+ Research the kinds of handmade soaps on the market.
+ Test market your soaps to see what sells and who is buying.
+ Have appealing and interesting designs and promotional literature to give out to your customers. Tell a "story" of the soap-making process on your label or tag.
+ Keep looking for markets for your soaps.
+ Make and sell related products: lotions, shampoos (check with your USDA extension office to see about labeling ingredients or other licenses or restrictions you need or adhere to).

For More Information
(See also "Arts and Handcrafts Businesses: General Resources".)

Books
The Complete Soapmaker: Tips, Techniques, and Recipes for Luxurious Handmade Soaps by Norma Coney. 1996, Sterling Publishing Co., New York, NY.

The Natural Soap Book: Making Herbal and Vegetable Soaps by Susan Miller Cavitch. Order from Storey's How-To Books for Country Living, Schoolhouse Rd., Pownal, VT 05261.

Soap: Making It, Enjoying It by Ann Bramson. 1975, Workman Publishing Co., Inc., New York, NY.

Additional Business Ideas
+ Aromatherapy products: Aromatherapy means healing through scent. Originating in France in the 1920s, aroma-

therapy is a form of alternative medicine used to treat such ailments as headaches, stomach disorders, fatigue, depression, colds, and other problems. People in our country use it to reduce stress and improve their general feeling of well-being. If you are interested in learning more about this fast-growing movement, here are some helpful resources for you.

People who are making money with aromatherapy are those who: make fragranced products to sell to individuals, retailers, health clubs, and by mail-order; give aromatherapy massage treatments; conduct seminars and courses; and publish books, newsletters, etc.

Association
National Association for Holistic Aromatherapy
P.O. Box 17622
Boulder, CO 80308-7622
A nonprofit organization not associated with any business interest. Membership benefits include quarterly newsletter, listings of aromatherapy sources, conference, and trade show. You can purchase several books on aromatherapy. Send a long, self-addressed envelope with two first-class stamps on it for membership information.

Books
Aromatherapy for Health Professionals by Len and Shirley Price. 1995, Churchill Livingstone, Inc., New York, NY.

Aromatherapy Plants and Oils: The Encyclopedia of How They Help You by Daniele Ryan. 1993, Bantam Books, Inc., New York, NY.

The Essential Aromatherapy Kit: A Full-Color Guide to Using Essential Oils for Health, Relaxation, and Pleasure by Carole McGilvery and Jimi Reed. 1995, Anness Publishing Ltd., New York, NY.

❖ Making your own perfumes:

The Essential Oils Book: Creating Personal Blends for Mind & Body by Colleen K. Dodt. 1996, Storey Communications, Pownal, VT.

Personalized Perfumes by Gail Duff. 1994, Simon & Schuster, New York, NY.

⚜ 99 ⚜
COLLECTIBLES SPECIALIST

If you have a knowledge of valuable collectibles—dolls, toys, baseball cards, coins, stamps, historical papers—you can earn money buying and selling these collector's items. One woman has an entire shop filled with old buttons, while another travels to England and other countries to buy vintage linens that she sells in her shop. People in this business say that you have to have a passionate interest in what you collect to succeed.

Start-Up Costs
$10,000 to $32,000

Pricing Guidelines
+ Refer to antique and collectibles publications and price guides.
+ Check with other collectibles specialists and brokers in the country for pricing updates.
+ Prices of some collectibles can change with fads and popularity, while others are more constant.

Essential Equipment
+ A computer for inventory, a modem for online searches; fax machine, copier, telephone system.
+ Storage and shelves; alarm system; packaging and mailing materials.
+ Liability insurance; business cards, flyers.
+ Subscriptions to antique and collectibles publications.

❖ A vehicle for traveling.
❖ Reference books and price guides.

Marketing and Advertising Methods and Tips
❖ Advertise in trade publications related to your collectibles, in antique and collectible publications, and in the "wanted" sections of local newspapers.
❖ Exhibit at trade and collectible shows
❖ Network with other collectibles brokers.
❖ Teach a course on collecting or write a column in a local paper.

Recommended Training, Experience, or Skills
Comprehensive knowledge of your specialty collectibles and the markets for selling them.

Income Potential
❖ You can start part-time in your free time, and then go full-time when your business demands it.
❖ Part-time: $10,000 to $20,000 per year.
❖ Full-time: $60,000 to $80,000 per year.

Best Customers
Other collectibles specialists and brokers, auctions, antique shops, individual collectors and antique lovers.

Helpful Tips
❖ This is an ongoing business involving traveling and searching your neighborhood, state, country and even overseas if you can afford it and your business demands it.
❖ It is easy just to start in your area going to flea markets, auctions, rummage sales, and thrift shops.

For More Information
Books
The Rummager's Handbook: Finding, Buying, Cleaning, Fixing, Using & Selling Second-hand Treasures by R.S. McClurg. 1995, Storey Communications, Inc., Pownal, VT.

Selling Your Stuff: From Tiddleywinks to Diamonds by Jeanne Sigel. 1996, Bonus Books, Inc., Chicago, IL.

Business Guides
Entrepreneur's Start-Up Business Guide, "Collectibles Broker." (800) 421-2300; $69.50 plus shipping.
National Business Library's Start-Up Business Guide, "Collectible Store." (800) 947-7724; $39.95 plus $5 shipping.

Additional Business Ideas
❖ Finding classic cars for collectors
❖ Buying and selling old records
❖ Repairing collectibles

≤ 100 ≥
GRAPHOLOGIST/HANDWRITING ANALYST

According to the American Association of Handwriting Analysts, "Handwriting is also called brainwriting." Graphology is the study of the complex act of handwriting and how it relates to the personality of the writer. Graphologists analyze handwriting to determine personality characteristics to assist in counseling, teaching, personnel decisions, medical and psychological profiles, and criminal rehabilitation. There are two types of analysts: questioned document examiners, who examine for forgeries, anonymous letters, etc.; and analysts, who do personality profiles.

Start-Up Costs
$500 to $2,000 for courses, seminars, and business cards.

Pricing Guidelines
❖ $25 to $250 for an analysis, depending on the clientele.
❖ Questioned document examiners and personnel screening graphologists fare best.

Essential Equipment
❖ Telephone system, fax machine, copier; typewriter, word processor, or computer with word processing software.
❖ Business cards, brochures, reference books from accredited courses.

Marketing and Advertising Methods and Tips
❖ Ads in the Yellow Pages and local and business newspapers, publications.
❖ Community presentations.
❖ Word-of-mouth referrals.
❖ Direct mail to law firms and businesses.

Recommended Training, Experience, or Skills
❖ Attend accredited courses (see "Schools," below), seminars, and correspondence courses. The National Society of Graphology recommends at least three years of training to be competent in the field.
❖ Join a professional society or association and study with a highly qualified teacher.

Income Potential
$25,000 to $100,000 per year working full-time in a medium or large-sized city; income depends on experience, number of contacts, etc.

Best Customers
❖ Attorneys; courts for help in jury selection.
❖ Businesses for personnel handwriting analysis.
❖ Job counselors for vocational guidance.
❖ Individuals wanting to know about a future spouse.
❖ A person wanting to know their hidden talents.

Helpful Tips
❖ Graphology requires concentrated study and practice. You should take accredited courses with qualified teachers.

❖ Adhere to the profession's code of ethics. Graphology is a respected profession and not to be associated with psychics or the occult.
❖ Strive to build up your reputation for professional work.

For More Information
Associations
American Association of Handwriting Analysts (AAHA)
820 W. Maple St.
Hinsdale, IL 60521
A nonprofit association of graphologists for novices and advanced. Newsletter, information on current aspects of graphology, news on workshops, seminars, conventions. Send SASE for information.

National Society for Graphology (NSG)
250 West 57th St., Room 1228A
New York, NY 10107
Founded by Felix Klein, "Dean of American graphologists"; a gestalt-theory-oriented organization emphasizing the psychological interpretation of handwriting. Sponsors seminars, professional certification, correspondence courses. Send SASE for membership and correspondence course information.

Books
Graphology by David V. Barrett. 1995, D.K. Publishing, Columbia, MO.
Graphology: The Science of Character in Handwriting by Henry Frith. Garber Communications, Inc., Hudson, NY.
Handwriting Analysis for Business and Personal Success by Henry O. Teltschen. 1995, Sure Sellers, Inc., New York, NY.

Schools with Accredited Courses
❖ Massachusetts Bay Community College in Wellesley Hills, MA 02181-5359.
❖ Felician College in Lodi, NJ 07644.
❖ There are also schools in London and Paris.

Additional Business Ideas

Mail-order personalized handwriting analysis: place ads in women's magazines to do a personalized handwriting analysis for $15 to $20.

⚔ 101 ⚔

PRIVATE INVESTIGATOR

Private investigation is not the glamorous life that is often portrayed on television programs. Much of the work of a private investigator involves library, online, and other research, as well as checking facts and conducting telephone interviews. Investigators are required to be licensed in most states, with requirements varying from state to state. Most require experience in some type of investigative work. Check with your state for the specifics.

Many private investigators specialize in one or two fields, and target the related industries. If being an independent investigator appeals to you, talk with investigators, and work in an agency or related business to get both the experience and the real picture of what a private investigator does.

Start-Up Costs

$3,000 to $8,000

Pricing Guidelines

$25 to $120 per hour, depending on the clients and the area where you are working.

Essential Equipment

+ A computer with fax/modem and business-related software; separate fax machine and phone line; copier, inkjet or laser printer; telephone headset; tape recorders for interviews.
+ Business cards, files, contracts, folders for reports.

Marketing and Advertising Methods and Tips
* Network with people you have worked for.
* Get word-of-mouth referrals from satisfied clients.
* Take out ads in the Yellow Pages.
* Direct mail to your targeted customers in your specialization; follow up with a telephone call to make an appointment.

Recommended Training, Experience, or Skills
* Gain several years of experience working in law enforcement, for a private investigation firm, for a collections agency, doing insurance claims investigations, or as an investigative reporter.
* Fulfill state licensing requirements and register with local officials if required.
* Be familiar with the legal process.
* Be able to work with people and understand their motivations.
* Have common sense, persistence, and the ability to process information until you find what you are looking for.

Income Potential
$25,000 to $55,000 per year.

Best Customers
Depends on your area of specialization: attorneys, insurance agencies, and individuals for personal investigations; businesses for competition research and personnel research.

Helpful Tips
* Concentrate your private investigation in the areas in which you have an interest and experience: missing people, background and credit checks, security evaluations for businesses, etc.
* Be able to talk with all kinds of people to get the information you need.

For More Information
Books
Be Your Own Dick: Private Investigating Made Easy by John Q.
Newman. 1993 Loopanics Unlimited, Port Townsend, WA.
How to Make $100,000 a Year as a Private Investigator by Edmund
J. Pankau, CLI, CPP, CFE. 1993, Paladin Press, Boulder, CO.
Private Investigation: Methods & Materials by 1991, Charles C.
Thomas Publisher, Springfield, IL.
Private Investigator by Jack Rudman. 1994, National Learning
Corporation, Syosset, NY.
Private Investigator's Guide to the Internet by Joseph Seanor.
1995, Thomas Publications, Austin, TX.

Business Guide
Entrepreneur's Start-Up Guide, "Private Investigator." (800)
421-2300; $69.50 plus shipping.

Courses
Nick Harris Detective Academy
Nick Harris Bldg.
16917 Enadia Way
Van Nuys, CA 91406
Not a correspondence course; write for information if you
can attend in Van Nuys, CA.

Additional Business Ideas
Security consultant (see "Personal Security Consultant," in
"Personal Services").

Still More Miscellaneous Businesses

FLEA MARKET BUSINESS

It's possible to make $40,000 to $100,000 a year at flea markets selling items on consignment or selling items that you buy low and sell high.

Books
Flea Market Price Guide, 5th ed., by Robert W. Miller, Wallace-Homestead Book Co., 1984, Lombard, IL.
How to Make Money in Flea Markets by Roger K. Williams. 1994, Roger's Specialty Products Co., Coshcoton, OH.
(See also "Collectibles Specialist.")

≥ ● ≤

HOLIDAY MONEY-MAKERS

Some people are so organized that they shop for Christmas gifts the year 'round. Many, though, wait until that first Christmas commercial on television soon after Halloween or after Thanksgiving. You can profit from both kinds of holiday shoppers by offering gifts and decorations all year long and during those hectic last-minute shopping days right before Christmas and Hanukkah. Of course, do not forget the other popular gift-buying holidays: Valentine's Day, Easter, Passover, Mother's Day, Father's Day, Labor Day (not a holiday for gifts, but does often mark the time when people do start buying for the Christmas holidays), Halloween, and Thanksgiving.

If you are selling a product, handcraft, or special service for one or all of these holidays, you have to plan and prepare far ahead in advance to be ready to sell or serve on those days—just as do retail stores and other businesses. Give yourself plenty of lead time to get ready for that buying season, working six months or more before the actual holiday.

Keep current on what is selling, and try to come up with creative and unique gifts or service ideas by reading trade publications, attending craft and trade shows, and networking with others in your line of business. Have a mixture of your best sellers and new items, and a range of prices to fit within everyone's budget. Sometimes, those $1 and $2 items might make the most profits for you.

It helps if you enjoy talking to people, and have fun to keep in the mood of the holiday. People like to see a friendly face, even at a holiday's hectic pace. Kindness, patience, and a smile will go a long way to make things go smoothly, and might just help your sales, too.

✤ Selling to catalogs:
"How to Sell to Catalog Houses Kit"
Success Publications
3419 Dunham, Box 263
Warsaw, NY 14569
$22.50 post-paid.

✤ Kiosk or cart in malls during the holidays
✤ Seasonal holiday boutiques:
   Seasonal/Holiday Boutiques/Directory
   from *The Learning Extension Catalog*
   The Front Room Publishers
   P.O. Box 1541
   Clifton, NJ 07015-1541
   A directory of places to sell your holiday items.
✤ Seasonal holiday open house: during the Easter and Christmas holiday seasons, many handcrafters hold holiday open houses. One or more handcrafters use one person's house to sell their craft, foods, and holiday decorations. It requires good organization and record keeping—not to mention being inconvenienced by having one's house used to sell the items. It is not uncommon for profits to exceed $1,000 to $2,000 per person over a weekend. Check first with your local officials and neighbors regarding any necessary permits and parking considerations.
✤ Wreaths—holiday and seasonal:
   "Make 22 Herbal Gifts for the Holidays," a Storey Country Wisdom Bulletin. Order through Storey's How-To Books for Country Living, Schoolhouse Rd., Pownal, VT 05261; write for catalog.
   The Wreath Book: Celebrate the Holidays...Over 100 Magnificent Wreaths to Make and Enjoy by Rob Pulleyn. 1996, Sterling Publishing Co., Inc., New York, NY.
✤ Year 'round Christmas shop: popular items are angels, custom-designed saints, creative Christmas cookie cutters, unique Christmas-tree skirts, wood crafts.
   52 Holiday Wood Projects by John A. Nelson. 1995, Sterling Publishing Co., Inc., New York, NY.
   Holiday Woodworking Projects by Joyce and John Nelson. Order from Stackpole Books, 5067 Ritter Rd., Mechanicsburg, PA 17055-6921
   Leisure Arts, Inc.
   P.O. Box 56089
   Little Rock, AR 72215-6089
   Christmas crafts books. Write for details.

+ Baking special Christmas foods
+ Being a Christmas Santa
+ Tree trimming and outdoor decorating service

⊾ • ⊿

ENTERTAINMENT BUSINESS IDEAS

+ Historical impersonator: For school assemblies, folk fairs.
+ Storytelling: School assemblies, family activity events.

⊾ • ⊿

KIOSK AND CART BUSINESSES

Start-ups run from $10,000 to $25,000, but you can earn $50,000 and up in the right location. Retail and sales background is helpful.

Business Guide:
Entrepreneur's Start-Up Guide, "Kiosks and Cart Businesses." (800) 421-2300; $69.50 plus shipping.

≈ ● ≈

OFFICE, HOME OFFICE, AND WORKSHOP DESIGNER

If you have design background, education, or training, you may want to plan home offices, small offices, and workshops, as more people start their own businesses from home.

Books

The Complete Guide to Building & Outfitting an Office in Your Home by Jerry Germer, A.I.A. 1994, Betterway Books, Cincinnati, OH.

Designing the Home Office by Random House Value Publishing, Inc. Staff. 1996, Random House, New York, NY.

Home Offices and Workplaces by Sunset Books Staff. 1986, Sunset Books, Menlo Park, CA.

Workplace by Design: Mapping the High-Performance Workscape by Franklin Beckar and Fritx Steele. 1995, Jossey-Bass Publishers, San Francisco, CA.

≈ ● ≈

HYPNOTHERAPIST

If you are interested in this as a career, get training and practice with a licensed hypnotherapist, join associations, and talk with hypnotherapists to learn what their careers are like.

Association

National Association of Transpersonal Hypnotherapists
1168 First Colonial Rd., Suite 12
Virginia Beach, VA 23454
Send SASE for more information.

Books

Hypnosis by Ursula Marham. 1993, Charles E. Tuttle Co., Inc., Boston, MA.

Hypnotherapy: A Handbook edited by Michael Heap and Wendy
Dryden. 1991, Taylor & Francis, Inc., Bristol, PA.
Hypnotherapeutic Techniques by John G. Watkins. 1994, Irving-
ton Publishers, New York, NY.

Training
Eastern Institute of Hypnotherapy
428½ Third St.
Marietta, OH 45750
Send SASE for listing of locations of certification programs.

Hypnosis Motivation Institute
18607 Ventura Blvd., Suite 310
Tarzana, CA 91356
Resident and correspondence courses; write for information.

· ◣ ● ◢ ·

PHOTOGRAPHY BUSINESSES

Here are some photography business ideas:

❖ Obtain old photographs of towns and sell reproduced copies
to individual collectors, restaurants, and public buildings.
❖ Offer construction photos: before and after photos of pri-
vate and public buildings.
❖ Take garden photos of private and public gardens.
❖ Sell slide collections of certain subjects.
❖ Take portraits of family and friends with an old-fashioned,
tintype format.

Books
Freelance Photographer's Handbook by Fredrik D. Bodin. 1993,
Amherst Media, Inc., Amherst, NY.
How You Can Make $25,000 a Year with Your Camera by Larry
Cribb. 1991, Writer's Digest Books, Cincinnati, OH.
Photographer's Market (an annual guide). Writer's Digest Books,
Cincinnati, OH.

◁ ● ▷

SHARPENING SERVICE

Have a mobile sharpening service, sharpening and polishing knives, slicers, pinking shears, beauty-shop scissors, ice skates, etc. You need around $10,000 to $12,000 for machines, van, and advertising. Train with a person who has a sharpening business. Income can be $35,000 to $36,000.

Books

The Complete Guide to Sharpening by Leonard Lee. 1995, Taunton Press, Newtown, CT.

Sharpening Basics by Patrick Spielman. 1991, Sterling Publishing Co., Inc., New York, NY.

Business Tips and Resources

Starting a business may be the easiest part of having a business; managing, running, and staying in business may be the most difficult. The following is a list of helpful resources with ideas, solutions, and problem-solving tips to help you be a success. Of course, every business owner should have her own list of experts—insurance brokers, lawyers, consultants, networking friends, and contacts—who can help her if she should face obstacles. Do not try to do everything yourself.

Persist, and do not give up. If your first business fails, keep trying to find one that works for you. Expect to make mistakes and wrong business decisions; everyone does. This is how we learn and grow and still go forward to success.

Books

Business for Profits by Allan Smith. Order from Success Publications, 3419 Dunham, Box 263, Warsaw, NY 14569. Send SASE for catalog.

The Entrepreneur Magazine Small Business Answer Book: Solutions to the 101 Most Common Small Business Problems by James Schell. 1996, John Wiley & Sons, Inc., New York, NY.

The Home Office Computing Handbook by the editors of *Home Office Computing Magazine* (David Langendoen and Dan Costa). To order, call (800) 325-6149; ask for Item #ZND 17330.

The Small Business Survival Guide by Robert E. Fleury. 1995, Sourcebooks, Naperville, IL 60540.

The Small Business Troubleshooter by Roger Fritz. 1995, Career Press, Franklin Lakes, NJ.

101 Home Office Success Secrets by Lisa Kanarek. 1994, Career Press, Franklin Lakes, NJ.

Software
"DecisionMaker"
Palo Alto Software
144 East 14th Ave.
Eugene, OR 97401
This is a decision-analysis program for business owners and managers. Write, or call (541) 683-6162, for information. $129.95 for Windows or Macintosh version.

General Resources

Associations

American Business Women's Association
P.O. Box 8728
Kansas City, MO 64114-0728

American Entrepreneurs Association (AEA)
Entrepreneur Magazine Group
2392 Morse Ave.
P.O. Box 57050
Irvine, CA 92619-7050
(800) 421-2300
Membership: $29.95; benefits include savings on insurance, small-business development guides, fax-on-demand business information, etc.

American Women's Economic Development Corp.
71 Vanderbilt Ave., 3rd Floor
New York, NY 10169

Independent Business Alliance (IBA)
P.O. Box 1945
Danbury, CT 06813-9643

Membership organization of about 30,000 members formed to give small-business owners and home-based entrepreneurs an array of products and services to support their businesses; $49 per year membership

> National Association for the Self-Employed (NASE)
> 2121 Precinct Line Rd.
> Hurst, TX 76054
> (800) 232-NASE

Benefits, advocacy for the self-employed.

> National Association of Women Business Owners
>   (NAWBO)
> 110 Wayne Ave., Suite 830
> Silver Spring, MD 20910-5603

Support of women business owners. Its research branch is the National Foundation for Women Business Owners; send SASE requesting membership information.

> National Federation of Independent Business
> 53 Century Blvd., Suite 300
> Nashville, TN 37214

> Entrepreneurs' Association (for Central Texas)
> 7501 Highway 290E, Suite 101
> Austin, TX 78723

Provides a small-business center, referrals, and services for small businesses in the Austin area.

Franchises

> Women's Franchise Network
> International Franchise Association
> 1350 New York Ave. NW, Suite 900
> Washington, DC 20005

Regulations and information on franchises for women.

Government Resources
Federal

Cooperative Extension Service: Part of the Department of Agriculture, this service usually works in conjunction with a university. There is an office in every county; call your county seat for the office nearest you. Provides information on animals, plants, and farming; in the past few years, many offices have held seminars on small businesses and crafts marketing.

Department of Commerce
(800) USA-TRADE.
Information on U.S. trade.

U.S. Small Business Administration's Answer Desk: (800) U-ASK-SBA
Online: (800) 697-4636, or on the Web: *http://www.sbaonline.sba*. Obtain the numbers for the nearest SBA office, Small Business Development Center, or relevant state agency.

Office of Women's Business Ownership (OWBO)
Small Business Administration
409 Third St. SW, 6th Floor
Washington, DC 20416
(202) 205-6673
Provides a free Women's Business Ownership kit.

SBA Publications
P.O. Box 30
Denver, CO 80201-0030
Write for listing of business publications.

Small Business Development Centers (SBDCs)
Small Business Administration
1300 Chainbridge Rd.
McClean, VA 22101-3967
Write for the SBDC office nearest you, or look in your telephone directory's white pages under "Small Business Development Center." SBDCs usually work in conjunction with universities or SBA branch offices and are available in 46 states, the District of Columbia, Puerto Rico, and the Virgin Islands. They provide free services, counseling, and low-cost seminars to prospective and existing business owners.

SCORE (Service Corps of Retired Executives) is a group of volunteers who offer management counseling and advice to small-business owners. Call the SBA at (202) 205-6762 or write to 409 3rd St. S.W., 4th Floor, Washington, D.C. 20024.

WNET—the Women's Network for Entrepreneurial Training—is a mentor program that matches experienced and new women entrepreneurs. Contact the nearest SBA office or Small Business Development Center.

Free Tax Publications:
Write or call (800) 829-1040.
Also offers "Your Business Tax Kit," a free kit for new businesses; call (800) TAX-FORM.

Trademark Search Library
Patent & Trademark Office
U.S. Dept. of Commerce
201 Jefferson Davis Highway, Room 208
Arlington, VA 22202
(800) 786-9199
Contact this office to apply for a trademark, and the library staff will tell you if the name is already taken. If not, the office will award you the trademark.

U.S. Fax Watch: (202) 512-1716
A free service of the U.S. Government Printing Office; if you have a fax machine, you can receive faxed information on a number of U.S. documents. Call the number and follow the automated instructions.

Publications About the Federal Government's Business Services
Books
Government Contract Negotiations: A Practical Guide for Small Business by David C. Moore. 1996, John Wiley & Sons, Inc., New York, NY.
Government Giveaways for Entrepreneurs II by Matthew Lesko. 1994, Information, USA, Kensington, MD.
Winning Government Grants and Contracts for Your Small Business by Mark Rowh. 1992, McGraw-Hill, Inc., New York, NY.

Video
"Your Guide to SBA Loans and Programs"
IWS, Inc.
24 Canterbury Rd.
Rockville Centre, NY 11570
$49.95 plus $4 for shipping and handling.

Getting Contracts
✤ Register with the SBA's Procurement Automated Source System (PASS). Call (800) U-ASK-SBA.
✤ Read the *Commerce Business Daily*, which lists available contracts (available in some public libraries). $277 per year from United Communications Group, P.O. Box 90608, Washington, DC 20077-7637.
✤ Read the annual *U.S. Government Purchasing and Sales Directory*, which lists more than 4,000 items the government buys.
✤ *Government Contracts and Subcontracts Leads Directory*, Government Data Publications, Inc., 1155 Connecticut Ave. NW, Washington DC 20036. $89.50.

State
State Representative or State Senator:
Visit your local state elected official's office for information on state agencies such as the State Department of Commerce, State Tax Agency, a women's entrepreneurial office, etc. for business start-up information, state regulations and licensing requirements, state business and sales tax information.

Also check out *Starting and Operating a Business in... (there is one for each state)* by Michael D. Jenkins. 1994, The Oasis Press, Grants Pass, OR.

Local
Check your local Chambers of Commerce, business associations, SBDCs, County Extension Office, local libraries, local colleges, and county business development agencies for local business start-up and support information.

Book Clubs

These clubs carry books on small business, gardening, handcrafts, sewing, etc. Write for catalogs.

Betters Homes & Gardens Craft Club
P.O. Box 8824
Camp Hill, PA 17012-8824

Many arts and crafts books plus occasional business and gardening books.

Chester Book Co.
4 Maple St.
Chester, CT 06412

Many fine art and handcrafts books.

Jeffrey Lant Associates
P.O. Box 38-2767
Cambridge, MA 02238

Many low-cost entrepreneurial reports.

"The Learning Extension Catalog"
The Front Room Publishers
P.O. Box 1541
Clifton, NJ 07015-1541

Craft business books, directories, plus other small business books.

Pilot Books
127 Sterling Ave.
Greenport, NY 11944

Publisher of budget travel, small business, and personal guides.

Storey's How-To Books for Country Living
Schoolhouse Rd.
Pownal, VT 05261

Many country living, crafts, and business books.

Success Publications
3419 Dunham Rd.
Box 263
Warsaw, NY 14569

Business and craft books and reports for entrepreneurs and home-based businesses.

"Whole Work Catalog"
The New Careers Center
1515 23rd St.
Box 339-CT
Boulder, CO 80306
Many books on self-employment and careers.

Writer's Digest Book Club
P.O. Box 12948
Cincinnati, OH 45212-0948
Books on writing and being a professional writer.

Small Business Books: General Business Information

Dive Right In—The Sharks Won't Bite: The Entrepreneurial Woman's Guide to Success by Jane Wesman. 1994, Upstart Publishing, Dover, NH.

The Entrepreneur's Relocation Guide by Kimberly Stansell, Research Done Write!, Suite B261-PH, 8726 S. Sepulveda Blvd., Los Angeles, CA 90045; 32-page guide, $7.95 plus $1.50 postage ($10.28 for CA).

How to Run a Small Business, 7th ed., J. K. Lasser Institute. 1994, McGraw-Hill, Inc., New York, NY.

Making It Own Your Own by Paul and Sarah Edwards. 1991, Jeremy P. Tarcher/Putnam Book, New York, NY.

The McGraw-Hill Guide to Managing Growth in Your Emerging Business by Stephen C. Harper. 1994, McGraw-Hill, Inc., New York, NY.

Second Careers: New Ways to Work After 50 by Caroline Bird. 1992, Little, Brown & Company, Ltd., Canada.

The Woman Entrepreneur by Linda Pinson and Jerry Jinnet. 1993, Upstart Publishing, Co., Inc., Dover, NH.

Working Solo: The Real Guide to Freedom & Financial Success with Your Own Business by Terri Lonier. 1994, Portico Press, New Paltz, NY.

Small Business Resource Books

77 No Talent Businesses by Kelly Reno. 1996, Prima Publishing, Rocklin, CA.

100 Best Retirement Businesses by Lisa Angowski Rogak with David H. Bangs, Jr. 1994, Upstart Publishing Co., Inc., Dover, NH.

The Big Instruction Book of Small Business (a series; one for each state including Washington, DC) by Carole Marsh. 1994, Gallopade Publishing Group, Atlanta, GA.

The Idea Entrepreneurial Business for You by Glenn Desmond and Monica Faulkner. 1995, John Wiley & Sons, Inc., New York, NY.

Mancuso's Small Business Resource Guide, revised and updated, by Joseph R. Mancuso. 1996, Sourcebooks, Inc., Naperville, IL.

Small Business Encyclopedia, 1996, Entrepreneur Magazine Group, $149; (800) 421-2300.

Working Solo Sourcebook by Terri Lonier. 1995, Portico Press, New Paltz, NY.

A self-employment survival guide is currently being researched and written by Kimberly Stansell. The book will provide tactics and strategies necessary for starting and running a business on a shoestring budget. For more information, contact Kimberly Stansell at the address below (see "Bootstrappin' Entrepreneur" under "Newsletters").

Reference Books

Gale Research Resource Books, International Publishing Company, Detroit, Michigan, publishes the following books and directories, which are found in the reference section of public and/or college libraries, especially those schools with business courses or degree programs:

Business Organizations, Agencies, and Publications Directory, 1996.

Encyclopedia of Associations; lists trade associations across the country.

Encyclopedia of Business Information Sources, 1995-96, 1994.

National Directory of State Business Licensing and Regulation, 1994.

Small Business Sourcebook, 1st ed., 1995; information in many industries.

Start Smart Business Advisor, 1994; profiles resources available to small businesses and to those who advise them. CD-ROM.

Here are a few from other publishers:

Business Information Sources by Lorna M. Daniels. 1993, University of California Press, $39.95, (800) 822-6657.

The Thomas Register of Manufacturers. A huge, multi-volume directory listing thousands of manufacturers, both light and heavy industry.

Educational Sources and Courses

"Hire Yourself and Work From Home"

An eight-week program developed by Paul and Sarah Edwards, offered by colleges in many cities. For the location of the nearest college, contact Home Business Services, 1540 Race, Denver, CO 80206.

Center for Entrepreneurial Leadership, Inc.
Ewing Marion Kauffman Foundation
4900 Oak St.
Kansas City, MO 64112-2776

A nonprofit organization offering various educational programs in different areas across the U.S. for new and established entrepreneurs.

Business Week's Guide to the Best Business Schools, 4th ed., edited by John A. Byrne. 1995, The McGraw-Hill Companies, New York, NY.

Distance Education (Home Study/Correspondence Courses)

Directory of Accredited Institutions
Distance Education and Training Council
1601 18th St. NW
Washington, DC 20009-2529

Write for free pamphlet listing many distance education schools accredited by this council that offer small-business and specific business courses and training.

Graduate School USDA (U.S. Department of Agriculture)
Ag Box 9911, Room 1112
South Agriculture Bldg.
14th St. & Independence Ave. SW
Washington, DC 20250-9911
Correspondence courses on accounting, auditing, computer sciences, editing, law and paralegal studies, library technology, and others. Write or call for a copy of the catalog: (202) 720-7123.

Internet Information
Books

101 Businesses You Can Start on the Internet by Daniel S. Janal. 1996, Van Nostrand Reinhold, New York, NY.

The Complete Idiot's Guide to Modems and Online Services by Sherry Kinkaph. 1994, Alpha Books, Indianapolis, IN.

Gale Guide to Internet Databases, 1996, Gale Research, Detroit, MI. A reference book telling how to access and retrieve nearly 3,000 Internet databases.

Internet Business 500: The Top 500 Essential Web Sites for Business by Ryan Bernard. 1995, Ventana Communications Group, Inc., Research Triangle Park, NC.

"The Internet Business Kit" by Matthew Ellsworth: includes CD-ROM plus two books: *The Internet Business Book* and *Marketing the Internet.* 1994 and 1995, John Wiley & Sons, Inc., New York, NY. (800) 225-5945; $69.95.

The Internet Business Primer by Wayne Allison. 1996, Source-books, Inc., Napierville, IL.

Internet for Dummies, 4th ed., by John Levine. 1996, IDG Books Worldwide, Indianapolis, IN.

Launching a Business on the Web by Deborah Sellers and David Cook. 1995, New Business Enterprises, Prentice-Hall Computer Publishing, Indianapolis, IN.

Making Money on the Internet by Alfred and Emily Glossbrenner. 1995, McGraw-Hill, Osborne, New York, NY.

Periodical

Internet World
P.O. Box 713
Mount Morris, IL 61054-9965
$14.97 per year, 12 issues.

Online Services

(Call for prices and to ask about their business forums.)

❖ America Online: (800) 827-6364; "Small Business Center." Also *Home Office Computing's* "Small Office/Home Office Center (key word: "soho").
❖ CompuServe: (800) 848-8199; "Entrepreneur" and "Working From Home" forums.
❖ Delphi: (800) 695-4005
❖ Genie: (800) 638-9636
❖ Prodigy: (800) 776-3449
❖ Yahoo's "Business Sources": *http://www.yahoo.com*

Mail Order

Associations

Direct Marketing Association
1120 Avenue of the Americas
New York, NY 10036
World Wide Web site: *http://www.the-dma.org*
Seminars, library and information services; conference and exhibition.

National Mail Order Association
2807 Polk St. NE
Minneapolis, MN 55418-2924
Excellent for small mail-order businesses; monthly newsletter: "Mail Order Digest."

Books

101 Great Mail Order Businesses by Tyler G. Hicks. 1996, Prima Publishing, Rocklin, CA.
101 Tips for More Profitable Catalogs by Maxwell Sroge. 1995, NTC Publishing Group, Lincolnwood, IL.

Building a Mail Order Business: A Complete Manual for Success,
4th ed., by William A. Cohen. 1995, John Wiley & Sons,
Inc., New York, NY.
How to Create Catalogs That Sell by Research Education Staff.
1995, Research Education Association, Piscataway, NJ.
Mail Order Selling: How to Market Almost Anything by Mail, 3rd
ed., by Irving Burstiner. 1995, John Wiley & Sons, Inc.,
New York, NY.
Mail Order Success Kit, $49. Order from Success Publications,
3419 Dunham, Box 263, Warsaw, NY 14569.
The Upstart Guide to Owning and Managing a Mail Order Business by Dan Ramsey. 1995, Upstart Publishing Co., Dover,
NH.

Mailing Lists
The Polk Company
1155 Brewery Park Blvd.
Detroit, MI 48207-2697
See also "Mailer's Software," below.

Mail Order Software
Mail Order Wizard
Haven Corp.
802 Madison St.
Evanston, IL 60202-2207
Write for information about IBM-compatible software for mail-order businesses. Prices start at $495. Help line available.

Mailer's Software
970 Calle Negocio
San Clemente, CA 92673-6201
Direct mailing software, mailing lists.

Software Information
The Software Directory—Software Buyers Handbook by H.T. Wrobel. 1991, Tactical Technologies, Harvard, MA.
The Software Directory, 1995 edited by R.R. Bowker staff. A
Reed Reference Publishing Company, New Providence, NJ.

Can be found in larger public and college libraries. Has fully annotated listings for more than 18,000 new and established software programs.

Small Business Periodicals
Business Start-ups
Subscription Dept.
P.O. Box 50347
Boulder, CO 80321-0347.
$19.97 per year, 12 issues.

Entrepeneur
P.O. Box 5484
Pittsfield, MA 01203-9350
Home Office Computing

P.O. Box 53543
Boulder, CO 80323-3543
$19.97 per year, 12 issues.

Income Opportunities
P.O. Box 55207
Boulder, CO 80321-5207
$9.97 per year, 12 issues.

Self Employed Professional
462 Boston St.
Topsfield, MA 01983-9917
$19.97, eight issues.

Small Business Opportunities
Harris Publications, Inc.
1115 Broadway
New York, NY 10160-0397
$9.97 per year, six issues.

Small Business Success
Pacific Bell Directory
Communications Dept. CWS, Room 429
101 Spear St.
San Francisco, CA 94105

WorkingWoman
P.O. Box 3276
Harland, IA 51593
$14.97 per year, 12 issues.

Newsletters
"The Business Woman's Advantage"
921 Gregory Lane
Schaumburg, IL 60193
$26.95 per year; a 16-page newsletter for women with "entrepreneurial spirit."

"Bootstrappin' Entrepreneur"
Kimberly Stansell, editor and publisher
Suite B261-PH
8726 South Sepulveda Blvd.
Los Angeles, CA 90045-4082
E-mail: KmberlyNLA@aol.com.
A 12-page quarterly newsletter teaching people how to use cost-cutting strategies to boost profits. Published by Kimberly Stansell, small-business expert and columnist. Back-Issue Bundler Pack: $16.50 ($17.86, CA), includes four past issues.

"SOHO America"
P.O. Box 941
Hurst, TX 76053-9952
(800) 495-7646
A nonprofit organization for the small office.

Start-Up Guides
Entrepeneur Magazine Group
2392 Morse Avenue
P.O. Box 57050
Irvine, CA 92619-7050
200 guides for specific businesses. Call (800) 421-2300 for a copy of the "Small Business Development Catalog."

National Business Library
P.O. Box 928
Los Olivos, CA 93441

Over seventy business development guides. Call (800) 947-7724 for a copy of their latest "Small Business Catalog."

Supplies and Equipment
Anthro Corp.
Technology Furniture
10450 SW Manhasset Dr.
Tualatin, OR 97062
Economical computer carts and work stations. (800) 325-3841.

Sauder Woodworking Co., (800) 523-3987; economical, space-saving computer cabinet.

Platronics Headset, (800) 544-4660; durable headset that is helpful if you do much work via the telephone.

Earth Care Paper, Inc.
P.O. Box 14140
Madison, WI 53714-14140

NEBS, Inc.
500 Main St.
Groton, MA 01471
Computer forms and checks, software.

Paper Direct
100 Plaza Dr.
Secaucus, NJ 07094-3606

PC Magazine 1996 Computer Buyers Guide edited by John C. Dvorak. Ziff-Davis Press, Emeryville, CA.

Quill Monthly Office Products Catalog
100 Schelter Rd.
Lincolnshire, IL 60069-3621

Viking Office Products
13809 S. Figueroa St.
P.O. Box 6114
Los Angeles, CA 90061-0144
(800) 421-1222

Miscellaneous

Dun & Bradstreet
899 Eaton Ave.
Bethlehem, PA 18025
Business information, research; source of a "Duns No," which is needed to gain a federal contract.

Lefty's Corner
P.O. Box 615
Clarks Summit, PA 18411
Sells writing supplies, etc. for left-handers. $2 for catalog, refundable with first purchase.

QVC/Vendor Relations
1365 Enterprise Dr.
West Chester, PA 19380
Write for application for selling your product.

Radio Show

Paul and Sarah Edwards discuss business and technology on the "Home Office Show" (Business Radio Network); (719) 528-7040. Sundays from 10:00 to 11:00 p.m. ET.

Television Shows

❖ CNN's new financial network, CNNfn: *Home Office Computing* editors appear Tuesdays, 3:00 to 4:00 p.m. ET to discuss small-business topics and technology.

❖ "Working from Home with Paul and Sarah Edwards" (the Home & Garden television network); check your local listings, or call (615) 694-2700 for more information.

Directories

The following directories can be ordered from DK Unlimited at P.O. Box 306, Blooming Glen, PA 18911.

Books by Donna Kosling:

❖ *Home Based Business Help Directory, Vol. 1, 1996 (HBBHD1)*. $19.95.

❖ *Home Based Business Help Directory, Vol. 2, 1996 (HBBHD2).* $19.95.
❖ Special for both directories, Volumes 1 and 2: $34.90.
❖ *Women-in-Business Help Directory (WIB1).* $14.95.
❖ *Disabled in Business Resource Guide (DIB1).* $14.95.
❖ *Injured Worker Resource Guide (IWRG1).* $14.95.

Add $4 in shipping and handling for the first book and $2.50 for each additional book. Send check or money order payable to DK Unlimited.

Index

Bridal businesses
  sewing gowns/accessories, 329
  shops, retail, 248
Brochure writing, 362
  real estate brochure writers, 372–374
Broom-making business, 175–178
Builder's clean-up service, 120–121
Business cards, 43
Business consultants, 125–126
Business cost reduction services, 89–91
Business description, 39–44, 59
Business experience, 17–18
Business idea books, 31
Business knowledge, 8
Business niche, 40
Business plan, 11
  defined, 35–36
  evaluation of business, 18
  in start-up, 26
Business referral services, 125
Business structure, 41
Business trainers, 265–268
Butterfly-raising business, 232
Button jewelry, 171

C
Cake baking/decoration, 216
Candy stores, 255
Canvas repair/custom work, 318–319
Capitalizing business, 12
Career counseling services, 287
Caricaturists, 154–157
Carpool coordinator, 281
Cart businesses, 390
Cartoonists, 154–157
Catalogs. *See* Mail-order businesses
Cat boarding/grooming, 67–69
Catering businesses, 216
Centerpiece-making businesses, 230
Chambers of Commerce, 10
Chauffeur services, 281
Checklist for start-up businesses, 25–27
Chefs
  personal chefs, 216, 308
  sewing uniforms, 328
Child-proofing services, 133–135
Children. *See also* Toy-related businesses
  book illustrators, 167
  child-proofing services, 133–135
  creative learning centers, 135–138
  as entrepreneurs, 145
  fitness centers for, 129–132
  miscellaneous services for, 144
  personalized children's book business, 354

services for, 129–145
sewing for children, 320–323
summer camp information/referral services, 138–140
taxi service for, 283
Chocolate factory business, 216
Christmas
  gifts, 388–390
  pets, ornaments for, 83
Classic car collectors, 381
Cleaning services, 125
Clip-art services, 163
Clipping/information retrieval services, 91–94
Clocks
  repair businesses, 283–285
  wooden clocks, 187
Cloth dolls, 180–183
Clothing consignment shop, 246–249
Clowning, 180
Coffee shops, 252–255
Collectibles specialists, 379–381
Collection services, 94–96
Columnists, 374
Community theater groups, 180
Commuter services, 281
CompuServe, 43
Computer businesses, 146–149. *See also* Software businesses
  cleaning businesses, 308
  consultant businesses, 147
  data backup services, 102–104
  database consultants, 104–106
  graphic designers, 161–163
  instructor/trainer businesses, 262–265
  multimedia services, 147–148
  online services, 118–119
  resources, 148–149
  software designers/publishers, 148
Confidence, 7
Consulting services
  book proposal/consultation/writing, 346
  career/vocational counseling, 287
  credit counseling, 287
  expert consultants, 49
  garden problem-solvers, 222–225
  job counseling for disabled persons, 305–308
  marketing consultants, 287
  personal security consultants, 302–305
  property tax consultants, 302
Containers, creation of, 233–236
Cookbook authors, 212–216
Cooking schools, 216

I
Illustrators, 167
Import/export business, 106–109
Income potential, 60
Incorporated businesses, 41
Independent publishing businesses, 349–354
Indexing, 374
Information retrieval services, 91–94
Information specialty, 369–372
Inns
bed-and-breakfast inns, 330–333
country inn/restaurant, 206–209
Insect-raising businesses, 230–233
Instructional businesses, 256–268
business trainers, 265–268
computer instructors/trainers, 262–265
disabled persons, teaching driving techniques to, 308
resources for, 257
videos, instructional, 259–262
Insurance
agents, 290–292
borrowing from policies, 52
fees, 49
restoration services, 292
Internet
general resources, 406–407
online services, 118–119
Interpreter/translator services, 359
Introduction services, 296–299
Invention businesses, 190–193
disabled persons, devices for, 308
security devices, 305
Investment counseling service, 287
IRAs, borrowing from, 52

J
Jewelry
making business, 168–171
sewing travel pouches, 329
Job counseling for disabled persons, 305–308

K
Keepsake organizing business, 308
Kiosk businesses, 390
Knife sharpening services, 393

L
Ladybug-raising businesses, 230–233
Language teachers, 268
Language translation services, 357–359
Lawn signs makers, 198
Legal business name, 43

Legal services, 293–296
Licensing products, 193
Life-size doll making, 183
Limited liability companies, 41
Limousine services, 281
Literary agents, 344–346
Llamas
raising as specialty, 73
for wool, 77–79
Loans
obtaining loans, 51–52
payments on, 50
Locksmiths, 305

M
Magazines for small businesses, 409–410
Magnetic signs makers, 198
Mailing list services, 110–112
Mail-order businesses
books by mail, 354
coffee/tea sales, 255
food businesses, 215
general resources for, 407–408
handwriting analysis, personalized, 384
holiday gift businesses, 388–389
mailing list services, 110–112
personal security devices, 305
planters, sale of, 236
used/rare book sales, 251
Manufacturer's agents/representatives, 112–115
Marine retail businesses, 336
Marketing consultants, 287
Marketing plan, 4, 13
Marketing research, 45–48
analysts/consultants, 115–118
Mary Kay, 21
Matchmakers, personal, 296–299
Mature adult services, 279–281
Mealworm-raising businesses, 232
Medical businesses, 269–272
data research business, 270–271
halfway homes/centers, 272
illustrators, 157
records consultant, 272
Millinery business, 325–327
Mobile fitness vans, 132
Mobile medical laboratories, 272
Moonlighting, 52
Moving/unpacking services, 279–281
Multilevel marketing (MLM), 21–22
Multimedia services, 147–148
Mushroom growing, 230
Music boxes, 201